KEEPING IT CHEERY

Rave Reviews

"A classic. Bill is an unrivalled anecdotist and this book about his ministry in the East End of Glasgow will still be read a hundred years from now - if he is still around to read it."
George Galloway, Baghdad T.V. Times.

"This is a very funny book altogether. Read it churself some time. It is a book for giving away."
Sorley Mist, deceased Gaelic poet.

"Outshines my own Bull."
Pope InClement the Last, Jewish Chronicle.

"The golfing section is a great advert for my new Hippo driver with jumbo head and titanium club covers."
St. Augustine of Hippo, Golf Monthly.

"The best thing since wholemeal, stone ground, vitamin fortified unsliced bread."
Rev. Amos B. Crackers, 'Life & Work'.

"Groundbreaking theology"
Grave-digger's Review.

For all the Reviews of *Keeping It Cheery* see the Court Circular of *The Big Issue.*

ISSUES
raised by "the book they don't want you to read":

1. Is the world a safer place now than it was under Nancy Reagan ?

2. Is a limited nuclear war better than no war at all ?

3. Why do the banks cancel Mexico's debts and then demand you pay your overdraft ?

4. Should Britain have invaded Iraq or had another go at the Crimea ?

5. Are CH_3 gases from hymn-books the cause of global warming ?

TESTIMONIALS

"I read your book and in a week lost ten pounds - it was a miracle!"
Ida Bottomly, Aviemore.

"I used to cry myself to sleep after attending Kirk Session and Presbytery meetings, but after reading your book, I am no longer depressed and realise it is their problem and not mine. Many thanks."
Rev. D. Creppit, Ceud Mile Failte Towers, Torquay.

"The greatest pleasure I know, is to do a good action by stealth, and to have it found out by accident. "
Charles Lamb.

St Francis-in-the-East, in the 1970s
(formerly Barrowfield Parish Church;
now Bridgeton St Francis-in-the-East.)

KEEPING IT CHEERY:
ANECDOTES FROM A LIFE IN BRIGTON

Bill Shackleton

Covenanters

Published by
Covenanters Press

the joint imprint of
Zeticula
57 St Vincent Crescent
Glasgow
G3 8NQ
and
Scottish Christian Press
21 Young Street
Edinburgh
EH2 4HU

http://www.covenanters.co.uk
admin@covenanters.co.uk

First published in 2005

Text and Photographs Copyright © Bill Shackleton 2005

Cover design by Heather Macpherson

ISBN 1 905022 00 x Paperback

ISBN 1 905022 01 8 Hardback

For my Grandchildren and old friends

Church House, steeple gone and re-roofed, 1975

Acknowledgements

My thanks are due to Sally Magnusson, for her advice on the editing of the manuscript, and for her long-standing interest in Church House Youth Club.

Harry Reid, former editor of The Herald, was another great help with his suggestions, and the contribution of a Preface to the book.

John Finch, the club's personal computer expert, was also invaluable to me - as far as I am concerned, the p.c. of God is beyond all understanding.

Janet de Vigne of Scottish Christian Press has guided me through the complexities of publication, and I am most grateful to her.

Finally, I am grateful to my wife, 'the unsinkable Maggi Brown', whose boundless energy and abundance of talent have not only saved her husband from a life of idleness and ministerial failure, but delivered him from an early death by malnutrition.

Bill Shackleton
December 2004
Deo Gratias

P.S. I should also acknowledge that, with my memory in its sere and yellow years, names and places, dates and times should only be considered reasonably accurate.

Illustrations

Preface

The life of a working journalist is very different from that of a Royal, but there is one common denominator: journalists and royalty both have, from time to time, and in the line of duty, to visit schools, hospitals, factories and the like. In 32 years in the Scottish Press, I got used to such visits. You are usually shown only what your hosts want you to see, and the trick is to be inquisitive and even investigative, without causing offence. But as often as not, despite your best efforts, you are left only with the most bland and unremarkable of impressions.

When Bill Shackleton invited me to visit Church House in Bridgeton, early in 2003, I agreed readily enough, though I did not expect that this would be any different from many other such visits. I knew that Church House was a youth and community centre in the 'badlands' between Bridgeton Cross and Parkhead in the east end of Glasgow. Further, I knew that it had been founded by the Rev. Arthur Gray during the second world war, but not that the minister most associated with it had been the Rev. Bill Shackleton himself.

Bill asked me to address the Bridgeton Business Club, of which he is a leading spirit, and he suggested that we should spend ninety minutes or so before the meeting, which was held at Celtic Park, visiting Church House, which is situated a few hundred yards to the west.

When I arrived at Church House I was not, in truth, expecting anything particularly unusual or illuminating or enlightening.

Well, I was in for a surprise. Although it was empty at that time in the morning, Bill's remarkable capacity for entertaining reminiscence and his mastery of the pointed, effective anecdote made the visit utterly compelling. Quite simply, he brought the place to life. He had a myriad of stories, some them really funny, some of them tragic, some of them heroic; he managed to convey a history of aspiration, of struggle, of dogged endeavour and persistent courage, of sheer practical goodness in the most hostile of environments - and all this without being in the slightest self-serving or self-important.

Something of the flavour of that most rewarding of visits is constant in this wonderfully entertaining book. Bill's style is couthy and chatty, but there is seriousness too. He is too clever a writer to labour his points, but he has plenty of serious messages to communicate. He can write with insight about break-ins, intimidation, delinquency, illness and death, deprivation, funerals, prisons, courts, hospitals, football and goodness knows what else without losing his upbeat, yet always realistic, spirit. Indeed, this books contains many pertinent reflections for our times.

Thus I hope and expect that Bill's book will amuse and enlighten many readers. It will also serve, incidentally, as a superb primer for tyro ministers and young teachers and novice youth workers. There is here much practical and sage advice, imparted lightly and without the slightest pomposity, about how to work with alienated or difficult young people. Altogether, this is the best kind of pragmatic Christian document: it is sensible, sensitive and helpful. It is a book rooted in reality and knowledge of the world, and it is the fruit of rich experience.

It is also, magnificently, a book about Glasgow, that most chancy, defiant, cheeky, and life-enhancing of cities.

Another point. The Church of Scotland is far too beset by doom and gloom. Bill Shackleton is a tireless enemy of doom and gloom. In short, it is easy and necessary to commend this book, for it is witty and wise, considered and kind.

It is also full of jokes, very good ones, so I will not attempt one here, for I would instantly be shown up. All I can say is that anyone who does not laugh constantly when reading this book must be a truly dull and dreary soul. If laughter is the best medicine, this book must be just what the doctor ordered.

Bill Shackleton is that most valuable of human beings, one whose constant task is to cheer the rest of us up.

Indeed, his title says it all.

Harry Reid,
Edinburgh,
October 2004

Introduction

I write this at the long-time urging of folk who have said to me over the years, "You should write a book". Maybe they thought this was the best way to stop me retailing anecdotes about my old days as a Church of Scotland minister in Bridgeton; on the other hand (as the Irishman said when he lost a glove), maybe they were anxious that my contributions to the annals of the humble poor be not lost forever. Anyway, here goes ...

This is a purely personal story. It is not a social history of the East End of Glasgow, and it is not an analysis of the Kirk's problems; first and foremost it is a light-hearted look at a lengthy ministry in a working-class parish church, namely St. Francis-in-the-East, and its offshoot, Church House Youth Centre. It is fifty years since I first became involved there and in my heart, I have never left it. Being retired, all I can do nowadays is raise money for the Club, and, by writing down my experiences, show that the ministry can be a great life. It is said that those who know most about the Kirk are those who least attend it, so if this book helps focus a truer picture then it will have been worth the writing.

A man from the Men's Regnal Circle in Gateshead once wrote me a letter in which he posed a question: "Why does God become real to me when I visit St. Francis-in-the-East in a way He doesn't seem to be as real elsewhere?" As you read what follows, you will find that he has not been the only one to have that experience. People from all over the world, and from every walk of life have found something in the Church and the Club which brings them back.

I get a telephone call from a sixty-five year old lady living in the Midlands of England, a former Church House member. We met recently when, here in Glasgow, I conducted the funeral of an old friend of hers from the days when they were bright young ladies in the Club over forty years ago. She talks in minute detail about the old days, and goes on to tell me that her daughter has recently suffered a tragic death. When she herself dies, she wants me to travel down south and take her funeral. At my age this is hardly likely, but I realise that for her I am still the young minister of yester-year. Like so many in whose lives the Club played a big part in their formative years, time stands still. She wants me to know that she is very active in her local church. Everywhere I go, I meet people like her, once Bridgeton kids and now members of congregations all over the place. We were in 'the export business', sending folk all over the world to do good.

Long ago I saw a film called 'The Deptford Boys' about a youth club there. The man in charge said the most sensible things about youth work: "Don't over-estimate yourself: you can do very little for the really bad boy, and the good boy doesn't need you; but for the great mass of boys in between, you can do far more than you realise." Wise advice! it has been the Church House Creed down the years. I like the saying of James Joyce, "God is a shout in the street", for it reminds us that the Kingdom of God is bigger than the church.

To keep it cheery, now read on folks - my adventures rival those of Candide! By the time you've finished, you will understand why Brigton Cross is believed to be the original site of the Garden of Eden (keep that to yourself or these New Age types will set up a nudist camp there).

The most important part of a book is its title (few read more than the title so it has to be a good one). I thought of calling it: "The Wit & Wisdom of William Shackleton", but the book would be too short; then I considered "Forty Years of Hell in an East End Parish", but that would frighten younger readers; "Pride and Prejudice" sounded a great title, but I'm told a lady author, called Jane Eyre, has already used it. How about "With Flag and Whistle through Sunny Brigton"? - that should appeal to train spotters - now there's a good title, "Train-spotting". A title I fancied was "Minister on the Roof", having spent a good deal of my ministry nailing down slates on the Club and the Manse roofs. Then I thought of calling it "Keeping It Cheery".

After Arnold Bennett died, somebody said of him, "Well, Arnold cheered us all up". If this cheers folk up it will have been worth them reading it. So here it is then: "Keeping it Cheery" (the expurgated edition).

Bill Shackleton
Glasgow,
October 2004

Chapter 1

*"I have tried in my time to be a philosopher; but
I don't know how, cheerfulness was always breaking
in."*
(Oliver Edwards to Dr. Samuel Johnson).

1929 - THE NEW START -
A POTTED HISTORY OF ST.FRANCIS-IN-THE-EAST

St. Francis-in-the-East is one of the best known kirks in Scotland,
but for those unfamiliar with Bridgeton, here's the background ...

Originally called 'Barrowfield Parish Church', it began in 1873
as an offshoot of Calton Parish into the new housing area being
developed around the old Bridgeton village. By 1929, Bridgeton
had become the industrial heart of the city, with over two hundred
industrial plants, some very big, like Sir William Arrolls who built
the Forth, London Tower, and Humber bridges. That year the Rev.
Sydney Warnes came to Barrowfield Parish Church; it was the height
of the Great Depression. Industry had stopped, there was poverty
everywhere, and the congregation was reduced to thirteen members.
Because he had no keys to get into the disused church, he held his first
Kirk session meeting up a close with his only two elders.

One of the first things Sydney did was change the name of the
church to signify a new start; he called it St.Francis-in-the-East, taking
the name from a newspaper article which read, 'The Rev. Sydney
Warnes has gone like a modern St. Francis into the East End'. It must
be the only church in the world to take its name from a newspaper!

A dynamic wee man, 'Pal Warnes', as he soon became known,
went across the street to the 'corner boys', handed out Woodbines,
and took them off for a game of football. He somehow got money
from the wealthy Park Church, and floored off the gallery to create
a sanctuary above, and halls below. He then moved the unemployed
in to start the "Pals' Club" out of which would later spring Church
House and the Men's Regnal Circle. He put baths into the cellar and
you got a bath, a cup of tea, and bun for tuppence. Old photographs
show Sydney, in his frock coat, organising impromptu concerts - he

was a first rate pianist - boxing matches, and competitions on the billiards table he got from the H.L.I. Little wonder that after four years he was exhausted. He bequeathed a flourishing congregation, with a very good name in the community, to his successor, another brilliant minister, Arthur Gray.

A simple story (one of many) illustrates 'Pal' Warnes ministry in Bridgeton. Having no manse, he and his wife rented a flat near the Kelvin Hall. On his way back there, while standing at the tram stop in the rain late one night, a man approached him wearing worn out shoes and asking, "Can you get me a pair of shoes, Mr Warnes?" Taking off his own shoes, "Try these", said Sydney. They fitted, so the minister went home in wet stocking feet, leaving his shoes with the man.

1935 - CHURCH HOUSE

In 1935, Arthur Gray, coming to his first charge, found there was not enough space for all the activities and people Sydney left him. He needed extra premises, but it would not be until 1942, when the old London Road East Church was united with his own in nearby Queen Mary Street, that he had his wish fulfilled. London Road East became Church House - hardly a purpose built youth and community centre, but good enough once adapted.

No extrovert like 'Pal Warnes', Arthur was a wonderful pastor, and completely suited to carry on where his predecessor left off. Before leaving for Aberdeen in 1950, he had carried the burgeoning congregation through the war years, found many men jobs, and bought a manse for the church (thanks to George MacLeod for the £600).

The kindliest and politest of men, Arthur Gray was the complete Christian gentleman. A story he liked to tell against himself is worth recording for posterity before it is lost from memory. One frosty night, while proceeding along London Road, he slipped on one of those steel trap doors you used to see in the pavement outside pubs, and which opened up so that beer barrels could be lowered into the cellar. Falling heavily, and lying stunned at the pub door, two old ladies passing by peered down at his prostrate body and one said, "Oh my! it's Mr. Gray, the meenister - the poor sowl's mauroclas!"

Standing with him outside the wee St. Francis-in-the-East church

The old London Road East Church
(Church House from 1942; the cost of turning it into a Youth
Club: £1,300 including blackout material)

one day, he said to me, "Providence has been good to this place, Bill". It was certainly good in sending him there. Arthur taught me the true meaning of faith: when Church House began he boldly employed two youth workers, although the congregation was too poor to pay his own stipend and it was in the middle of a war! All he had was financial support from an enlightened Home Board. He took a colossal gamble. "I went into the Club an hour before it opened, and stood there all alone, and I said to myself, 'Arthur, what if nobody comes?'" Until you have had that feeling, you do not know what faith is. The trend today is for consensual and democratic management, but that is the road to failure; only a small number of people have the long-term vision to lead, act with authority, and accountability. Sydney Warnes and Arthur Gray were fishers of men. How short we are of such ministers these days.

Arthur used to call Church House "the vestibule of the church." Abraham Lincoln was told during the American Civil War that the city of New York, which called itself "The Vestibule of America", intended leaving the Union and going its own way. Old Abe tersely remarked, "Well, that will be the first time a vestibule has existed without a house!" Church House's Youth Club work and the Kirk are inseparable. We have never had an 'in-your-face" kind of evangelism, the vestibule is open to all, remembering what Dietrich Bonhoeffer said, "It is better to speak to Christ about your brother, than to your brother about Christ."

Arthur needed and loved the common people; I used to see photographs of him in the homes of the local matriarchs, wartime hand-tinted photos of a youthful, handsome Arthur. He suited his times: the pre-war poverty, wartime stresses. He enthusiastically talked football (essential in Glasgow), smoked Woodbines, and understood people's needs. An early supporter of the Iona Community, Arthur was a man of vision, and courage. He was a dear friend to me when I became the minister of his beloved former charge, and I had the chapel in the rebuilt Church House dedicated to his memory in 1974.

When the new Eastern Division police station was built in the mid-Seventies, in my dedicatory speech I pointed out that the building was forty years late arriving. Ground had been promised to Arthur in the Thirties by the owner of Anderson's mill to build Church House, but when Mr Anderson suddenly died, his two sons withdrew the offer, saying the land was earmarked for a police station.

This information was not well received by the V.I.Ps assembled to congratulate each other and exchange gifts. Where Arthur would have got the money to build a new Church House in those days I know not, for the congregation was so poor that the linoleum in the vestry was paid for with farthings brought by the ladies of the Guild, and any bread left over from Communion was gratefully received by folk glad to get it. But knowing Arthur, he would have found the money somehow.

We often complain about the stress of ministry these days, but it must have been far greater in the 'good old days'. Even in my own early ministry there was real poverty in the Victorian slum tenements with ancient spiral staircases. It was common for ladies to say they couldn't come to church because they didn't have a good coat. Later, Marks & Spencer would change this so everyone could afford good clothes for the first time. Looking now at old slides I took of the streets, I wonder why I was so blind to the conditions around me, but when you live in a place you really don't see it until you take pictures.

I saw a great deal of Arthur after I became parish minister in 1960, but I had to go looking for Sydney Warnes. I found him in his old age retired to Douglas, Lanarkshire, and brought him to the centenary of the church in 1973. He still had that twinkle in his eye which spoke volumes about a young minister who went to Bridgeton (without a shirt to his back, I have been told), and in four years resurrected a dead cause. I went with Alex Mair to his funeral, and was saddened to see so few folk there to honour his memory. Space does not allow me to tell all I know of these two fine ministers, but perhaps Oliver Goldsmith says it for me in 'The Deserted Village'.

"There where a few torn shrubs the place disclose,
The village preacher's modest mansion rose.
A man he was, to all the country dear,
And passing rich with forty pounds a year;
Remote from towns he ran his godly race,
Nor e'er had changed, nor wished to change his place;
Thus to relieve the wretched was his pride,
And even his failings leaned to Virtue's side;
But in his duty prompt at every call,
He watched and wept, he prayed and felt, for all.
And, as a bird each fond endearnent tries,
To tempt its new "fledged offspring to the skies;

He tried each art, reproved each dull delay,
Allured to brighter worlds, and led the way."

THE REV. JOHN SIM
AND MY ARRIVAL AS HIS ASSISTANT IN 1955

Arthur Gray moved to Aberdeen, but in spirit he never really left Bridgeton, and during his very many appearances on television, for which he received an Honorary D.D. from Glasgow, he constantly referred back to his time there.

Following Sydney and Arthur came my 'bishop', John Sim, who was (and is!) an organiser. He took all the work of his predecessors and gave it shape and direction. Medium height, slim, blunt spoken, John hard-worked himself into a severe skin condition. One of the old Iona school of ministers, who earned their collar and title 'Reverend' the hard way, John did not wear his heart on his sleeve, but he was a loyal friend to have when you needed one.

During his ten years in Bridgeton, he had to operate Church House without the later government funding of youth work which came in with the famous Kilbrandon Report. When I arrived, I attended a meeting of forty voluntary leaders, under his chairmanship, to discuss how on earth the Club could pay a £200 debt which a previous Boys' Leader had left behind - a fortune in those days. During his time at St. Francis-in-the-East, John Sim effectively organised the, by now large, congregation so that it became, for the first time, self-supporting; something I insisted upon maintaining when I eventually followed him.

My son likes to remind me how fortunate I was to go as Assistant to St. Francis-in-the-East and enter into the ethos and history of such a dynamic Iona parish. John Sim recorded the church's story in a booklet called 'A Light in Bridgeton', and got the University Art Department to paint a huge mural on the wall of the chancel, showing the founding of St. Francis-in-the-East. Not a sentimental man, when John left Bridgeton he did so without a look back, and I hardly saw him again for the next thirty-five years. I have an abiding memory of John dealing at a Kirk Session with one of those obnoxious elders you seem to find in every Session: a nasty, runt of a guy. John listened to this exasperating nark, took off his clerical collar, laid it on the table and pointing to it said, "Sir, you may not respect me, but you will certainly respect this!" Nobody ever put one over on John Sim!

In 1958, after three years as the Assistant to John, I considered joining the newly formed Gorbals Group. Wisely, I decided there was no future for me there, and resolved to become a 'worker priest', living on in the Club with Mr Hay, the caretaker, and doing an outside job. The idea of worker priests was in vogue at the time, a French attempt to place the ministry *in situ* in the work place (Industrial Mission was all the go then). Unfortunately, *in situ*ing was hard to come by, and for twelve weeks I unsuccessfully sought employment in local factories.

The problem was that I usually ended up in the manager's office trying to explain why on earth I wanted a job - any kind of a job. The manager would be an acquaintance through an industrial chaplaincy I had been doing, or even a pal through the Bridgeton Business Club. They did all they could to help me. In other words, they politely refused to employ me for my own good, and that of their own business!.

When a friend in Templeton's huge local carpet factory finally phoned me offering a job, I was highly relieved (being penniless). However, as I went there I met one of the Club Senior boys coming out of the place. It turned out he had been sacked, and I was his replacement! I took the despondent young chap back into Templeton's and persuaded them to re-employ him, thus sacrificing myself in a good cause. So much for my career as a 'worker priest'. It seemed like a good idea at the time, but when I look back my real motive for staying on at the Club was because my football teams were doing very well, and I couldn't live without them!

The £6 a week I earned as an Assistant Minister had not enabled me to save up for a rainy day, and, being self-employed, I got no benefits. So I had to reconsider my noble plans and ideals. When the headmaster of the local Bernard Street Secondary School, where I had acted as school chaplain, suggested I join his staff temporarily for a couple of months, it was an offer I could not refuse. Once finished there, I was then passed on to another Secondary: Wellshot School, Shettleston. So for, the next two years, I stayed on living in the Club, running my football teams, and trying to pass myself off as a school teacher.

In Wellshot School (where my wife-to-be was teaching too), the headmaster was a Mr Drummond, a small man in a black gown who welcomed me into my new job by handing me a time-table of maths and science. When I protested my utter ignorance of both these subjects, he placed a kindly hand upon my shoulder saying, "Go forth and teach". Such a great act of faith on his part moved me deeply, and I went forth to teach maths and science. The interest in these subjects on the part of my pupils was minimal, and my experiments and lectures proved less than inspiring, but if the boys and girls didn't learn much, I certainly did. To teach in a Junior Secondary School provides more instruction in human nature than all the theological, philosophical, and psychological studies put together. All ministers should be compelled to teach for two years before they are released from captivity into the wild.

Teaching in the Art department was a young man called Alasdair Gray. At the time he was painting a wonderful mural on the walls of the old Greenhead Church (now demolished, mural and all, alas!). The mural depicted the whole Bible and it covered every nook and cranny of the church interior, and I enjoyed going along with him to see it. Alasdair has since become famous as a painter and novelist, and I am mentioning him here so I can get in a bit of name-dropping. Later on, I will mention God, and that will really impress you!

John and Jean Sim passed ten demanding years in St. Francis-in-the-East. Money was a huge problem at the Club, he had a very busy parish, a congregation of over six hundred, and every organisation imaginable! No wonder John's nerves and health were not in great shape when he left. Typical of the man's matter-of-fact outlook, he put all that behind him and moved forwards to pastures new. In 1960, he accepted a call to Kirkcaldy Old Parish. He claims I hung around waiting him out, but I was not the first to be invited to fill the vacancy. Eventually, I was called upon to fill John's 'vestry-creepers' (shoes to you), and I did so with alacrity. I had long walked the mean streets absolutely certain this would one day be my parish, and so it turned out in the end, as it was meant to do.

ELEVATION TO THE PARISH MINISTER'S JOB,
AND THE END OF A BACHELOR LIFE.

I moved out of Church House and into the manse overlooking the Glasgow Green. Those five years of living in a shoebox-sized room in the Club's insalubrious environment had left me looking pale and haggard - so folk anxiously told me. Now I had a new abode: a nine apartment flat with enormous rooms.

My pal from University, Tom Skinner, moved in with me. Tom worked for the Clyde Shipbuilders' Federation, and spent his days trouble-shooting up and down the river. Teddy Taylor, now an M.P., was Tom's office junior. We were joined by Sandy, a Cairn terrier possessed of an uncertain temper and a taste for human flesh. There was plenty of space for the three of us, as the flat was a veritable Versailles of a tenement flat: it had a hall forty feet long, a ballroom, a maid's room, a kitchen with a bed recess for a live-in cook, plate-glass windows, nine fireplaces, and an average winter temperature of minus ten degrees. The apartment was a left-over from the era when the Green was fashionable and lined with wealthy merchants' mansions. I remember overhearing a young couple pointing up at the windows and saying with awe, "That's Mr Shackleton's mansion". Well, manse sounds like mansion!

I lived in the kitchen with my few possessions and the dog, and soon discovered that I had not moved up the social scale as far as I thought I had. The man in the flat above played his piano through the weekend nights and the only tune he knew was "Shine on Harvest Moon". With the exception of the phantom pianist, the neighbours were pleasant enough, and scratching rude remarks about Glasgow Rangers on my front door amused some of the younger Irish among them. Gradually, Pakistani families began to move into the close, bringing the odour of curry, and invitations to the Muslim Mission were shoved through the door. Two Pakistani brothers were first to come, and they were not enamoured at the sight of some of their fellow countrymen moving into our close. They explained to me that they definitely did not know these other people, and were not encouraging them to come and join some sort of conspiracy to take over Scotland. I suppose they worked on the theory that two's company, three's a crowd!

A decent, hard-working Irish neighbour used to ask me to go and tell his boys that they ought to behave themselves and attend mass! Another Irish lady neighbour thought her flat was haunted, so she filled it with the most ghastly religious pictures and had the priest in to exorcise the ghost. A young man from along the street came to see me about taking literacy classes; he was very clever but came from a remote part of Ireland and, being a Protestant, he said he had never been to school. As an old Bridgeton lady said: "It's hard these days to know if you're in Bengal or Donegal!"

My salvation from death by malnutrition came in the form (and very nice form too) of Margaret Brown, daughter of Dr. & Mrs James Brown of Dennistoun. Margaret had returned from teaching in the African Girls' High School, Kenya, during the Mao Mao terror. I tried to lure her into the Girls' Leader's job at Church House, and she was so impressed, by my designs and charms, that she took off to the United States for a year, leaving me to pine away in her absence. However, when she returned, the scales fell from her lovely eyes, she saw my potential, took out adoption papers and married me. We had known each other from a distance on Iona, but it was not until I saw her in a friend's manse that I fell for her on the spot. Selfishness divides, they say, but love multiplies, and in due course our son Scott and daughters Alison and Joy turned up to seal the deal.

With Margaret in, and Tom out, the flat began to take on a civilised appearance. Infant Scott was taken along to a playgroup in nearby Community House where he rubbed toys with the weans of Richard Holloway, now a celebrity T.V. bishop, who was in those days priest of a wee, red-brick Episcopalian church in the Gorbals. Scott would come home speaking of his friend 'Suzy-Wendy', the early version of Wendy Alexander, MSP. I had become a family man and, through my son, was becoming socially very well connected.

CHURCH HOUSE - GOOD TIMES. BAD TIMES.
AND 'WE SHALL REBUILD'

Geoff Shaw came to Church House as Boys' Leader in the same year as I did, and, when he left after two years, he was replaced by the Assistant at Glasgow Cathedral, George Buchanan-Smith. When George left in 1960, he was followed by John Webster, Assistant at Wellington Church. John left for India in 1965, and the Girls' Leader, Joyce Campbell, departed a year later. There followed a troubled period for the Club, with no settled leadership, and dry rot.

One Friday night in September 1969, having struggled on for four years, I sat alone in the vestry, despairing of keeping Church House from demolition. We had no fulltime leaders. The dry rot had not been eradicated. It looked like the bitter end. Then a 'coincidence' - a miracle! A young stranger appeared from the far side of the city; he did not know me, had never seen Church House, and knew nothing of its problems. He brought with him an old Club Annual Report and had come to offer his services as a voluntary leader. Thus did the good Lord save his servant's bacon in the hour of need! Had Tony Ireland not walked into the vestry that night, Church House would not be here today. He brought a glimmer of hope.

Coincidentally, the following Sunday, Alex Mair turned up at the church. A former Club boy, I hadn't seen Alex for a long time and I asked him what he was doing. He replied that he was taking a Local Authority course in youth work. I snapped him up! With Tony and Alex, two keen young men, I decided to run the Club myself, telling the congregation they would see me Sundays, etc., but I would be at Church House every night of the week henceforth. The three of us soon got the place up and running. But that still left the tremendous problem of saving the building.

This was achieved (another miracle), and in 1974, the rebuilt Club opened its doors. In 1971 I offered Alex the full-time job, and shortly afterwards, another former Club member, Margaret Beaton, was given the Girls' Leader's job. In 2001, we celebrated Alex's thirty years service. Stunned by his sudden death shortly after this, a new computer area was dedicated to his memory. Alex is a great loss to the Club and to me personally - one of the few men I could talk to in mutual respect and understanding. Margaret Beaton is still there, carrying the flag for us.

It was a sacrificial decision for both Alex (and his wife, Cathie), and Margaret to give up their jobs for an uncertain future working at the Club with virtually no reliable income. Training for the diaconate at St. Colm's, Edinburgh, gave them security but not much of a stipend. I told them that once they had set their hand to the plough at Church House they would never be able to return to their old lives. There is no looking back in the Kingdom of God.

Many Minister's Assistants have come and gone over the years - at first, like myself, through the Iona Community, then later through the generosity of Newlands South Church, the members there sharing their own Assistants with us in Bridgeton. So we have had Assistants from Australia, America, Holland, even Fife! The interesting thing is that the Club youngsters thought that, no matter their accent, all these

Alex Mair's first day as warden,1970

Queen Mary Street, opposite the church

incomers came from a mythical land called 'Edinburgh'.

We have had voluntary leaders from all the 'airts and pairts', folk of all ages, from all walks of life, all parts of the country: Charles Pilkington, of Pilkington Glass, taking gymnastics; Tor, a Norwegian, running the football. The Club was an international meeting ground, and local helpers and youngsters experienced the wider world church. It is not the atheists, the agnostics, or the do-gooders, for all their talk, who turn up and turn out, night after night and get the job done. It is the humble Christians.

The history of the church is one of repeated deaths and resurrections (as Calvin pointed out), and the wee kirk in Queen Mary Street died and rose again to be blest with an 'apostolic succession' of dedicated, able leaders. As P. T. Forsyth said, "The true archbishops are the archbelievers". The constitution of Church House states that its aim is to incarnate the Gospel so that Christ is seen amongst His people. The years have tried and tested that aim and purpose, and there are lessons here to be learnt. So many congregations today are going the same way as the nine Church of Scotland charges which did not survive in Bridgeton during my time there, To them add the Methodists, Baptists, Salvation Army, Episcopalians, Congregationalists, who were all wiped out. Today, of the seventeen parish churches in 1929, only one remains - St.Francis-in-the-East (now Bridgeton-St.Francis-in-the-East following the union in 1986, with the former Bridgeton Parish Church). Once regarded as the Cinderella of local churches, why, then, has St. Francis-in-the-East survived where so many others have vanished?

Sometimes, a chaplain in Barlinnie would telephone to say he had one of our church members inside. The Club boys did not distinguished between membership of the Church and of the Club - and that made me feel proud! Pride can be a good thing: when Frankie Vaughan visited Easterhouse, bringing a lot of television publicity to the wayward youths there, one of our own Club boys complained to me sourly, "Why has he gone there? We're bigger hooligans in Brigton than them!" There's local pride for you, and a good thing too! When an outsider said one night in the Club, "Bridgeton is a dump", an offended boy snapped, "Aye, it's a dump - but its a good dump!" *Hear, hears* all round! To commend the boy for his loyalty, I awarded a free penny-snake from the canteen.

Chapter 2

"Some gods are angry with fortunate men, as the goddess Nemesis seems to be to most people. But the statues of gods should be made cheerful and smiling so that we may smile back at them rather than fear them."
(Epicurus. 341-271 B.C.)

ARRIVAL

A funny thing happened to me on the way to the pulpit ...

One September Sunday in 1955, as I waited to follow the beadle into the church to start my first Service in St. Francis-in-the-East, he turned and whispered to me, "Keep it cheery, Bill, keep it cheery". Resolving there and then to take his advice to 'keep it cheery', both in and out the pulpit, I little realised how difficult it would be at times to keep cheery during the wild and wonderful years that lay ahead of me in Bridgeton. Here I was, standing on the threshold of the ministry, fresh from university, an impressively sincere young man if ever there was one, proficient in Greek and Hebrew, but sadly innocent of the hazards of youth club work in Glasgow's East End. I had a lot to learn about refereeing on the bloody fields of Glasgow Green!

As a new recruit to the Iona Community, I had been sent to serve for a two years Assistantship under the Rev. John Sim, ministering to a densely populated parish notorious for its appalling housing conditions. John had an Assistant, two full-time Club Leaders, and an elderly caretaker, Bobby Hay, who lived in Church House. Mr. Hay's wife had been recently knocked down and killed in an accident, and hoping my company would keep him from depression, it was arranged for me to lodge with Bobby in his wee flat.

It was a sunny morning as I arrived, carrying all my worldly goods. I picked my way along the rubbish strewn lane which led to the battered door of Church House. A small boy sitting on a high wall fell off as I passed and landed at my feet. As I anxiously picked him up, he rubbed his cropped skull and moaned, "Ah hiv stoatet ma heid aff the grun!" As neither his 'heid' nor 'the grun' seemed any the worse for the collision, I proceeded on my way and knocked the door. Scripture states, "Knock and it shall be opened unto you" - but I soon discovered that at Church House for 'knock' read 'kick'. After considerable kicking, the big, blistered, scarred door opened, and Mr Hay, welcomed me into my new home.

Church House was a huge old church with a very high steeple, the walls blackened, the windows boarded up and covered with tattered blackout material left over from the war years when the Club began. Entering took you into a pitch-dark cavern around which ran a dusty gallery, half stripped of its pews and timbers to provide fuel for the Club's boiler. The floor space below the gallery was divided off by rickety wooden partitions into a chapel, games rooms, toilets, and a canteen. The upper and lower halls of the former church building had been turned into a gym for floor soccer, a 'library' room (with piano but no books!), an office, and the caretaker's flat which I was to share with Mr Hay.

The flat consisted of a small kitchen with a bed-recess, a parlour (full of jumble sale junk), a wee bedroom, and an inside toilet. Mr Hay slept in the kitchen, and I occupied the iron-lung sized bedroom which contained a wardrobe, a card-table, a chair, and a wall-to-wall double bed. It was just possible to squeeze into my room sideways, and to get into my bed by climbing over the footboard. A window in my Lilliputian cell relieved the claustrophobia. As it overlooked the lane's crumbling brick wall and the middens of a back court, it was a scene in which only L. S. Lowry could have found artistic inspiration. However, one must try to keep cheery at all times, and I was assisted towards this desirable end by the sight of a burst water main which shot a fountain high in the air from the day I arrived to the day I left Bobby's flat some five years later.

To continue this conducted tour, Mr Hay's kitchen formed the living room in which the two of us lived, moved (where possible), and had our being. It had a jawbox sink under a window from which could be seen, in all its glory, Willie Wilson's scrapyard, a tottering stockade built from sheets of rusty corrugated iron and broken doors into which had accumulated every kind of human discard from old ovens to broken prams. Mr Wilson's backcourt shanty town was surrounded by crumbling tenements and, even on the sunniest day, the view from our kitchen window did little to lift the spirits. Nights were even more dispiriting, tormented and sleepless, owing to the melancholy howlings of Willie's Alsatian guard dog. A small, reclusive man, Willie was one day stabbed to death in his yard, a tragic event which made the dog howl all the more. Tossing restlessly, the Alsatian howling and the mice scrabbling around under the bed, how I wished that the murderers had stabbed the Alsatian instead of its owner! And there was another handicap to peaceful slumber ...

On my first night in Church House, I was finally about to fall into the relief of a blessed coma, when the bed springs began to vibrate with increasing intensity until, after climaxing at 9.5 on the Richter Scale, the earth-shaking, body-racking tremors gradually subsided. I lay there trembling, lathered in sweat, panic stricken - Good Lord! had I suffered a heart attack? With daylight came the good news that I had not had a coronary; and the bad news that a railway tunnel ran directly below my bed. Every night a train passed beneath my fatigued, recumbent body, dragging millions of tons of pig iron to destinations unknown. One night a tremendous explosion left me wondering if the train engine's boiler had exploded, but it was probably only someone testing a hydrogen bomb and nothing to worry about.

To the nocturnal visitations of the 'ghost train', the dog's laments, and the scampering mice were added the nightly visitations of the midden men, phantoms who arrived with darkness to hurl empty ash cans around the backcourts and bellow instructions to each other amidst the deafening din. Into this infernal cacophony mixed the evensong of pneumatic drills as road repair gangs dug up tram lines under brilliant, blinding arcs lamps. I had more sleepless nights than MacBeth!

Having survived my first night, my first breakfast also turned out to be an alarming experience. Mr Hay had a mentally disturbed, mangy cat, and before breakfasting, he would go to the fishmonger's and return with a big, smelly herring for this ferocious feline's *petite dejeuner.* As the beast screamed and clawed up the nearest trouser leg, Mr Hay would slap this fish on the linoleum floor with a sickening thwack fit to put a walrus off its breakfast. With much tigerish tearing and crunching, the fish went down well with the pussy, but not with me and my cornflakes. Fish and I have never got on well together since.

A further reason for my distaste for fish was due to the cooking of our Girls' Leader, Monica Morris. My main meal of the day was one prepared by Monica in the canteen for the voluntary leaders who came straight from work before the Club opened. For a hungry bachelor like myself, this arrangement seemed a good thing; that is it did until I tasted Monica's cooking. Indelibly imprinted on my memory is the fish dish she laid on the table at my first evening meal in Church House. Entombed in an impenetrable rubbery substance purporting to be a white sauce, Monica had buried, alive and in the raw, some sort of marine creature. Managing to conceal deep fears that culinary martyrdom would go with my new job, I politely did the 'curate's egg' act and assured Monica that my portion of her cuisine was 'good in parts'. Anyway, the cat enjoyed it. The experience proved to be a useful preparation for visiting church members. On one such visit, I was kindly invited by the lady of the house to dine with the family. She set before me a plate containing nothing but a mountain of cold cauliflower which, somehow, I managed to choke down with a ghastly smile on my lips. My advice to young bachelor ministers is, therefore: time your visits to avoid mealtimes. Play safe and eat alone; Scotch pies and Ambrosia rice pudding make a most satisfactory diet, and will see you through until you can make arrangements, as I did, to marry a teacher of Home Economics.

In all the five years I shared the small flat with Mr Hay, we never exchanged a disagreeable word. That we got on so well was due to Bobby's tolerance, something which I considerably tested from time to time. One night, having been to the cinema with Geoff Shaw, we returned to discover that I had gone out and left on the electric iron; this had not only burnt its way through the ironing board, but also through the floor of Bobby's flat and was hanging by the flex from the ceiling of the room below - still switched on! Luckily, the lack of oxygen, the result of closed doors, kept Bobby's flat from bursting into flames, but the house, like Isaiah's temple, was filled with dense smoke, to the ruination of most of Bobby's possessions. He never complained to me, which was quite remarkable under the circumstances. You could truly say that Mr Hay and I got on like a house on fire! I should add that it did occur to me that had I burnt down Church House, the fire insurance would have built a fine, new Club - but one must resist such regretful, tempting thoughts!

I think that our both being staunch Socialists, and lovers of 'the beautiful game' bonded us both together like father and son. When I became parish minister, replacing John Sim in 1960, a lady friend from a posh part of the city remarked how odd it was to hear the minister refer to the caretaker as 'Mr Hay' (never 'Bobby'), and everyone else call the minister 'Bill'; but I never could bring myself to say 'Bobby' to a man my father's age. He died watching a game at Hampden Park, and was no mean footballer himself, even in his sixties. Whenever I see Fred Astaire in an old film, I see a look-alike for Bobby Hay: neat in appearance, slight of build, light on his feet, dancing round the floor playing floor soccer.

I guess that just about cleans up my living conditions in Church House, which I managed to conceal from my mother! I should add that my father received the news of my appointment to a church in Bridgeton with a noticeable lack of enthusiasm, for he seemed to regard the district as a death trap. His attitude surprised me, as he and Mum were from Kinning Park, beside Govan, and not a part of the city which looked to me to be any different from Bridgeton. In the event, I had providentially arrived in exactly the right place for me to be at the right time. Increasingly, I sensed that all my past life had been a preparation for coming to Bridgeton. 1 was at home in these dilapidated surroundings; amidst the whirl of youthful activity; it was exciting to find myself working with some of the greatest people I have known - intelligent, healthily motivated, dedicated. The work rate was killing, and the expectations were so high that I have never settled for lower standards since. Many other young ministers never had the opportunity which came my way.

St. Francis-in-the-East Kirk was three streets away from Church House, and a concert was held there to introduce to the flock the new Minister's Assistant (note, *not* Assistant Minister, you knew your place in those days!). Everyone was Glasgow-friendly, and the concert boisterous and jolly. When it finished, I was on a 'high'. Then Mr Sim took me aside and brought me down to earth, telling me to remember two things: firstly, that I was not doing him a favour by coming and, secondly, that I was being paid to perform the tasks which he assigned. John then handed me a pencil and a pad and told me to go round writing down all the close numbers of the parish. Having just completed seven years of advanced education, this affronted my dignity no end. However, having laboured in a shipyard, unquestioning obedience to authority had been instilled into me, so I meekly submitted. It turned out to be one of the best things I ever did; to this day I can identify people by the close in

Bobby Hay, John Webster and Sandy

The lane to the club door, 1958

which they stayed. Do ministers walk round their streets these days, as John Sim made me do at the beginning of my ministry? It is a very valuable training exercise.

Years later, when returning with a colleague from a conference in Rouen, we went into a very big café in central London. It was early morning, around 7.30 a.m., so the place was empty. Eventually, a man entered and sat at the far end near the door. On our way out, passing him, I said to the man, "I can't remember your name, but you stayed at 14 Marquis Street and you owe me three quid!" He was dumbfounded to be caught in such an unlikely place at such a unlikely hour! His name was Campbell, and no, I didn't get back the three quid he cadged out of me to pay his electricity bill!

So, sporting my Edinburgh University green and white striped scarf (a garment I quickly discarded in deference to local sentiment), I settled in to my new home and job. The summer days on Iona, living in and helping to rebuild the Abbey, were past. I had arrived in Brigton. A nice, quiet chaplaincy in a lighthouse would probably have suited my modest talents better than the inner-city of Glasgow, but there I was, George MacLeod's cannon-fodder, and there I would remain, one way or another, for the next fifty years.

Chapter 3

Containing the story of how I visited St.Francis-in-the-East, its daughter Church House, and Iona Abbey for the first time, while working in a shipyard to ensure Britannia rules the waves.

"I take care to travel only on Italian ships because,
in the event of disaster, there is none of that nonsense
about women and children first."
(Noel Coward).

The day I moved into Church House was not my first visit. During the summer of 1953, Penry Jones, Industrial Secretary of the Iona Community, ran what was called The Student Work Community. His idea was for the group of theological students joining the Community to work in industrial jobs of various kinds, and share their incomes as an experiment in 'economic witness'. I knew Penry before he went to work for the Community, and was glad to join the project and find a job during the University vacation.

We lived in the old Community House in Clyde Street, a rambling warehouse of a building with sagging floors upstairs, and a big, public restaurant downstairs. We were to sleep on army-type bunk beds, but I slept on a couch as far away as possible from a Welsh bloke whose snoring, like John Peel's famous horn, 'would awaken the dead'. I was sent by Penry to work in Fairfield Shipyard, Govan, as a humble labourer. After the first week, the upper-class Anglican in our group announced that he was departing to attend to "urgent business in Lincoln"; adding, as he departed, that working nightshifts in a bakery is "not much of a life". The plan to share our incomes did not last long either.

As part of the programme, we were to visit an 'Iona parish' in Bridgeton called St. Francis-in-the-East; so, one Friday evening, we visited St. Francis-in-the-East Church House Youth Club. We hiked past Glasgow Cross, then along London Road, a canyon-like thoroughfare lined with black tenements and faintly menacing 'corner boys' and, a few hundred yard short of Celtic Park, I got my first view of the Club.

The sight was daunting - outside, a run-down old church building; inside, a very rowdy dance. A few moments after our arrival, a flustered Monica Morris began shooing everyone outside - seemingly, some of the youths had made off with the gramophone records. After the records (old '78s') mysteriously returned, I waltzed around with a young lady, bumping into a Teddy Boy who growled, "Hey! watch it, you!" This was my first encounter of the third kind with a Club member.

Making the two mile walk back to Iona Community House, I little suspected that in the near future I would be living in the Club I was happily leaving behind. When the time came, George MacLeod pointed a Lord Kitchener finger at me saying, "Your Community needs you on the Eastern Front". Of course, I pleaded with him for a posting as chaplain to Devil's Island, or as padre to the Foreign Legion (where I could forget), but to no avail - it was to be "Church House, Bridgeton, here I come!"

The Sunday visit to St. Francis-in-the-East church introduced me to the Rev. Mr. Sim, and his Assistant, a handsome young fellow called Ian MacLeod, over whom the girls were swooning. Ian preached on the text, "Take up thy bed and walk", and I was not long in learning that beds were not the only things which 'walked' in the parish! It was fascinating to see the Community's 'Four Emphases' of Mission, Healing, Politics, and Liturgy operating in what was a very busy, vibrant congregation. I was quite captivated, and also fascinated to learn about the remarkable history of the church.

THE SHIPYARDS - ALL THE THINGS I LEARNT,
AND PETER THE GREAT FAILED TO LEARN!

Together with the student from Wales, I was sent to Fairfield's in Govan - he to the engineering shop, myself to the shore park. Shores are used to shore up a ship being built in a berth. The huge ships we were building stood on row upon row of these timber supports made from cut up sections of old telegraph poles. Cutting and stacking these in the 'shore park' (our domain), was our job and, when required, we positioned them upright in the immense, dark cave under the ship's bottom. I laboured at this task from 7.45 a.m. to 5.30 p.m., with two nights and a Sunday thrown in for good measure. The Welsh student soon threatened to leave his allocated job, for he was a pacifist and had learnt the engines being produced in Fairfields' were for warships. I pointed out to him that he had money in the Post Office Savings Bank, and could not but contribute to armaments production, so he decided to stay under protest.

My arrival created something of a stir amongst the gang of a dozen men I was to join, and they were very curious to know what I was doing there. I first saw them sitting on a pile of logs eating their lunch, and they established communion with me by offering me a share of their 'pieces' and tea. They were all R. C.s and Celtic supporters, except for a speechless old shipwright who, being our only tradesman, I presumed to be a 'Prodie'. With commendable ecumenical generosity, I was sort of adopted by the gang as a kind of pet student in whom they took a certain degree of pride. Our foreman, an Irish Atlas of immense strength, possessed a remarkable immunity from pain. When our antique mobile crane came off the rails and let its load fall on one of his hands, crushing it, he simply stuck it under his oxter, and walked away for treatment saying, "Carry on, bhoys, Oi'll be back in a wee while." They were a tough lot.

The shore park was on the river bank, close to Govan Old Parish Church, a swampy corner of the mile-long shipyard, a rickety shed providing cramped cover during the frequent downpours. The first thing I noticed in the shed was the powerful body odour; after a week in the job, I was adding to the pong myself. Washing and toilet facilities were medieval, to say the least. Arrangements for making tea were equally primitive. It was my job to gather all the tea cans and take them into the welding shed, where boiling water could be obtained by plunging a red hot iron bar into each can. This manoeuvre had to be carried out unobserved by the gaffers patrolling around in bowler hats, and this was not easily done while carrying ten boiling hot cans of tea! Detection could have meant dismissal at one hour's notice, but I was never caught, owing to my woodcraft training in the Boy Scouts.

After several weeks outdoors, my face was so dark from exposure that a friend gasped when he saw me! I was so tired at the end of the day that I just could not read a newspaper, or pay attention during our meetings to discuss the merits and problems of a communal life. The merits stemmed from the realisation that Christianity is a lot easier in theory than it is in practice; the problems from sorting out relationships and equitably distributing worldly goods which, even in a small group, did not come easily. Sharing out our incomes fairly (what we called in high-falutin jargon, 'economic witness') was the main bone of contention. Some, like myself, worked lots of hours, while others had it easy. Ergo, why should we all get the same share out of the common pot? Our wages were all different, so why should some subsidise the others? The old maxim, "Christianity stops at the garden gate" came home to roost. We were learning the only way anybody ever learns - the hard way - learning how to preach meaningfully to people who had to relate what they heard on a Sunday to the world in which they lived and worked on a Monday. In the end, we agreed to keep our own overtime, and share the rest, illustrating George MacLeod's favourite quote from Peguy: "All things begin in mysticism, and end up in politics."

Life in the yards was, I soon discovered, very dangerous; a chap was decapitated by a loose raft, which slid over the ship's side as he stood looking down from the deck. And a young laddie was drowned in the dock while I was there. One Sunday I came pretty close to the Grim Reaper myself, when one of the lofty cranes touched and dislodged the scaffolding around a half-built ship, and down came the lot. We were underneath, unloading a lorry when this avalanche of planks and steel fell, and I watched it all cascading upon us as if it were dropping in slow motion. Fortunately, one of the gang quickly grabbed me and pulled me under the lorry, or I would have been killed. The lorry was wrecked, and I was physically sick with shock for a long time afterwards. I was there in summer; how men worked in winter conditions high up on the scaffolding, or on the exposed, icy steel decks, beats me!

The shore park, overlooked by the tenements of Govan Cross, was surrounded by a barbed-wire topped wooden wall. A shipyard and prisoner of war camp had much in common - particularly a great interest in escaping. When an evening football match was on there would be a Great Escape, lines of men climbing the walls and making a run for it. Another dodge was to avoid work by hiding in piles of wood, and I saw two electricians do this successfully for a fortnight. My gang had a very comfy 'secret garden' of its own, in which we played cards snug and undetected. In such a vast area as the yard, it was easy to get 'lost'.

I had just got into the natural rhythm of playing hide and seek with the gaffers, seeing to it that we did as little work as possible, enjoying a life of leisure and, most importantly, staying alive, when, on one disastrous afternoon, we were despatched to unload lorries filled with keel blocks and then carry these to the far end of a vacant berth in which a new liner was to be built. Keel blocks are what the hull sits upon, solid oak, not too big to be lifted up and carried on the shoulder, but as heavy as lead. I staggered under the weight of hundreds of these blighters for hours until my shoulder was black and blue and my legs were collapsing. I fully earned my whole summer's wages in that one go!

Lateness in the yard was serious business, and being inside the gates counted for nothing. You had to go the full distance to your area time keeper's hut and collect a numbered metal disc. This you returned to him at lunchtime, and he gave it gave back to you when work restarted. I forgot to hand my number in one lunch break, causing great consternation amongst my shipmates, this being, in their eyes, a grave offence. The problem, it seemed to me, could quite easily be solved by my simply explaining to the time keeper my mistake; this innocent proposal was received by my colleagues with gasps of horror! No! what I had to do, ordered my gaffer, was go to the box after lunch, drop my numbered disc on the ground, bend down, pick it up, and tell the guy I had handed it in at lunchtime, as required, but that it must have fallen off the shelf of his hatch. This embarrassingly unlikely tale I told, with the accompanying actions, and to my relief, all went well. I had done the right thing, and everybody was happy, including the time keeper who could not have believed a word I said! It was brought home to me that there was a code, a system in the yard which everyone accepted because it resolved problems and brought harmony to all: the system has a name - it is called 'deception'. I learnt that honesty is not invariably the best policy in life, and that a little deception, in a good cause, can sometimes prove beneficial.

THE CYCLIST'S TALE

We were not the only pole cutters and shore handlers on the block - there was another and rival gang. I heard the foreman of this band of cut-throats was selling a bicycle, and, as inspection showed the machine to be in perfect order, and the tyres brand new, I bought it. A bike would enable me to pedal to work from Community House, without depending on the subway. However, after collecting it, I saw that the vendor had pulled a fast one and switched the new tyres for old worn ones. Buying the bike was my first mistake; trying to get my money back was my second.

Next day, at lunchtime, crowds of men were sitting in a circle enjoying the sunshine as I pushed the bike into the arena, drew a bead on the guilty party, and indignantly demanded the return of my investment. The temerity of this confrontational approach seemed to render him speechless, but he soon girded up his loins, gnashed his few teeth, and refused my request. I had not expected this. I awaited an explanation. The massed onlookers breathlessly awaited a fight. I found myself in a situation of considerable peril, and was giving urgent consideration to running away, when, mercifully, I was saved by the bell, so to speak! The blast of the yard's siren was sweet music in my ears as it summoned everyone back to their labours, and sounded a welcome 'all clear' for W.S. I cleared off swiftly, and still in possession of the bike.

Wars are often sparked off by small incidents, and so it proved in the "Mysterious Case of the Unreturned Bicycle". My own gang members were outraged at the behaviour of the rival gang's foreman, and sought revenge with perturbing enthusiasm. I had unwittingly provided them with an excuse to open hostilities with their old enemies; 'All for one, and one for all' - nobody was going to mess about with their student, poor innocent abroad that he was! I pleaded for peace and reconciliation in vain - the gang went on the warpath, and the 'War of the Bicycle Tyres' was declared. Mercifully, though sharp, the conflict was brief, and at the end of it we seem to have won, the opposition agreeing to refund my cash. The reason for their capitulation was that the misinformation had been circulated that I was a trainee priest, news which influenced the situation greatly to my advantage. My opponent, being an Irish R.C. had no wish to detract from his good prospects in the after-life by stealing from a holder of the keys to heaven!

When I took a day off to graduate Hons M.A. in the McEwan Hall, my gang kindly threw a party for me in The Vine, a wine shop of low reputation in Govan. When I left, after four months, they took me back there again, showing their affection by plying me with many drams which I could not, in politeness, refuse. I somehow wandered back to Community House not a little inebriated.

I can still vividly picture those men with whom I associated so closely day after day in the muddy shore park. As I took my leave, wee Alex said something I have never forgotten: "Bill," said he, "one day you'll drive past the gates of Fairfield's in your own car, and you'll not give a thought to us still in here." He was wrong about that: I have, indeed, prospered sufficiently to own a car, and I have often driven past the gates of Fairfield's, but I have never done so without remembering Alex's words, and giving him a passing thought. It is for such men that I have never abandoned the hope that one day every kirk will have a Regnal Circle.

During my summer time in the yards, the Iona Communion Service in the small chapel in Community House meant a great deal to me; indeed, Iona has provided me with a starting point for all my thinking and working ever since. The original purpose of the Community, the training of young ministers was of tremendous value, providing a daily discipline as well as a wide vision of the Creator. There is an urgent need for this today. The Iona Community must never lose sight of the special, unique purpose for which it was founded.

As part of the Student Work Community we visited Iona - my first trip there. The present cloisters and dormitory-refectory block were not built then, and we lived in a wooden hut, individual bedrooms being reached by a corridor running the length of the building as in a railway carriage - this gave it its nickname, the 'Rome Express', the destination to which its many critics believed the Community to be heading. It is difficult now to understand the hostility which the Community aroused in many quarters, and to be a Community minister could make obtaining a charge difficult. The 'Four Emphases' are pretty well welcomed by many people these days, but it was not so then.

As the summer of 1953 turned to autumn, I drew my wages of £21 for working two weeks, four nights and two Sundays, and, as rich as a tea biscuit, I went to Bradford for my final eighteen months there. Another stage in my preparation for a ministry in Bridgeton had passed, and, though I did not know it, I was right on course.

Chapter 4

When the news leaked out that I intended entering the ministry, one of my pals nearly fell off his bike! Ever since, I have been frequently asked, "Bill, how on earth did you ever become a minister?"

This chapter reveals that the rumour that my father was First Lord of the Admiralty (before becoming Warden of the Cinque Ports), and that my mother (or was it my nanny?) was a Duchess of the Austro-Hungarian Empire is not entirely true. The following is from recently released classified material.

I was born in Govan, not far from Fairfield's shipyard, in 1927. That was the year film star James Stewart astounded mankind by flying the Atlantic solo in 'The Spirit of St Louis'. 1927 was also the year when the 'talkies' came in, puzzling Harry Warner of Warner Bros., who asked, "Why the hell would anybody want to hear actors talk?" I was too young at the time to hear him say this, so I got off to a flying start in life, and started talking. However, sad to say, I had hardly got beyond saying "Mama" and "Papa" when Wall Street crashed, causing World War II and the demise of the British Empire. Through it all I have retained my own hair and teeth - which is no small achievement.

My father was an iron moulder. Like many men of that era, advanced education was impossible, so he spent a lifetime, proud of his skills (Glasgow was renowned for iron moulding), but personally unfulfilled. An easy-going soul, my abiding memory of him is of a cheerful man toddling homewards of a summer's evening in his sand-stiff working clothes, stopping in the street to talk to some wee children.

Dad was what Burns called "a man o' independent mind" - not half he was! He absolutely refused to clock on or off at work, considering it an indignity, and he would pack his tools and leave rather than make things he considered unworthy of his skills. Whenever he felt like a smoke, he sat down and stopped work. Bosses did not exist for my father, and they for their part wisely accepted his egalitarian ways for they knew he was their ablest worker. During his some thirty years of living in England, nothing would get him to go to work on a New Year's Day. I guess my own reputation as an anti-Establishment man goes back to Pop.

I am rather proud of the famous surname I acquired at birth, passed down from my Dad's great-great-grandfather, a certain Jonathan Shackleton, a muslin manufacturer from Airedale, who was residing at 93 Virginia Street in Glasgow city centre in 1848. Thus the Shackleton name came to my native city. His son opened a confectioner's shop in Eglinton Street, in the newly built upper-class Gorbals. There he earned the gratitude of children everywhere by inventing the sugar mouse and toffee whistle. He died in 1884 and, a century later, I was conducting interments in Sandymount cemetery unaware of the proximity of his remains.

My father's father was the master upholsterer responsible for the furnishings of Glasgow City Chambers. A great Queen's Park supporter, he saw them play in the English F. A. Cup. He also ran a Juvenile football team called 'Park United' which won just about everything in 1932. He married Isabella Sinclair, an Orcadian from South Ronaldsay. As a baby, having been found lying in the arms of her dead mother, she was raised by the Linklaters - the famous writer Eric Linklater and my father played together as boys. My Grannie's fisher folk parents were 'Muckle Jock', and 'Peedie Jeanie'. Widowed, Jock remarried and his second family helped crew the Longhope lifeboat which went down in the 1950s with the loss of all hands.

My father served throughout the Great War in the Royal Naval Division, an infantry unit formed by Churchill in 1914 from the Navy, R. N. V. R., and Royal Marines. He was eighteen. He won the Mons medal, with bar, and was wounded three times (the Somme, Arras, and Passchendaele). Before the battle of Gavrelle in 1917, while he was waiting to go 'over the top', he heard his aunt's voice saying, "You'll be all right". Taking cover in a shell-hole with a dozen or so others, a shell fell amongst them, throwing him in the air and killing every one of his mates. After the battle, shellshocked, he received a letter from home saying that the aunt whose voice he had heard had died in Orkney. By the armistice, he was the only man of his original 1914 battalion still on active service. Had he not taken pneumonia *en route* to Gallipoli, he would almost certainly have been killed there, his Collingwood Battalion being virtually wiped out during the fighting. While visiting Gallipoli recently, I conducted worship at the Cape Helles Memorial, not realising that my son, Scott, now Senior Corps Chaplain to the Royal Marine Commandos, had taken the Remembrance Sunday Service there the previous year. Dad would be proud to know that a grandson of his honoured the memory of such a fine Division.

Like other men who experienced the war, my father rarely mentioned it, but contrary to the popular view of the Great War he did not think it was 'futile' - like A. P. Herbert, another R. N. D. man, he believed that preventing the Kaiser winning was a good thing. Nor did his harrowing experiences disillusion him. He supported the inter-wars 'Peace Pledge' Movement, yet when war came in 1939 he snorted, "So, they want another go!", and was disappointed to find he was too old to enlist!

The Great War has made deep impression on me, and been a very important factor in my life and ministry. As a child, I was fascinated by my father's volumes about the war. The Great War was not long past during my boyhood, and in the local rag-store you could swop rags for Uhlans' helmets and French bayonets! The long lists of names on the war memorial drew me. A local pacifist shop window was completely filled with gruesome pictures of dead soldiers. Consciously, and subconsciously, I lived with the Great War. As we inherit our physical characteristics, so we inherit the extraordinary psychic experiences of our forebears. In some sense I was there in the Great War - one reason why I have been drawn to Regnal, a movement which began amongst the troops in the trenches. When Dad died, my mother threw out his sailor's 'ditty box', containing his records, and gave his bayonet to the police. Luckily, she kept his medals - his R.N.D. Mons Star with bar being rare these days. I guess his badly scarred leg and arm, and who knows what troubled dreams, had haunted her married life.

When my son Scott was taking some cadets on a visit to the Normandy beaches and battlefields, a Wren asked him who we were fighting against. Surprised, Scott told her it was the Germans. She looked puzzled: "But you said this is France. What were the Germans doing here?" Has the ugly shadow of the past now dispersed for new generations? I hope so. My daughter Joy teaches history and tells me that her pupils haven't heard of Vietnam, the Falklands, or even the first Gulf War.

My father's joke was that my mother was 'auld' when she married him (she was Annie McCulloch Paterson Auld). They were engaged for seven years. Dad tried his luck playing for a football team in New Jersey, and newly wed Mum was to join him there, but he returned home so I wasn't born a Yank! While working in Harland and Wolfe's Govan shipyard he was offered a job in a foundry in Preston. Glad of any employment in those days, he jumped at it. So, a babe in mother's arms, I was baptised into the United Free Church of Scotland, and transported ninety miles south of the border.

The Reformers called what we call coincidence, 'Prevenient Grace'. Chancing to be last out of the foundry that day, Dad was the one offered the job in Preston. I look back on my life as a series of remarkable coincidences and if "coincidence is the random plus the necessary", then I have done all right thanks to 'Prevenient Grace'.

THE LONG ROAD TO BRIDGETON

"There's a Divinity that shapes our ends,
Rough-hew them how we will."

I had the happiest boyhood possible. My father neither drank nor gambled, nor lifted a hand to me or my two young brothers (he had hands like iron too!). Mother was always short of money, but we were not poor, like some of my school mates who could not afford to buy one of those expensive new comics - *The Dandy* and *The Beano*. Our terrace house had three bedrooms, a front parlour, a cold water kitchen, and a lavatory outside in the yard. This mattered little to me as, like all the boys of my generation, I was only indoors to eat and to sleep. The Cubs and Scouts, football in all weathers, my £3.10s bicycle to go fishing, or north to the Lake District, or west to Blackpool and the seaside. Looking back, I am surprised I survived jumping dykes, shooting arrows, rafting on canals, and subjecting life and limb to every hazard. Dark winter evenings were spent reading, and listening to a wet-battery wireless under the light of the gas-mantle. Finally, Dad reluctantly abandoned his belief that the mellow glow of gaslight was beneficial for the eyes, and installed electricity. Saturday afternoons were spent at Deepdale watching 'North End', a team of Scotsmen in whom Dad delighted; all things Scottish being beyond his praise. He would cycle all the way home to Glasgow whenever possible.

We stayed near Preston railway station and Dad sometimes came home from work to find his homesick new wife gone, taking me with her to Glasgow. Eventually, mother settled; a typical housewife of those days, she rose at dawn to put her man off to work, shopped, and did the chores without complaint. I doubt if she ever slept; a tap at the door got her up! She was kindness personified - but cross her and you were black-balled forever!

The story which best typifies my mother's personality concerns the time she was buying toffees in the local Co-op: the manager weighed them on his scales, unwrapped a toffee, cut it in half, put half into my mother's poke, and half back into the sweetie jar. She never bought another thing in that shop! Sir Ernest Shackleton had the same temperament: those who had made trouble for him on his famous expedition to Antarctica received no honours, even McNeish, the ship's carpenter, who was with him in the *James Caird* on the epic voyage to South Georgia.

Having had her younger sister Betty commit suicide, due to a bad husband, Mum had very definite views on morality and the church: in those days the wording for the funeral service of a suicide was slightly different from the normal, and Betty's funeral left my mother with a lasting resentment against 'religion'. She did not speak to me for weeks after I decided to train for the ministry. At the same time she would not have allowed into her house the 'low-lifes' portrayed in today's T.V. 'Soaps'.

Mam loved theatre plays, and the music hall, and never entered a cinema. She had an aversion to making tea, put off by a nasty mouthful of tea-leaves as a girl, so I never drank anything but percolated coffee until in my late teens. She was also 'teetotal', often saying, "Alcohol has never passed my lips; in company, I just take a *Baby Cham*." She never knew that a *Baby Cham* was champagne, and we hadn't the heart to enlighten her. So Mam had the best of both worlds: she was a teetotaller who enjoyed a tipple at the same time!

From my father I got my love of books and learning. Every Saturday night, he took me to the library; and when war was declared in 1939, he handed me *Mein Kampf* to read though I was only twelve! Starting work at 7.30 a.m. and finishing at 5.30 p.m. I don't know how he found time for reading, and his hobby, collecting stamps. As a trade union branch treasurer, men called at the house for him to fill up forms, or write letters for them in his fine hand.

It was while walking together to the Saturday football that I broke the news to him that I intended entering the ministry and

Edinburgh University. I thought this would amaze him, but how you underestimate your old man! He had already read my mind full well! As Mark Twain put it, at seventeen you think your father knows nothing and by twenty-one you are amazed at how much he has learnt in four years! As a true Scot, Dad was a great believer in education, and I guess I had disappointed him when I dropped out of the Grammar School - but that story belongs to another chapter.

Chapter 5

In which I get a bit closer to examining how I came to be in Bridgeton and Church House through a series of remarkable 'coincidences'.

Of my infant's school I have but two memories: one of sharing lunch on my first day with my oldest pal, Arthur Nunn; the other of a boy (age seven) having his bare bottom skelped before the class for wandering into the girls' toilets. These days the young lady teacher concerned would be placed on the sex offenders' list!

At Primary School, thanks to the driving force of Miss Evans, I passed the eleven-plus and went on a scholarship to the fee-paying Preston Grammar School - Richard Attenborough made a film about a boy like me called *The Guinea Pig*. I found myself in a strange world of mullioned windows and ivy-clad walls, mixing with boys from wealthy homes in parts of town unknown to me. I missed my pals.

Like the rest of the boys, I lived through the war without noticing it very much. We were taught by masters brought out of retirement, and with so many younger men teachers away, and adults taking so little interest in the young, we boys often went over the limit. This helped me understand juvenile delinquents, for I was one myself (in an amateurish kind of way), and a useful experience for later in Church House.

Our boyish dream was that the school would be burnt down in an air raid by one of the 'Gerries' who peered down upon us from time to time from their Heinkels and Dorniers. No luck! What I did see, however, following Dunkirk, was the railway station with hundreds of French soldiers lying on stretchers - when they were moved, thousands of fag ends littered the platform. The Atlanta railway station scene in *Gone With Wind* always reminds me of it.

On the morning of 22nd June, 1941, Mr Lamont, the French master strode in to announce that the Germans had invaded the U.S.S.R., and predict the Russians would only last six weeks. It certainly looked that way at the time. The exciting thing for us boys was to sneak into an American airforce base and wander amongst the aircraft unchallenged! But of much greater interest to me was the white mouse I kept in my desk at school; and the joy of taking home a puppy - 'Rags'. My wife Margaret tells me that boys are boys, no matter where you go in the world, and she has been around.

One playtime, I looked over the playground fence into the adjacent park, which contained a huge army transit camp, and there was my cousin, Jim Tennant! He was moving south with the Highland Division, and he and his pal came home with me for the night. How Jim bewailed being a "silly wee laddie" for volunteering - sharing a bell tent with a bunch of drunks disgusted him! He thought the H. D. were going to invade Europe, but they went to El Alamein instead - where his pal was killed.

Over the same hedge, we boys often saw huge numbers of American soldiers in the transit camp; sloppy dressed but glamorous guys from the land of Hollywood, who gave us gum. Some negro soldiers were amongst them, and I remember one white G.I. saying to us, as some of these went by - "See them negras, they're trash, jist black trash!"

Then along came a major event in my life: after a Scout camp in 1941 I went to the pictures with some pals, crawled home in agony, finished up with a burst appendix, and took peritonitis (usually fatal in those days). I must have been in a bad way because it was reported in the street that 'that little Scotch lad has passed away'. But the reports of my death were greatly exaggerated! I had not, in fact, snuffed it; we Shackletons are survivors.

The illness left me a nervous wreck and I was sent to Glasgow for several months recuperation in the care of an aunt. Owing to losing a year at school, I was kept back in the Lower Fourths, so I left for a job as an apprentice printer. Printing was interesting, and it has been of value to me in the ministry, but it was not for me.

At the age of sixteen, I know not why, I suddenly developed a thirst for knowledge and began reading everything from T. S. Elliot to algebra. The tedious hours feeding a printing machine turned out to be ideal for studying, and by another one of those strange 'coincidences' which have shaped my life, the owner of the business (a Colonel Blimpish gentleman) happened to attend the same church which I had started attending with my pal, Arthur Nunn. On our first Sunday there, the very big organ's power supply failed and the minister, the Rev. John Gibbs, asked the two of us to pump it manually. When we emerged from the dusty interior, my boss was astonished to behold one of his apprentices! Thereafter he turned a blind eye to my surreptitious studies on his machinery, time, and premises.

"I AM THE DOOR"
JOHN 10:7

I started attending the Rev. John Gibb's Congregational church by pure chance (or by 'Prevenient Grace'). Arthur and I were keen on badminton, and a ginger-headed pal took us along to play in the hall there one evening. The following week, we hoped he would take us again, but he wasn't going so we went without him. As non-members, we stood outside a long time, hesitant over going in. Taking a chance, we pushed open the door and entered, and on that small decision my entire future life has hinged!

A Spitfire pilot on leave welcomed us, and awed us by throwing a screwed up chip paper right across the hall and through an open window! This convinced us the war was in good hands and that this badminton club was the place to be.

John Gibbs was a Southerner, come to Preston to be part of a 'team-ministry' involving several churches (where have I heard that one before?). After two years of no team-ministry appearing, he moved on to London to become Study Secretary of S. C. M. I did not hear of him again for thirty years, when I learned he had become an Anglican and the Bishop of Coventry.'

The entrance exam for London University could be taken in Manchester, so I studied old exam papers, took time off work, and passed all the subjects except maths. Having taught myself, I was very glad to have Marion Gibbs, who was a mathematician, tutor me through the maths resit. I had no intention of going to London University (I thought a University was for geniuses), and no idea what to do with my life, but as I spent more and more time with John and Marion Gibbs, it began to occur to me that there might be something in this Christianity after all.

During my post-peritonitis nervous collapse period, I had been converted in a tent on Eaglesham Green (I had family connections with the Tent Hall in Saltmarket), but once back in Preston with my pals the conversion soon wore off. It was when the Gibbs entered my life that I had presented to me for the first time the one version of The Faith which attracts me: an intellectually stimulating one (in those days Congregationalists, e.g. C. H. Dodd, were said to be all head and no tail, whereas the Baptists were said to be all tail and no head!). It was possible to be intelligent and highly educated and a Christian all at the same time! John Gibb's Reformed theology and worship emotionally appealed to me too; my father was right - "some things are in the blood".

During a quiz held in the manse, a quote came up and I identified it as from John Ruskin. This impressed John Gibbs (who hadn't known the answer), and he began considering this youth, with his rag-bag of knowledge, as a potential recruit for the holy ministry. I was nineteen, and now knew what I wanted to be: a minister.

Having turned eighteen shortly after V. J. Day, I had taken the medical for National Service. One of my pals (mastoid and all!), was soon packed off to Israel and a nervous breakdown, while I waited to be called up. Nothing happened. Fretting at losing the chance to serve king and country, I wanted to know why I had not heard from the Army, but my father's wise advice was 'let sleeping dogs lie'. My guess is that the Armed Forces were too busy at the time to drop me a line. Maybe one day I will belatedly get papers conscripting me into H. M. Chelsea Pensioners' (Regimental March: 'Cockups of the North'), or I will be shot for desertion!

All set to go to college, and enter the ministry, there then occurred the most astonishing coincidence of my life. John Gibbs was friendly with an Australian named Professor Cunliffe-Jones, who was the Principal of the Yorkshire United Independent College, Bradford. By an arrangement going back to the 18th century, when Dissenters were barred from Oxford and Cambridge, the Bradford college was part of the Divinity Faculty of Edinburgh University. Students went to Edinburgh for an M. A., returned to the college to study for the Edinburgh B. D., and sat Divinity exams at New College. Had John Gibbs not known Cunliffe-Jones, I would not have returned to Scotland and, eventually, arrived in Bridgeton. This was another of those 'life-determining' coincidences which, looking back, still amaze me!

The college was a long, two storey Gothic structure, surrounded by extensive grounds and millionaires' mansions. It had some twenty-five students, one of whom, Stuart Jackman, had had a novel published by Faber & Faber, with a foreword by no less a literary giant than T .S. Eliot! The local librarian was John Braine, author of 'Room at the Top', a novel which he got published after thirty-seven rejections and which later became a famous film! I determined to become a famous author myself, but had a few other things to attend to first - like passing exams.

I enrolled in the Bradford College - and hit a snag. Edinburgh would not recognise my London University entrance qualifications, and that meant me sitting the Edinburgh University's Entrance Exams. Teaching myself, completely unaided, all five Highers for a second time, while concurrently studying for the first year B.D. was a bit much! The Greek I did with that great New Testament scholar W. D. Davies, a Welshman; the theology lectures were by Cunliffe-Jones (a Ralph Richardson look-alike); and I was taught Hebrew by that wise and learned Scot, Jimmy Stewart.

I was in digs with an older student called Cecil Clyde, who came from Belfast, and we lived under the eagle eye of two formidable retired ladies who had served in the Salvation Army (as military policewomen, no doubt). Cecil ate like a vulture and was a negligent payer of his rent so the two demobilised Sally Army ladies disliked him. Happily for me, the more they spurned Cecil, the more they mothered innocent, loveable me.

Cecil slept in the attic above my bedroom, and we were both freezing cold. My request for an extra blanket was granted, but Cecil's was denied. That night the rugs beside my bed and on the landing disappeared and I found Cecil snugly tucked up under a rigid pile of carpets and rugs! I have never met anyone as carefree, and unorthodox as Cecil. He was full of the blarney, and when I asked how and when he got the B. A. which he displayed after his name, he beamed at me and replied: "Sure it means Born Again, Bill, Born Again."

Cecil was short, strong as a bull, and had a broken nose from his days as a boxer. In his cheerful Irish way, he loved a fight. When he disappeared for a week one time he explained he had been home to Ulster to train with his Loyalist machine-gun unit! Late Friday nights he would whisper at my bedside, "Bill, the pubs are scaling, come on, there's a fight". I would reluctantly follow him out into the street to watch him wading into the conflict, enforcing Christian reconciliation! Just walking along with Cecil was hazardous, for he would stop and upbraid passing rowdies for using bad language; his broken nose and body language made clear the advisability of taking his good advice. He pulled me one day into a house packed with mourners bewailing some man who had died, and commanded all present to 'turn to the Lord' and kneel in prayer. To my astonishment, they all knelt down, though they had no idea who Cecil was, or why we were present in their house.

It was the custom at the college meals for the Senior Student to sit at the top table with the staff, while we lesser beings took turns serving as stewards. Cecil was stewarding one evening when the Senior Student called for more coffee. A hushed fell over the company, for we all knew that Cecil deeply disliked and resented that particular individual, though no one knew why. Grimly striding the length of the silent hall, Cecil lifted cup and saucer, opened the window, threw them out, closed it and returned to his seat! We all agreed that he had let the Senior Student off lightly by not throwing him out the window with the crockery.

"Mr Clyde," wearily remarked the Principal at lunch one day, "I am unable to discover where you have been for the past thirteen years." Cecil's past and age remained a mystery. While a lady from the Social Security was giving us a lecture one day, she looked closely at Cecil and stated that his face looked familiar to her. His denial of her accusation that he was augmenting his college grant with Social Security payments did not go down convincingly with the college bursar and, inevitably, Cecil 'left', thus concluding a troubled career. To be fair to Cecil's reputation, more than one student of my acquaintance had financial 'sidelines' - one I knew worked on the buses until the unhappy day he sold the Principal a ticket! I am recording these various anecdotes about Cecil because I remember him very, very fondly. He is the only person I have known who received Holy Communion with tears rolling down his cheeks. Years later, I asked an Ulsterman if he knew a guy called Cecil Clyde; he pointed to a gap in his teeth saying, "Cecil Clyde! he knocked out that tooth!" The Church Militant right enough! Wherever he is, I wish Cecil well.

We were free spirits in those days: one Divinity student of my acquaintance used to duck down in the pulpit for a quick puff during the offering - rising cigarette smoke eventually gave him away, and led to reprimands. Students were older than they are today; most had been in the Forces, and had too much experience to be pushed around. At Bradford college I met Ziko Provulovic, a tall, thin, grave, silent Serbian Orthodox student priest who had escaped Tito's massacre of

Mihailovich's Chetnik partisans and fled to Britain. At New College, one student had been a prisoner in Colditz, and at the close of the war held as a bargaining hostage by the S. S. who thought he was related to Churchill. An independent-minded lot, we usually had a job to go to in the summer, and a profession at the end of our studies.

We paid no tuition fees (the State saw us as an investment), and local authorities gave us grants. How different today for students who have to find their own fees. However, on the other hand, school children and students are better cared for these days; I never knew I was short-sighted until my army medical (no wonder I couldn't see the blackboard at school); and all the interest anyone took of us at University was an initial fresher's two minute meeting with the Director of Studies - after that, you were one your own, sink or swim.

After a year in Bradford, I moved to Edinburgh and digs in Easter Road - where I was strategically placed to watch Hibs' glorious 'Famous Five' on Saturdays. Moving in with Bill Stevenson, now a world authority on William Blake, we shifted to Pilton, then to Stockbridge where the landlady claimed to be a spiritualist. She held spooky seances, and gave us the creeps by accusing us of tramping round the flat in the wee small hours ripping up her garments. We soon realised she was a fraud and left her with the student's farewell: a kipper nailed under the table. ("I know what it is, and I know who put it there, but, for heaven's sake, where is it?")

How I loved Edinburgh University! You met so many wonderful people there. Julius Nyere, later the highly regarded Prime Minister of Tanzania, was just another student taking coffee in the Old Quad canteen of the University, always shivering in chilly Edinburgh. Great men were never far away: Neils Bohr, Danilo Dolce, John Baillie, such as these conversed with us in small S. C. M. groups, men of impressive presence. John McMurray taught Moral Philosophy, and the brilliant Prof Pares, totally paralysed, taught me Honours History for four years. Prof Tom Torrance's lectures on Church History were memorable, and I particularly recall his enthusiasm for Calvin's scheme for a 'Church Without Walls': the idea was for pubs to provide a Bible, so that, while knocking back their pints of *Bière d'Alsace*, the patrons could pour over the Scriptures. Tom, highly regarded for his immense intelligence and knowledge, is not noted for a sense of humour, and he was somewhat non-plussed when the class burst out laughing.

One of the Americans in the Hebrew class was a conjurer. When asked for some word from the Hebrew vocabulary he never knew the answer, but whenever Prof Stalker called upon him to come forward and write the same word on the blackboard he always wrote it correctly. Our mystified lecturer never twigged that this wily student had the vocabulary written on concealed small cards, flipped to the required word and then copied it on the board. Prof Stalker was very popular, but we had a lot of fun at his expense. He liked to pounce upon the class demanding to be told the Hebrew word for something or other, and one time he sprang upon us crying, "A woman, a woman, I want a woman!" Much student hilarity ensued.

I moved into Cowan House in George Square, a male-only residence for about a hundred students, selected on a quota system to represent all the different faculties. Dinner was an Oxford style affair: Latin Grace, long tables, Warden's high table. I was given the usual rookie's initiation: told the wrong time, I arrived late, skidded on the polished floor, flew up into the air and, to hoots and jeers, crashed down sending much cutlery flying. For the next three years I sat at a table full of medical students, and ever since have treated doctors with caution..

Apart ftom those pre-exam weeks when gloom and silence fogged Cowan, life was spectacularly happy. George Square was ideal for 'chariot' races, and we would circle round on assorted means of transport, bombarding and being bombarded with flour bombs and fire extinguishers. My friend George Buchanan-Smith owned a tiny open-topped car, ideally suited for this purpose; his wee dog, Bran, perched on the rear end, and would go flying off if we cornered sharply. By coincidence, George and I found ourselves working together at Church House when he followed Geoff Shaw (another of my fellow students) as Boys' Leader.

Anyone who has dined in the officers' mess of the R. M. Commandos will know what I mean when I use the word 'boisterous'. As students, we were a boisterous lot: before one Political Economy lecture, we put some foul tasting substance into the elderly Profs glass of water and whisky. After the liveried servitor led him in all his majesty, he took his seat, took a sip from the glass and cried out, "Good God, man! they've tried to poison me!"

We did not spend all our time poisoning the lecturers; one time a group of us put on clerical collars, took a box at a theatre showing the *Folies Bergere*, and examined the posing beauties closely through telescopes. All went well until some sailors in the audience decided to take a closer look and invaded the stage - to the considerable alarm of the ladies.

By going on strike against the food at Cowan House, we went over the score; the Warden gave us a dressing down and repression followed. Our ring-leader was John Cumming, an unlikely revolutionary who, when not protesting against Scotch Eggs, smoked a leisurely pipe and ambled through life pretending to be studying history. Cumming was expelled, so we arranged for him to win the annual "Principal's Race", a run from Cowan House to the Old Quad, the prize being dinner with the Principal of the University. Dressed in frock coats and top hats (I raced on crutches), we trailed behind the martyred Cumming as he toddled along at one mile an hour in a cloud of St. Bruno, pausing for frequent rests. He was expelled from Cowan and dined with the University Principal on the same day!

Cumming's nickname was 'Nutshell'; on the night before an exam he would ask me what it was about, and if I had a book putting it in a nutshell. Students (male ones) often boast that they never do any work - in Nutshell's case he truly never did. Like Norman Mair, the rugby pundit, I never saw him at a class in four years - a record for absences which beat my own score. Last I heard of Cumming, he was selling ice-cream in Canada. Is Norman Mair still a student?

After the horrors of Hons. History Finals (eight three hour papers over four days), I returned to Bradford to do two more B. D. years, having decided to transfer to the Church of Scotland at the end of it, and join the Iona Community. Before leaving Cowan House, my rugby-playing thespian room mate, Pete Hanna, and I took leave of the Deputy Warden, remarking to him that the room we were vacating had a spongy, sagging floor. His room was directly below ours and he replied in a hollow voice, "Yes, but it had to suffer a great deal of pounding during your occupation". Pete went off to teach in London and introduce the brand of Christianity in which I had long been instructing him. His teaching went off much better than his preaching.

Chapter 6

"And further, by these my son, be admonished: of making many books there is no end, and much study is a weariness of the flesh. "
(Ecclesiastes 12: 12).

A famous rabbi once taught that the Bible is so important that God Himself has to study it!

A chapter in which I finish studying, work on the railways, meet two guys who play a big part in making me a scintillating preacher, help rebuild Iona Abbey, and arrive at Church House.

Back in college in Bradford, I moved into digs with my dear student pal, Winston Roberts. We were welcomed by a nice widow lady who was being terrified by spooky, silent, anonymous telephone calls - she was receiving these every night for months at precisely 9 p.m. We gave her company and the calls ceased. Winston and I missed the bright lights of Edinburgh University, and things had changed during the four years since our first year at the college. Professor Davies had left for Duke University, and his replacement was Dr. Aubrey Vine, a tall Londoner, who treated us like secondary school pupils. Dr Vine became to us what Sir Roderick Glossop was to Bertie Wooster.

Our hero was Prof Jimmy Stewart; moustached, small, portly, approaching retirement, he had a dry wit, and was a teacher of Socratic merit. Having been a wartime chaplain in the R.AF., as well as a young soldier in the Great War, Jimmy knew how to treat high spirited young men, and it was obvious that he didn't like the incoming Dr. Aubrey any more than we did. Over lunch they would, ever so politely, verbally joust, and when at table one day Jimmy claimed that every action carried a meaning, Dr Vine scoffed and turned his empty glass upside down saying, "There, what does that mean?" To our delight, Jimmy replied, "Ah, it means something of great significance: have you never read in Omar Khayyam "turn up the glass" - it is the symbol of death".

Prof Stewart was from a farm in Perthshire, and one of his father's farmhands had been John Dewar, founder of the famous "Dewar's of Perth" whisky firm. His wide, liberal knowledge greatly influenced me

- he knew as much about Social Anthropology as Hebrew. I am much indebted to Jimmy's teaching methods and care for students,

Another Stewart, Donald Ogden Stewart, the American humorist, wrote of Robert Benchley: "He was Humour, with its instinctive humanity, toleration, wisdom, non-competitiveness, non-aggressiveness, democracy (not in the political sense). I myself warmed at that fire and what I wrote always was, unconsciously, for his approval. It still is." Professor Jimmy Stewart, like the great Robert Benchley, epitomised Humour. I still preach for his approval.

Our student pranks did not go down well with Dr. Vine: one morning it was the turn of one of his student toadies to read the brief lesson during college prayers, so we switched the reading to Psalm 119 and the dimwit ploughed through all 176 verses! This aroused ill-feeling on the part of the said Aubrey towards Win and myself, his main suspects in these covert operations. When Dr. Vine published a learned article in a newspaper, the pair of us wrote a letter to the editor (under a false name) criticising the article extensively. Dr Vine took the bait, and answered us, and the letters began to fly to and fro across the correspondence columns until the subject became a lively topic of conversation at the college table. Aubrey scornfully questioned the sanity of his adversary with rising irritation as the debate intensified until, fear of detection prevailing, Winston and I withdrew from the contest. Victorious, Dr. Vine was left to display much triumphant satisfaction; but he never suspected what we had been up to and we reckoned, with quiet pleasure, that we were the ones who came out the winners.

DOING THE ROUNDS

On Sundays, we students were sent out to conduct services in small towns and villages all over the West Riding of Yorkshire. It was "Last of the Summer Wine" country.

The first Service I was sent to take was on a Remembrance Sunday morning, and I arrived to find that I was expected to conduct the official ceremony at the local War Memorial. Nobody had told me about this, and I was totally unprepared, but I had no other option than to lead the band and procession through the streets, in pouring rain, desperate for something to say when we arrived! My contribution to the proceedings was exceedingly brief, and therefore surprisingly well received by the umbrellas. Thus did I learn my first lesson: count on being caught out every time you go somewhere to preach.

My experience was further expanded when, having given out the text of my sermon one Sunday morning, a lady stood up in the pews and began bombarding me with Bibles and hymnbooks. The text (shall I ever forget it!) was: "And the ruin of that house was great" - a most appropriate verse in the circumstances. Some elders quietened her down, and, totally unnerved, I hastily delivered my homily. Shaking hands at the door as folk left, the lady in question thanked me most generously for my message! "She does that from time to time," explained an elder, "she is unhinged." An advance warning that she would be using me for target practice would have been beneficial, but I was grateful that at least she had not hurled a stool at the pulpit as did the late Jenny Geddes!

Another Sunday morning, bleary-eyed after a late Saturday night at a dance in a teacher training college for attractive young ladies, I rose late and rushed for the bus, grabbing *en route* my sermon. When I rose to preach, I was shaken to see it was a sermon for Christmas! As it was a hot day in July, the congregation showed signs of bewilderment at my dwelling at length on the three wise men travelling to Bethlehem, and, after the Service, I received some pointed remarks. Had I preached this fine Christmas sermon in the Southern Hemisphere it would have gone down a treat, but, alas, north of the equator it was not well received.

While on Iona, I was sent one Sunday to preach in a wee church in Mull, and discovered, to my utter dismay, that the lectern Bible was in Gaelic! As the congregation maintained a stony silence before, during, and after the Service, either they didn't speak English, or my Scripture quotations from memory didn't go down too well.

Catching an early morning bus to some far off unknown town usually meant being the sole passenger aboard. One Sunday, after asking the conductor for directions, he helpfully made sure I got off at the right place, and gave me detailed instructions how to reach the church. I gratefully disembarked, and carefully followed his directions: first right, second left, and so on. I finished up in a dead-end street facing a huge green gate with a big notice on it saying "Gas Works". The joke was on me: he is probably still telling the tale of putting one over on the gullible young preacher.

I conducted my first Communion Service one evening in a mining village. Nobody had told me I was to do this, and I was pretty sure that, not being ordained, I ought not to celebrate the sacrament. However, the humble few in the pews were indifferent to such fine points of church procedure, and the scene was set, so I had no option but to go ahead. Ginger wine is not a beverage one usually associates with the Lord's Supper, but, to my surprise, that was what was on the menu. I had never received ginger wine before, and said so to an old lady as she was leaving; "Aye, lad," said she sagely, "but it did me a fair bit of good that did. Ginger wine is real good for the wind!" Bearing this in mind, I trust kirk sessions throughout Scotland will consider using ginger wine for its beneficial effects.

One of my pleasanter duties was to assist the Rev. Geoffey Thrussell, an athletic, Oxford Blue, bachelor minister whose manse was across the street from a young ladies' college in which resided a French student named Marguerite. A friend had asked me to look her up, so I popped over to meet her.

The college had the aura of a convent ruled by a Mother Superior, so, as I introduced myself, I divined from the head mistress' chilly reception that I was not welcome to fraternise with one of her charges. On hearing of my intention to befriend Marguerite, the Rev. Geoffrey also regarded my visit across the street with considerable alarm. When I took her out several times, and began to speak glowingly about her considerable physical attractions, my boss grew increasingly distraught. It turned out he was secretly 'doing a line' with one of the teachers across the way, and I was blundering in, linking the manse to the college. To safeguard Geoffrey's romantic assignations, I did the gentlemanly thing and left, to his obvious relief, taking with me a photograph of Marguerite as a perpetual solace for my sacrificial loss.

Living for four years on a grant of £150 p.a., and for three years on a mere £60, like all my fellow students I was always 'skint'. A fag divided in three by a razor made life just bearable during term time, but in the vacation we were not only penniless but in debt. Luckily, apart from one summer when I could not get work, a job usually could be found to save the day. At Christmas there was always the usual student Post Office job. One of my fellow students used to brazenly shove his bag of mail back into the nearest pillar box and return home - he probably went on in life to become the Postmaster

General.

In summer, for me, there was always mainline Preston railway station, which had thirteen platforms and was extremely busy. I worked three shifts, earlies, lates, and nights, sometimes in the telegraph office, mostly as a lowly porter.

I had been told by George MacLeod that manual work, however humble, should be done to the glory of God, so I swept the mile-long, deserted platforms with my enormous brush, and shivered in the cold light of dawn with a piety worthy of Brother Lawrence. On night shift, ghost trains would arrive, engined by mighty, fire-glowing dragons belching clouds of steam, bright carriage windows displaying rows of lolling dead bodies as the wheel tapper rang his tocsin bells in the enveloping, sound-enhancing, chilling, eerie darkness. In the wee small hours, freight wagons carrying dusty mailbags, or frozen fish clanked to a stop for unloading. A railway station is an empty, lonely, place at such an hour, so I was much comforted one night to find myself unloading a box of fish intriguingly labelled 'To Iona Abbey'.

The worst thing about nights (for me) was the presence of huge rats which scuttled about. The porters' canteen was a miserable dungeon reached down a flight of steps at the bottom of which these rats (or their friends and relations) chased each other round and round in a ring, nose to tail. Closing my eyes, taking a deep breath, and making a run for it, I would dash down to safety, and join in a game of three card brag with my fellow workers. Brag, like poker, involves bluffing, and if everybody has a good hand, and you can beat them, then you are in for a big win. Three-threes is the best hand possible and when I got this one night, and everybody bid up and up, I scooped in 12/6d! This astounding success by a student of Divinity was widely reported to be the result of Divine Intervention, and this seemed to me to be a reasonable explanation.

A fellow railway student was an exceedingly clever chap who did *The Times* crossword with amazing speed (though not quite as fast as the old vicar who said he could fill it in while singing 'Onward Christian Soldiers' and boiling his three minute egg). In the dawn light, I remember this tall young man calling across the platforms that he had finished the puzzle, adding the information that Dien Bien Phu had fallen. Unfortunately, his information concerning train times usually fell under what is best termed the 'wild guess' category, and I was much alarmed one busy holiday to see him send a troop of Boy Scouts to Wolverhampton when they were aiming for Windermere!

He and I did most of our work carting piles of goods around on broad, low-slung, heavy iron-wheeled trolleys. One load was of chicken crates, and when we began larking around, before we could stop it, the lot tipped off the platform and the chickens were sent fluttering and clucking up and down the lines while we frantically tried to catch them, terrified a train would rush upon us. Luckily, we got off with it safely, and resolved to take more care. Railways are dangerous places, and a worker had been killed crossing the lines.

The trolleys were moved from platform to platform through a tunnel entered and exited by means of hydraulic lifts. These were simply steel plates onto which you ran the trolley and pulled a handle to operate the thing while you tried to stop the brakeless trolley rolling about and the piled high goods falling off. When one porter slipped on the wet surface and his leg got jammed between the rising lift and the entrance arch, the gruesome results fed my fear of suffering a similar fate, especially on rainy days.

My most unnerving job was in the telegraph office, tapping out signals and sending them down the line to warn approaching trains. My imagination worked overtime, dreading great disasters due to my incompetence, and how none happened, considering my perfunctory training, remains a mystery which still causes me to tremble.

There seemed to be a certain type of passenger who had it in for British Rail. Because much of the work was done before the general public arrived, people put in complaints that we were slacking. During one lull, I read the *Communist Manifesto* in a waiting-room, and was reported as a Russian spy! Not that nationalisation had changed the embedded LMS culture much, for the old pecking order remained intact. When I complained to an Inspector that one of the foremen came in drunk, slept in the carriages during the night-shift, and took tips when the morning papers arrived (*our* tips!), he glared at my impudence and replied, "He is an old servant of the company" — end of story! It was a sentiment I would hear later in life from elders protective of kirk Session pals.

My oldest friend, Arthur Nunn, worked in the station office, and we had a lot of fun. A dab hand at maths, Arthur was also extremely witty. Lancashire wit is sharp, like Glasgow wit - e.g. Ken Dodd, Eric Morecambe, etc. compared with Ricky Fulton, Andy Cameron,

Tommy Morgan, etc. We had a particularly odious and dopey porter known as 'Trapper Wilson' who hung around the taxi rank trapping passengers for their luggage and tips. We filled the biggest suitcase we could find with bricks, and got a taximan to drop it off with instructions to 'Trapper' to carry it to platform 13, where a passenger would meet him. Anticipating a large monetary return for his labours, he hauled the ton weight to the farthest platform, where he probably still is, awaiting the 'passenger' and the tip.

Arthur and I had no idea about horse racing, but when we talked up a horse one day, and it won, we acquired a reputation as tipsters. This false report we encouraged, and began selling our tips at 2/6d a time. We were amazingly successful, and Arthur decided to cut out the middle-man and back horses for himself. His keen mathematical mind, and a pile of form books, started him off on a subsequent career as a professional punter. In my penurious student days, he gave me a list of the first five horses in the Grand National - *in order*! I thought he was bluffing (who wouldn't?), and, indeed, he didn't believe his own words, because he didn't back his forecast. Amazingly, all five came in exactly as he said! Arthur was one of those guys who are remarkably lucky; he used to say to me, "Give me a fiver and I'll give you tenner tomorrow', and he would have, I am sure, had not my high principles disallowed me accepting filthy lucre. Perhaps I would now be ministering as chaplain to a leading race-course had I followed Groucho Marx's example and declared: "Those are my principles, and if you don't like them, well, I can always get new ones."

When I put university and college behind me and joined the Community, I arranged for Arthur come on holiday and stay in the Abbey. When 'A Nunn' appeared on the guest list, the staff went into flap over where to put such a creature in our all-male dormitory.

Chapter 7

When Mr Morrison, the Publications Manager of the Iona Community, went on a business trip to an office in London, the lady receptionist looked up from her desk. He introduced himself saying: "Iona Community". "Oh, do you?," said she, "where exactly is it?"

"I can see the red boats dancing,
Over the Sound of Iona;
I can see the white waves prancing,
Over the Sound of Iona.
Sail away, sail way,
Over the Sound of Iona."

In 1955, student days all past, alas!, Winston and I arrived on Iona to spend a whole summer as new, fully paid up members. The dormitory block was finished by then, and we shared a small room together. A dozen young probationer ministers were joining with us, and we were put to work alongside the craftsmen rebuilding the ruined cloisters and Abbot's House.

One of my companions on the previous 'Student Work Community' joined with us, Malcolm Duncan, and he was tragically drowned while out swimming in the Sound of Iona. In his sermon at the funeral Ralph Morton emphasised that this beautiful world, especially a place such as Iona, is also a dangerous place - something our present New Age 'back to nature' types choose to ignore. Another fatal accident occurred while we were working that summer. Charlie Kirkpatrick, one of the craftsmen in our team, was killed by a fall of timber as the puffer was being unloaded in Martyrs' Bay. This was a great sorrow, as Charlie was an islander and well liked. Before a dance in the village hall, Charlie took Win and me into his house for a dram - a Hielanman's 'dram' - a full tumbler of whisky! We couldn't stand up, never mind dance!

Winston and I came close to drowning while swimming in the 'scuddy' at the North End; we were caught out by some ladies appearing on the beach, and we were compelled to stay a long time in the very cold water to cover our blushes. Swimming back to shore in the strong current, we swallowed a lot of sea water, and just made it back to dry land. It was said that the old monks of Iona used to pray with eyes wide open, standing up to their necks in the sea in order to remember their mortality. This must have been one of those ideas which seemed all right at the time. How long they kept up the practice is significantly not recorded. My advice to anyone considering even a paddle in the Siberian waters around Iona is this: don't go in without a local anaesthetic in the lower limbs. I find that remembering one's mortality is just as easily done while lying in a cosy bed.

George MacLeod was at his peak in 1955 - majestic in the pulpit, a leader of men, a prophet. Personally I found him intimidating. If he had a buddy-list, I was never on it, but I still believe that he single-handedly saved the Church of Scotland in the Twentieth Century. He was a great man. Like the one or two other great men I have been privileged to meet, his was a dominant presence immediately felt. He could enter a room of a hundred men, many powerful personalities, and was the immediate focus of attention. I have never known anyone else could do that.

I had the temerity to disagree with him at times, and said so, and he didn't like it. One time we clashed at table (I told him he had been a pacifist in the wrong war!) and he was momentarily angry; but the following day he threw me a fag, a reconciling gesture saying much about the man. I will always be in his debt for, like many others, including my wife Margaret, the Iona experience was foundational to a confident Christian faith. It met the hopes of whole generations of young people. Community members were expected to minister in industrial parishes, and it is difficult to think how church extension charges could have been staffed without them. It has been truly said that the future of Christianity itself will be decided in the huge housing schemes of our great cities, and the contribution of the Community has been invaluable.

Margaret and I paid a sentimental return journey a few years ago, and attended the evening service in the Abbey. I was the only male present. Worship was held in the crossing, and we all sat in a circle, each of us holding a candle. A guitar played 'songs' for us to sing, and we were then invited to place our individual candles in the middle of the ring to form one big blaze of light. It was what is called 'atmospheric', nice, very nice. Suddenly a terrifying thought struck me - Good Lord! I'm sitting round a bonfire at a Girl Guide camp! We are all going to sing 'She'll be coming round the mountain when she comes', whoa back! But then, out of the darkness enveloping the distant High Table, there swam before my mind's eye a glorious vision of George, robed in all his majesty, his incomparably beautiful prayers rolling down the aisles as he distributed the Bread of Life, man and Reformed liturgy united at their purest and finest. Alas! the vision faded, and the sad fact dawned on me that I am a lingering relic of a bygone age. But there you are, that's life. As the Irishman said, "Everything is improving for the worse", and even nostalgia isn't as good as it used to be.

During thirteen weeks of hot, sunny weather that summer of 1955, there was not a drop of rain. The wee island reservoir at Lock Stonaig dried up, and the only water supply came from the well beside the Abbey front door (it occurs to me as I write this that the Abbey's well water could be sold as 'Iona Spring Water' - Del Boy and Rodney doing the bottling, and Uncle Albert the marketing). Anyway, this well was always full to a depth of one foot so, by forming a chain of buckets, we could nightly fill the water tank above the buildings and have just enough water for each day's cooking and toilet flushing. That meant washing was a serious problem - and not only for the Abbey but also for the youth camps. Margaret, cooking at the time for the village campers, had to wash dishes and clothes in the sea, prompting an observant lady day tripper to say to her friend, "Look, dear, the primitive natives wash in the sea!"

Every year George had a catch-phrase, and that year it was: "All our righteousness is as filthy rags". We got this ten times a day. In our party of new recruits to the Community was 'Big Frank', a Canadian of sleepy disposition and lumberjack physique. Like the rest of us, it was his turn from time to time to take morning prayers in the Abbey before we went off to work, and Frank's approach to the Almighty was via *ex tempore* prayer. His prayers were what my Uncle Alex once called "blin' sermons", that is to say, rambling addresses to heaven delivered with the eyes shut, and consisting of whatever topics occurred to Frank's torpid mind at 7.45 a.m. Often short of issues he could bring to the Lord's attention, Frank would say: "Yea, Lord, Thou knowest ... " and then punctuate his rogation with lengthy pauses while he thought up what further matters he ought to be bringing to The Lord's attention. One drowsy morning - they were all drowsy - Frank intoned from the prayer desk his usual "Yea, Lord, Thou knowest", chewed the cud for awhile, and then, suddenly, George's catch-phrase springing to his mind, he brightly exclaimed, "Yea, Lord, Thou knowest that all our garments are filthy!" To this we all said a fervent 'Amen'. Our garments were, indeed, filthy, not having had a wash for weeks. Living *with* one's righteousness as filthy rags is not nice, but living *in* filthy rags is positively disagreeable!

A team of archaeologists was digging away close beside where I was working with the stone masons, and I got to know one of these in particular. He was a tall, distinguished looking English chap, in his forties I guessed, and no archaeologist. Every Wednesday night there was an impromptu concert for the blue shirted community members and the youth campers, and at one of these this chap gave a very professional performance. One evening he and I went for a walk and I told him I knew he was an actor pretending to be an archaeologist. It turned out he was Eric Porter, the guy who played the part of Soames in *The Forsyte Saga*, the T.V. play which stopped the world on Sunday nights. He was avoiding publicity by being on the dig. I found him a fascinating and most agreeable companion, with an actor's eye for personalities. He heartily disliked several other famous folk in the theatre world - Claire Bloom especially! Thespians are not the 'luvvies' they like to pretend in public. (I found the same thing is true of politicians; when I met up with a very prominent lady politician, I found her a delightful person, but surprisingly open about what she thought of some of her colleagues). I asked Eric Porter what impressions he had about MacLeod and, with an actor's eye, he saw the Abbey building as an outward and visible extension of George's creative personality. Porter was right, of course. That is why, once the Abbey was completed, problems immediately arose. George had to redirect his formidable energy. In my opinion, he did not do so either successfully or constructively. Since his death, the Iona Community has been seeking a purpose to replace the rebuilding of the Abbey. What had once been novel and even revolutionary has become generally accepted. New ways to 'touch the hearts of men' must be found in a new situation which George did not foresee. Ralph Morton was the only one who looked ahead, beyond the post-war period to which George belonged. I recall sitting beside Ralph when George was telling a big meeting that unilateralism is "God's Will"; Ralph muttered quietly, "Who knows God's Will?"

I kept in touch with Eric Porter, and discovered he was a famous Shakespearean actor. He was very kind, and most helpful when a problem boy from Church House, who had heard I knew Eric, turned up at a London theatre where he was appearing. I read of his death not long ago and was saddened.

George MacLeod was one of those people who never get tired. Like King Henry II of England, who never sat down, and Winston Churchill, another man of boundless energy. In one week, George could write two hundred letters, give two broadcasts, go wandering round the Abbey at 2 a.m., telling people to go to bed and putting out the lights, then see people off on the 6 a.m. ferry! I remember him travelling to Edinburgh for a meeting, and on the way back catching up with a party of us climbing Ben More - he was seventy years of age at that time! His was a towering presence, but he had a very tender side, and he was a great pastor to Margaret at a point in her youth when she had severe family problems to face.

While working for Toc H between the wars, George MacLeod was much upset to discover that denominationalism continued to divide men, even after the overriding unity they shared in the comradeship of the Great War. He was refused Anglican Communion. I think this set him searching for a Christian authenticity which predated feudalism, and he found it in Iona's glorious submerged history, symbolised by the ruined Abbey. An older Scotland, before the Norman influence, before Canterbury, before Rome, began to speak again through George MacLeod. Never other than a loyal son of the Church of Scotland, he expanded the narrow theology of individual salvation to open it up into the whole of Creation. His pilgrimage tours of the unique island brought the dimensions of time and space into harmony with Salvation. His published prayers shine with poetry, and his sense of the presence of God. He really did sense the winds of God were conveying messages to him, because the world was alive with the Spirit for MacLeod, born into Highland second-sight. He was strange mixture of the Brigadier and the Mystic, so not an easy man to know. Lord MacLeod of Fuinary had his faults, but he was never stuffy!

Conducting one of the evening Services in the Abbey, a daunting experience for us novices, was made all the more gruelling because George sat right beside you, muttering, shuffling his feet, and grunting throughout. One evening, as I nervously led prayers before a packed congregation, the great man suddenly reached over and snatched away all my carefully written intercessions. Great man or not, I had no option but to grab them all back again in an unseemly tussle! I had heard of 'wrestling in prayer', but this was taking it a bit too far!

George did not seem to know how to handle Winston and myself - especially Win. We wrote scurrilous songs, like "Parading Round in Shirts of Blue" (Community members 'uniform'), a song to which others have fraudulently laid claim since. We also wrote pantomimes for the concerts, and these did not endear us to our Beloved Leader. On the door of our room we pinned up satirical notices which entertained passing groups of visitors, but did not amuse Lord MacLeod. He tried to make us take them down - but we just added to them until we ran out of door space.

Dear Winston, what a guy! He had the most incredibly complex family background you can imagine: a many branched family tree fit to out-rival the 'begats' of an ancient Israelite. I totted-up that he had twelve grandparents, then stopped counting! Of slender build, Win had a Jewish nose, a facial feature which doubtless helped him with his encyclopaedic knowledge of Hebrew. Indeed, if Sydney Smith could call Thomas Babington Macaulay 'a book in breeches', he would have most certainly have called Winston Roberts 'a dictionary in a kilt'. Win knew more languages than a Port Said taxi driver, and more Hebrew roots than the Chief Rabbi. This made him an invaluable room mate when it came looking up verbs.

In our student days together in Edinburgh, some of us went along to the synagogue to see a Jewish Service. We sat at the back and an official, curious to know who we were, came along to speak to us. Seeing Win's nose, he invited him to come forwards to read the Scriptures, which Win, being Win, cheerfully agreed to do. After telling the guy he didn't have a prayer shawl, one was provided, and Win read beautifully - until suspicions grew that he was not one of the chosen people. We were chucked out without ceremony, and it was typical of Win that he just could not understand why there had been such a fuss.

Winston was one of those extremely precious and rare birds you come across in life who are completely devoid of malice, jealousy, and conceit. When the same was said about David Garrick, Dr. Samuel Johnson's comment was, "Fond though I am of David, he lacks the merit to attract enemies." Johnson forgot that men like Garrick and Winston will always attract enemies, people who mistakenly see their inability to think evil of other people as a weakness to be exploited.

It was typical of my room-mate that, when told he was being falsely accused of keeping one of the girl campers out late at night, a serious offence for a big-shot Iona Community member, Win shrugged his shoulders. I insisted he immediately clear his name, but he just said, "If people want to think evil of others, that's up to them!" He was impervious to animosity.

If Winston had a fault it was lateness: he was always late because he took an interminable amount of time carrying out his ablutions. These began with him rearranging the furniture, then approaching the sink with a carrier-bag full of lotions, potions, brushes, etc. Only when groomed to perfection would he contemplate moving on. Vanity had nothing to do with all this - it was simply the tempo at which he passed through this world.

Once a week, after work, the Community members crammed into a small room at the end of the refectory to be given a talk by Brigadier McLeod. In a bad humour one time, George gave it to us long and strong about our lack of punctuality, As his scoldings drew to a close, heavy footsteps heralded the approach of Winston who clanked open the door, looked cheerfully around, and disturbed the whole assembly by making his way to a front seat. A chilly silence was followed by George hissing icily, "Come in, we are just discussing lateness". Win beamed. "Ah, good," said he, "in that case I'll stay, for it's a subject with which I am very well acquainted!" Winston was the only man in the world who could best George Macleod, and he did it every time!

The refectory was the scene one morning of a 'siege'. A mentally unstable guest staying amongst us had gone berserk during the night, desecrated the Abbey, and barricaded himself in the wee room mentioned above. He threw things at anyone who came near. Eventually, Attie Mackechnie, one of our workers from Bunessan and the complete Highland gentleman, soothed him down and persuaded the man to come out. The police and doctor were called from Mull, and the poor chap was given an injection. Unaware of what was going in the refectory, I was working nearby in the cloisters, in the middle of which stood a party of day visitors off the boat listening intently to one of the tour guides describing the daily life of the members of the Community who lived in the buildings enclosing the cloisters. "Over on that side," said the guide, pointing to the dormitory block, "is where the members sleep." Rubber-necking, the eyes of everyone in the party turned to stare in that direction and at precisely that moment, the door from the dormitory block into the cloisters opened, whereupon a policeman and two men in white coats emerged carrying a stretcher on which lay a lunatic, strapped down and screaming, "I'm not mad! I'm not mad!"

One sunny day, the Duke and Duchess of Argyll showed up as visitors, accompanied by their factor and several small dogs. In front of the Abbey is a small, fairly high mound on which Saint Columba slept in a hollow containing his round cell. Some of us were following this saintly example and snoozing on top of this mound when the Duke paraded below us. Piles of building material lay about on the ground and he waved his stick at these while loudly denouncing George and all his works. When this 'gawky' (to quote Burns) had finished his strutting and staring, and moved off with his entourage, George himself appeared on the scene so we eagerly recounted all we had seen and heard from our hiding place. He made no comment. I do recall, however, on another occasion, George grimly saying that until he came to Iona, he had no idea what hatred was.

As the long summer days floated by, time on Iona ceased to exist. No newspapers, radio, traffic, just work, Abbey services, sails to Fingal's Cave, football matches against the campers, lectures by Ralph Morton or some other highly admired parish minister. Life was wonderful! On the long strolls beside the white sands, deep in conversation, we dreamed of a new heaven and new earth with all the idealism of the time and of youth. We really did believe in nationalisation, believed the world could be changed, not by protest, but by involvement.

Chapter 8

"Unthinking, idle, wild and young,
I laughed and talked and danced and sung,
And proud of health, and beauty vain,
Dreamed not of sorrow, care or pain,
Concluding in those hours of glee
That all the world was made for me."

Attributed to Princess Amelia (1783-1810)

Years later, after I was married, I went for a walk to the North End of the island with John Morrow, my friend of many years from Northern Ireland. As we toddled along, like two on the road to Emmaus, pondering deep matters, my twelve year old son, Scott, listened for a long time, then suddenly began to join in the conversation. He not only gave utterance, but monopolised the talking, and for several miles! John and I couldn't get a word in edgeways. Our boy companion had, of course, a Gospel precedent where, in the Temple, another twelve year old put his elders in their place. Scott has since done nine operational tours with the Marines, and is now a Ph D. I would like to take all the credit for that, but in fairness should add that he had a mother as well as a father.

It saddens me that my son and two daughters (one a solicitor, one a teacher) never had the Iona experience which has meant so much to their parents. The unilateralist requirement for Community membership means my son, serving in the armed forces and a signatory to the Official Secrets Act, cannot be a member - only an Associate. That is a loss to both parties.

The first members of Church House I met were staying at a youth camp on Iona - St. Francis-in-the-East was very Iona centred. I tried hard to keep alive the close links between the Club and Iona, but by the Seventies, things there had greatly changed, and our Club Leader at the time, Alex Mair, felt that working class folk like himself were out of place in what had become a middle-class, politically programmed scene. After fifteen years membership of the Community, I myself decided to leave it, after much agonising over what I saw as a very important personal decision.

Dr MacLeod had called a special meeting and told us all to sign up for unilateralism or he would leave. I found myself a lone voice protesting at this threat, pointing out that, by definition, a community is a unity of differing opinions, and not an exclusive association. I felt this was George at his worst - like a child who, having built up his bricks, wants to knock them all down again. There was much heated talk about Hiroshima, so I mentioned Auschwitz, and that I saw nothing Christian about smugly sitting on the moral high ground while millions were being gassed. I got no support. I wasn't being what is known these days as 'politically correct'.

What was most disappointing was that nobody talked to me about my resignation; I just left, feeling that nobody cared. I was quite depressed, and might have despaired had not a nice man at the Inland Revenue kept writing to see if I would oblige him by paying my Income Tax. His endless flow of letters made me feel really needed. Bless him, whoever he is. I owe a lot to that man, including a debt of gratitude, so I really must reply to him him one day.

Looking back, I think that what was happening at the time was that George MacLeod was being overtaken by the Sixties, and didn't know what to do about it. The underlying assumptions of society, things taken for granted, were being assaulted by new, unforeseen forces. To those born and bred in the patrician era, and who considered themselves liberal progressives, the "Permissive Society" was something beyond the control they were accustomed to managing. Maybe George foresaw the Permissive Society would lead to more problems than it would solve (Pol Pot's 'Killing Fields' were the end result), but he offered no answers and simply fell back on his one great certainty - Ban the Bomb! True, this was not "Sit Down, Sit Down For Bertrand Russell", it was 'Stand Up, Stand Up for Jesus', but he had lost the initiative.

Books about George Macleod have told his story, so I have little to add except my admiration. He had his mischievous, unpredictable side (dogmatic unilateralism apart), and when Harold Wilson's big political debate about 'entering Europe' was going on, George did not scruple to tour the churches denouncing it as a Vatican plot, playing the 'Protestant Card' to the full. Ever his own man, at the same time George was being attacked by the Orange Order and openly accused of being a crypto-papist!

One unforgettable night, I went with some friends to the Orange

Halls in Springburn to hear George doing his 'Daniel in the lion's den act'; This took immense courage but a holder of the Military Cross and Croix de Guerre is not easily intimidated. The hall was packed and stacked, and as George began to speak, a voice from the gallery called out, "Go home, Father MacLeod". This reassured me I was in Glasgow right enough. The chairman was a minister called Alan Hassan, a luminary in the Orange ranks in those days. He raised his voice and a hand in solemn rebuke, but his pious words went unheeded and the heckling continued. Then it was that George rose to his finest hour: he quoted 1st Corinthians 13, off by heart, "If I speak with the tongues of men and of angels". The place grew quiet. I treasure the memory of that sublime moment and the man alone on the stage. When Luther's tormentor, Eck, was deserted and in trouble, it was to Luther that he turned for help. So too, when Alan Hassan ran into serious trouble, it was to George MacLeod that he turned. Neither Eck nor Hassan were turned away.

In 1974, when I invited George to re-dedicate the newly rebuilt Church House, I picked him up in my car and he said to me, "I've only been here twice, the first time to dedicate the place, and the second to re-dedicate it!" I found it an uncomfortable experience to be helping along this old man of whom I had been in such awe. The last time I saw him was when Margaret and I went to St. Boswell's Kirk in the Borders, into which charge George Buchanan-Smith was being inducted. Lord Haig was at table with us, and the numerous Fettes boys present provided me with a great audience - sharp as tacks! Lord MacLeod looked sadly frail, and he ate very, very carefully. There will never be another like him.

Parish ministers in those far off days were, on the whole, men of high quality, and through the Community I was in touch with a network of like-minded individuals. When the time came for me to do so in the early Sixties, it was largely through these ministers I was able to spread the Regnal League, a movement which, with its theology of 'Wholeness', fitted the Iona outlook perfectly. In that sense, I never really left the Iona Community. And I continued visiting the island.

To get there meant sailing on the shallow draught 'King George' round Mull. On board ship one day, I overheard an American lady explaining the Community to her female travelling companion. "It was started by Rev. MacLeod who is the minister of a church in

Go-van, a village near Glasgow."

Another time, while looking out from the boat over Tobermory Bay, where a search was going on for a sunken galleon, a barge could be seen sending up huge fountains of water. Tom Milroy explained to some American tourists what was going on, telling them, with a straight face, that the Bay was being drained to get to the wreck on the bottom - one tourist asked how long the draining would take!

During another sail on the 'King George', while sitting below decks in the wee saloon bar, two Americans ladies asked what the pictures round the walls were about. I told them they illustrated the ballad of Young Lochinvar - "O, Young Lochinvar is come out of the west ... " The ladies were delighted and one said, "Oh, gee! And we've come out of the West too."

You could also get to Iona via Tobermory, or by landing at Craignure and being ferried ashore in a small boat which came alongside the 'King George'. This was a very short trip, and when the ferryman one time mentioned there were sharks in the water as he went round collecting the extortionate fare, a lanky Australian remarked caustically, "And sharks in the boat as well!"

A wee bus took you from Craignure to the Iona ferry, and if you hadn't pre-booked it, you were left behind. Left stranded one time, I was rescued by Hugh Drummond and his motorbike. Hugh managed to run into one of those rarities on Mull - a tree. Having been a paratrooper, he landed as trained, but I hit the ground hard and saw stars and "the red boats dancing" long before we reached the Sound of Iona! Hugh later became a minister in Easter Ross, where he initiated revolutionary liturgical advances - such as uplifting the offering during the service instead of at the church door.

Travel to Iona is easy these days, but that hasn't spoilt the thrill of sailing over the Sound of Iona and landing on Columba's island, the burial place of kings, where Dr. Johnson and James Boswell went as pilgrims like the rest of us.

Chapter 9

Youth

"When all the world is young, lass,
And all the trees are green,
And every goose a swan, lass,
And every girl a queen"

from 'Young and Old' by Charles Kingsley

Iona to Bridgeton

At the end of a glorious summer, I took-up my appointment as John Sim's Assistant, and moved into Church House. Geoff Shaw arrived shortly after as the new Boys' Leader. Monica Morris had been holding the fort with the help of two theological students, Tom Milroy and Ian Renton (great guys), but she was leaving to marry one of our voluntary leaders, Roddy Campbell, a veterinary pathologist.

The Club had been going thirteen years before I arrived and in those days was only one of many youth clubs throughout Scotland. The Glasgow Union of Boys' Clubs, together with the National Association of Youth Clubs, organised a wide range of activities, including Saturday football leagues. Church House fielded four football teams, covering the different age groups, and there was no minibus then to carry us to far away places like Fifty Pitches in Govan (where young Sir Alex Ferguson's Club, Harmony Row, played), Possilpark, and even distant Kirkintilloch. All this organisation of voluntary youth work has long since vanished, alas!

Geoff had been in New York, where he had worked in East Harlem Protestant Parish for a year, and come back devoted to a life of uplifting fallen youths (those were the days of *The Cross and the Switchblade*). While Glasgow Presbytery gave pause and consideration to the setting up of the 'Gorbals Group' (along East Harlem lines), Geoff needed a job. John Sim was wary of Geoff, fearing he would bring in all kinds of undesirables and separate the Club and Church, but John really had nothing to fear, for Geoff was a conservative in all but name and reputation. While waiting for Presbytery to OK the Gorbals Group scheme, Geoff came to Church House, Walter Fyfe took a locum at Hall Memorial Church in Dalmarnock, and John Jardine started teaching. Of the three highly intelligent men, Walter was the dominant personality, calling all the shots.

Groucho once said that he knew the apple-cheeked, all-singing-all-dancing-gal-next-door Doris Day, "before she was a virgin!" Well, I knew Geoff Shaw before he was a Spartan! Edinburgh upper-middle class, close to the patrician Rev. Leonard Small of Cramond, Geoff was from a very different world than that of Bridgeton. As often happens with people from his background, Geoff seemed to try to make up for this by painful self-denial. He moved into a room and kitchen, with a stairheid lavvy, near the Club at 983 London Road. That was to be home to his successors, George Buchanan-Smith and John and Jennifer Webster. In those days, it was considered a good close, and London Road was full of shops, doctor's surgeries, etc., so it was no East Harlem, even if it was no Morningside.

I once accompanied Geoff to his mother's house in the West End of Edinburgh, close to the Episcopal Cathedral. His father had been a surgeon, and she was widowed. I soon noticed that Geoff's mother understood her son perfectly, for she was a very astute as well as charming lady. As we left his mother's flat and walked up the street, Geoff said to me, "I sometimes feel like going back there and smashing the place up!" I don't think he meant it for one minute, but he was trying to persuade himself he didn't belong there. You meet middle-class guys like Geoff who have a sort of guilt complex, and though they have never worked in a job where you receive life's basic education, namely "work or starve", they talk as if they are more working-class than the working-class! Geoff had an Edinburgh High School accent, and whenever I hear Magnus Magnusson's voice I am reminded of him. He also looked like James Garner, the actor, and whenever I see *The Rockford Files*, I see Geoff Shaw, urbane and charming.

Sitting one bitterly cold evening in Geoff's flat with some visiting bright young things from Cramond, he wouldn't light the fire, and we were frozen, shivering in his sparsely furnished monastic cell. The discussion came round to skiing and one handsome, athletic young fellow said he was eager to get out on the slopes. At this, the worthy Geoffrey tut-tutted and pontifically said that there are finer and more important things to do in life than amuse oneself. The prospective skier gave this earnest thought for awhile, and then pleaded, "But Geoff, I like skiing!" Dedication and grimness are never far apart, and, in Spartan mode, Geoff could be very grim.

Although I was very friendly with Geoff, it took me years to see what made him 'tick', and what he was up to. His role model was a famous priest called Father Birelli, who worked with poor boys in Italy, and this was Geoff's key interest: working with a small number of youths, no more than a dozen. Theologically, he believed that nobody is too low for the Cross and no matter how bad a guy was, if he was one of Geoff's chosen few, he would never be rejected. That was the great constant behind all Geoff did. It was the core of his being. Unfortunately, nobody pays a salary so you can do what Geoff wanted to do, so Geoff had to dress up his motives in various disguises. What confirmed my understanding of the man was his saying, at the pinnacle of his political elevation to the Convenorship of the newly formed Strathclyde Region, that he wished he could chuck it up and go to Vietnam to work with boys. Geoff was an ordained minister, not a politician. It was interesting to see that when he became Convenor of Strathclyde, he took great delight in putting up markers for his 'parish' boundaries, and printing a 'parish magazine'. I pulled his leg about that. Such a well educated and intelligent man was bound to rise to the top in the ranks of local Labour Party councillors, but he was never one of them. Tony Blair is lampooned as 'The Vicar' running the country as his 'parish', and it is a sly description which fits Geoff Shaw very, very well.

The only change Geoff made was that he re-admitted to the Club a gang of trouble-makers who had been banned, and they soon broke all the rules which Geoff, paradoxically, insisted that they keep. Result - conflict! This conflict went on inside Geoff himself, as well as within the Club, and it hardly made Geoff a happy man, or a team-player. After Monica married and left, Geoff brought Flossie Borgmann over from East Harlem to replace her. Flossie was a brilliant Club leader, a sophisticated, very attractive, elegant young lady. She had had a vast amount of experience of the New York street gangs - drugs, zip-guns, murders. In the many conflicts during Geoff's reign, she took the sting out of confrontations with consummate skill.

Flossie moved into a local single-end - one which her successors also later occupied. When Geoff left to start the Gorbals Group, she went with him. Her prediction that drugs would one day come to Scotland has proved only too true, though I considered that impossible at the time.

When a Club member was suspended for violent conduct, judicial inquiries would be instigated, sentence passed, and the matter fully explained to one and all during the Epilogue. It was all very serious. After the Club closed, late night group discussions were held to analyse behavioural problems, but whether the boys grasped the theological principles expounded by Geoff is doubtful. After one very long discussion in Geoff's flat to explain why a boy was being suspended for a month, one puzzled youth in the group said plaintively, "But Geoff, we're only a bunch of boys!" What was all Geoff's palaver about?

Inevitably it became a game, leaders versus the Senior boys. As was bound to happen, the gang of trouble makers began to rule the roost, disrupting the life of the Club, and causing much disquiet amongst the voluntary leaders, because Geoff would never take a leader's part, even when he or she were in the right. So Geoff made himself the sole source of authority, and playground bullying took over. Fortunately, Flossie often kept things from escalating into violence, but Geoff often showed the strain, and went into a huff.

The ring leader leader of the gang was Nick, 'Tricky Nicky', an egregious, thin, artful youth who made the bullets for the others to fire. Nick and his accomplices saw Geoff as a 'soft-tap', for no matter what they did, he would not bring in the police to sort them out. The one time he did bring in the police he sent them away again - a bad mistake. So we were left to deal with the nightly crises ourselves, and every night was a crisis. Confrontation became the name of the game. Geoff seemed to invite and encourage it. Maybe he was right - we only learn the hard way, and he was bringing to the surface all the issues and problems. I can see his noble purpose now that I am safely out of the battle, but at the time I thought Geoff was off his head. He would never admit that any of his swans were geese, an idealisation of some of these youths (OK - 'neds') which I could only attribute to some sort of vitamin deficiency in his diet.

Monica Morris (we shared the same birthday) used to say to me, "You and I are both Librans, Bill, so we take a more balanced view of things". It would be wrong to paint a black picture, as some still do, of Geoff's time in Church House, for we had a lot of fun, and when not masquerading as Father Birelli, Geoff could be a good laugh. One day we would be anguishing over the ethics of taking off Easter Monday and awarding ourselves a rest day; the next we would be off enjoying the Club Sports at Hogganfield Loch. The kids went on a fleet of tramcars, returning with jerseys bulging with rhubarb pauchled from the nearby rhubarb fields. In those days, life was great, exciting, and I was as happy as if I had just dropped a fourteen foot putt. The only dark spots in my life were those dreadful late nights in the Club office after the Club was supposed to have closed.

The office was a long, narrow room with a table, a telephone, and a locked door. Breaking into it was one of the Club's most popular activities, almost a part of an evening's programme! Everybody knew the office was where the nightly entrance subs, dance takings, and canteen goodies were kept for safety so there was considerable interest amongst some of our members in gaining an entrance. We went through a lot of doors and locks, and the members went through them too!

Living as I did only a few feet away from this Aladdin's cave, the habit Nick and his chums developed, of forcing an entry into the office and thinking up some pretext for settling down there for the night, did not suit my bedtime arrangements. Being kept up until they pushed off in the wee sma' hours did not appeal to me. Geoff may have relished these confrontations, but I did not. One night, on the pretext that someone had stolen Nick's 'jaiket', the gang occupied the office, and refused to leave until the garment was recovered. It was Geoff's night off. I was all alone.

Now the previous day I had seen certain "known thieves loitering with intent" - intent, that is, on breaking into a pub. The thieves knew that I knew, but what they did not know was whether or not I had shopped them to the police. That afternoon, when I answered a telephone call, a very cultured lady's voice informed me that she was telephoning on behalf of the Eastern Police Division, and required to know if I was the person who had offered information regarding the aforesaid crime. I replied I was not, and gave what information I had, names and all. She thanked me for my co-operation.

That night, at one of Geoff's late night 'getting to know each other better sessions' in his flat, Nick and the others were taking tea and fairy-cakes when Nick caught my eye and gave me a knowing look. I got the message: he had fooled me! How he did it I still do not understand, but the cultured lady on the phone had either been Nick, or one of his female friends. I had to hand it to the wily Nicky, he had put one over on me in our battle of wits!

On the night that Nick claimed to have 'lost his jaiket', and parked his buddies in the office. I had to take up the challenge - if they stayed until they felt like going I lost; if I got them out I won, game, set, and match. Smarting from losing the last round to Nick with his 'police lady' phone call, I suddenly had a brilliant brainwave, swiftly tuned into it, noted it down, printed it, packaged it, and issued it to the rest of my body. Picking up the office phone, I dialled a friend. When he answered I asked to speak to the C.I.D., and reported a 'jaiket' had been stolen in Church House. Putting down the phone, I let it be known to the boys that a squad car was on its way and would be arriving any moment. I then sat back, relaxed, and hummed a merry tune.

Sceptical jeers greeted my intimation, a quick poll of all present showing that nobody believed I had phoned the police station. Rising above the sneers and jeers, I casually threw Nick the telephone directory: "Look the number up for yourself - Eastern Division, 554 1113". This Nick did. A brief pause was followed by an immediate evacuation of the premises by my unwanted companions. I had got rid of them! One up to me in the Great Game!

The following night, sitting together in Geoff's flat, I gave Nick a 'knowing look'. He got the message: I had put one over on *him*. What he didn't get was that I had a friend with the number 554 1112, and despite their watchful eyes, I had dialled a two instead of a three. Of course, my answering friend thought I was crazy talking about police, and lost jackets, but he later offered me his future 'phone a friend' services should the occasion arise again. It never did when I was in charge of the Club, for Nick was never sure whether or not I was prepared to bring in the cops. And they did not like *that* one bit!

We used to put on Club shows, and for one these I was handed a script and asked to introduce Nick and his friends to amateur dramatics. I viewed this as quite a challenge; furthermore, when I viewed the script, I recognised that I had written it. When I told Geoff this, he refused to believe me, stating that he had picked the sketch up at a student show in the University of Pennsylvania, and brought it back to Scotland. I responded, with all the artistic dignity at an author's command, that I did not care where he got it, and could prove it was my very own work by quoting from it extensively. What had happened, extraordinary as it sounds, was that I had put on the sketch in Edinburgh, and an American student in the audience had picked up a script and taken it home to the States; then Geoff, in turn, had picked up a copy and brought it back to Scotland and to Church House, where he and I happened to be at the same time! Talk about coincidences! Anyway, I gave a brilliant performance as Pappy Zeke, and 'Tricky Nicky' was outstanding as Jesse James, with the others giving supporting actors roles as outlaws, Indians, and General Custer. The play's previous triumphs in Edinburgh and Philadelphia were repeated under the bright lights of our own East End production, photographic evidence of which I treasure to this day.

I could not have been more fortunate in the ministerial associates with whom I worked in those days: all very able men. Geoff's two years at Church House, were, I am sure, his happiest times, and when he left to form the Gorbals Group he did so under pressure from others, concealing his heavy heart. But Church House gave him an opportunity and set up which allowed him to do what he really wanted to do, and when he left he never had the same chance again and he knew it.

After leaving the Club, almost because he couldn't think of much else to do, and by chance, Geoff became a very prominent politician, a role for which he was particularly unsuited. His first attempt to stand in local politics resulted in him losing one of the safest Labour wards in Glasgow by saying he approved of the Abortion Act. When he did get a seat, it came about accidentally, owing to the death of somebody else. Having decided to get out of politics, and been reluctantly pulled back in, Strathclyde Region got him as its first convenor, and it cost Geoff his life while still in his prime.

It has been said that the worst fate that can befall a man is to fall into the hands of his admirers - one only has to think of Burns' Suppers and realise how true that is. Geoff, a man who wanted to disappear into the lowest levels of society, ironically received a 'state' funeral with all the trimmings! You could say that there is no use living a humble, obscure Christian life if nobody notices you are doing it; but I prefer to say that a person of great gifts and accomplishments, like Geoff Shaw, can never remain obscure for long. Ever disguising his motives, Geoff left an image of himself as a great youth worker and Labour revolutionary, which was completely inaccurate, and which persists to this day (there is a 'Geoff Shaw Centre'). After his death, I visited an exhibition in Edinburgh of the lives of saints down the ages and there, to round off the gallery, was Geoff's picture, his face alongside Martin Luther King, Mother Theresa, etc.! How fortunate he was not alive to see it for he would have thrown up!

We were very different personalities, yet so very close that I just could not bring myself to visit him in hospital before he died. The last time we met he turned up at the funeral of a school boy killed in an accident; he was surrounded by *apparatchiks*, and smoking a cigarette! To see Geoff with a fag was a shock - like seeing one's spinster aunt chewing tobacco! He looked worn out and unhappy - toughing it out, so to speak. I have dwelt at some length on Geoff Shaw because Ron Ferguson has written his biography and it is still widely read. I contributed information to the book. A book is one thing, but it is very different when you have known a man up close, and miss him as a friend and colleague.

Chapter 10

Taking the Wee Man aff the Cross

At floor level, wooden partitions divided Church House (the old church-turned-Youth-Club) into games and craft rooms; canteen, toilets, and a chapel to seat around sixty youngsters. All this work had been done by Mr Gray's original twelve boy members, so it was somewhat primitive, but they made a fine Communion Table for the chapel, and over it placed the St. Francis-in-the-East motto: "Rise Up and Build".

The Epilogue began with an analysis of the evening's proceedings, appropriate moral lessons being drawn concerning the wickedness of thieving biscuits from the canteen, and other demonstrations of anti-social behaviour. As many of the members saw nothing wrong with such conduct, the congregation inclined towards restlessness, and oft times the Benediction had to be abruptly administered. The nearest thing to preaching in Church House would be St. Paul's reception by the mobs of Ephesus, and I can claim, modestly, to be one of the few modern Christians to have been stoned. Yet, for all that, the most realistic preaching I ever heard came during our evening prayer time. No flannel! Preacher and hearers were truly 'engaged'. Geoff Shaw's epilogues were a 'rammy'; 'Big George' Buchanan-Smith's inspired just enough fear of his wrath in his hearers to get him through; John Webster began his Epilogues by telling everyone they had to be saved or they were doomed - his soft heart quickly qualifying that stern doctrine with convenient loopholes and exemptions. I myself tried mass hypnosis, but not with any great success.

When Church House was rebuilt in 1974, I named the new chapel 'The Upper Room'. The reason for this was not merely aesthetic, but also to get rid of the word 'chapel', and the old problem of having members saying, "I'm no gonnae go intae a chapel- I'm a Prodesant!" (for the uninitiated, an R.C. church is known in Glasgow as 'the chapel'). Mind you, religious issues were always somewhat clouded; I asked a happy laddie one time why he was wearing a crucifix when I knew he came from a prominent Orange family. "Och, it's OK" was his cheerful reply, "I'm gonnae take the wee man aff the cross!"

One thing I learnt is that one never knows the lasting influence of the Club and those epilogues, even on those you have chucked out. The best illustration of this concerned a young 'ned' who was a member in the Club's earliest days during the war. He was the type of boy who spat on the floor and hung about causing as much trouble as possible - the sort of boy who didn't play games and had to be watched. Called up into the army, he disappeared until, following V. J. Day, Mr Gray received a letter from him in the Far East. He had been a Japanese prisoner of war, and had soon found out that misbehaving with his captors was a very unhealthy thing to try, They pushed him into a kennel-sized, underground cell, and left him there in the suffocating heat and darkness, In the letter, he told how surprised the Japanese were to find him still alive when they opened it up after weeks in this oven. What filled Arthur's heart with joy was that he wrote to say that the only thing which kept him alive was the tiniest chink of light and the words of a prayer he had learnt during the Club epilogue: "Lighten our darkness, we beseech Thee, O Lord, and by Thy great mercy, defend us from all the dangers and perils of this night, for the love of Thy Son, Jesus Christ, Our Lord". The Japanese had been defeated by a far off place, of which they knew nothing, a place called Church House in Glasgow.

Following the Epilogue, after everyone had been shepherded outside, a blessed calm fell over the Club. The peace was disturbed for a while as a barrage of stones, bottles, etc., battered off the door, but once this bombardment subsided, the weary leaders escaped to their homes, locally, or all over the city and beyond - all I had to do was go upstairs. One night, as I sat in my mini-room, a missile came crashing through the window. I picked it up from the shattered glass and it was not a stone, but a heavy, bulbous car aerial. The strange thing was that I had been out that very day trying, without success, to buy an aerial for my old radio, so I plugged the thing into the set and it went a treat! They say the Lord will provide, but I had not expected Him to do so by express delivery! Many years later, Alex Mair confessed that he was the culprit who threw the car aerial through my window; and I thought young Alex was *such* a nice boy!

On Friday nights, some leaders stayed on after the Club closed to play indoor football in the gym, Mr Hay, light on his feet, showing his skills and not his age. He had been a very good player in his youth. He told me that during the Great War, having avoided conscription, he had to keep running away from the police half way through football matches on Glasgow Green. Bobby was a pacifist, a conscientous objector, and, more importantly, a good runner. He died spectating at a game one night at Hampden Park - a fitting place for Mr Hay's earthly finale. I took his funeral, a personal sorrow to me.

In winter the Club was freezing; it was freezing in summer as well. Any heat from the coal-fired boiler vanished into the vastness of the overhead darkness, and at times I had to save myself from an icy death by popping up to my room for blankets. One snowy night, we had a film show in the gym, and the big picture was *Scott of the Antarctic* - the memory still gives me the shivers, shakes, and chilblains! We sat there, huddled together for warmth, icebergs passing before our eyes, blizzards howling across the screen, and boy! did I empathise with Captain Scott. Dying of frostbite, I just made it back to my own base camp upstairs for an overcoat and blanket. I requested *Some Like It Hot* for our next film show. Saturday morning film shows for children were packed out, despite the cold; most popular were the *Sinbad* films with their terrifying monsters chasing about the screen. A total hush fell upon the audience during the more fearful scenes - not a crisp packet rustled, hair stood on end! However, moments later the din would start up again and disorder was restored. A frail old biddie used to turn up every week and sit amongst the weans; she was as deaf to the bedlam as she was to our request that she pay the tuppence entrance fee.

The film invariably broke, at which point the audience would shout at the operator, "Put a penny in the meter!", or some other pertinent message of encouragement. The sound-track was another problem - it came out in two modes, either sluggish or extra-sluggish. I obtained new loudspeakers to cure this, only to find at the next performance that the sound came out worse than ever: in a sort of slow, sludgy, slurp. Technical examination of the fault disclosed that some careless child had decanted lemonade into the speaker. At such moments, I experienced 'the dark night of the soul'.

It is one of life's mysteries how boys are as oblivious to noise as they are to low temperatures, tripping off to school in frost, hail, and sleet, scantily dressed, utterly indifferent to mother's plea to 'wrap up' In contrast, girls are always cold - as Shakespeare puts it: "Two women in the one bed make for a cold night". Perhaps this Divine arrangement was the Lord's providential way of helping the boys of Church House to survive our lack of heating. Since those days, the nearest I have

Rear of old Church House, 1955

Rear of re-built Club, 1975

been to the Club's icy conditions was during a Sunday Service in a venerable Anglican church on the Isle of Wight ("St. Hypothermia's"). This ancient edifice possessed a heating system installed during the episcopate of Thomas à Becket (1118-70). At forty degrees below, I offered a boy sitting in front of me £5 for his baseball cap, but there are limits to what even a boy can stand and he refused.

Every night, around midnight, Geoff would walk me to the famous 'Umbrella' at Bridgeton Cross for fresh rolls, and the early edition of the morning newspapers. We would eat the rolls sitting by Bobby Hay's coal fire, discussing politics, in amicable agreement about the evils of Toryism, and the blessings being bestowed on the nation by Socialism. Bobby and I would smoke Woodbines, the Shaw abstaining. They were, indeed, idealistic days, and we were, after all, in Bridgeton, a place fertilised for the Independent Labour Party by the speeches of the late, great Jimmy Maxton. It was during one such speech that the long haired radical M. P. shouted, "There are millions of unemployed in the country!", to which some wit in the crowd shouted back, "Aye, Jimmy, and they're all barbers!" Our nightly treks to the Cross gave us an opportunity to talk to people in the street - which just goes to show how determined we were in those starry-eyed days to go out into the highways and byways and compel folk into the Kingdom of God. We were young men of serious purpose.

At the close of an evening, alone in Church House, I used to idly wonder who the people were who built this huge church, with its tall steeple, away back in Glasgow's Victorian heyday. It was not hard to imagine the carriages drawing up on a Sunday morning, men in top hats and ladies in hooped skirts alighting at the door of the kirk as barefoot street children looked on. I pictured in my mind the Club's circling gallery filled with the faces of real people, each a person with a life-story to tell. What would those elders of old have thought of their church had they have lived to see it become Church House? I think they would be pleased that God's Word was still preached there, and His praises sung by succeeding generations. Mind you, when everybody had left, and midnight came round, and I was all alone in the Club, it was a pretty eerie place, with all sorts of creakings and bumps in the night going on - and not all the noises were made by burglars paying their frequent nocturnal visits. It was a spooky place in the dark.

Apart ftom Mr Hay and myself, two other species inhabited the

Club building: rats and pigeons. The former terrified me, as I have already recorded in the account of my railway days. For Mr Hay they held no such fears; he would corner them in batches and batter them to death with a shovel, all the while the poor beasts squealing and scrambling up the walls in search of escape. Anyone who can face up to rats without flinching gets my medal for bravery.

One afternoon I went to give a talk to a meeting for Pensioners in a Salvation Army Hall in Bridgeton. A huge rat began to walk around the stage on which I was sitting. As the platform was high up, the old dears could not see this intruder, but the shapely, gorgeous young Salvation Army lassie standing up beside me to open the proceedings certainly could - it scuttled around her feet. She never batted an eyelid! Hers was a martyr's courage worthy of bonus points in heaven and immediate canonisation. I have admired the Salvation Army ever since. Thankfully, the rodent did not linger to hear my speech which was delivered in a trembling voice.

I might add that rats were a common sight in the backcourts of those days. When, at an Easter Service, I asked the children what we can see gamboling about in the springtime (meaning, of course, little woolly lambs), the tiny hands shot up and they chorused - "Rats!"

I hate rats, but pigeons, recently described by the Lord Mayor of London as 'rats with feathers', don't scare me one wee bit! I don't wish to boast, but can stand up to a pigeon any time, look it straight in the eye, and say in my best Robert De Niro - "You cooing at me, eh? You cooing at *me?*"

Great flocks of pigeons resided in the Church House steeple, fluttering in and out as if they owned the place. On a policy of 'live and let live', I was prepared to tolerate this aviary (apart from the dive-bombing) but, unfortunately, the boys in the Club wanted to catch them and take them home. This involved scaling the towering peak of our spire, an enterprise defying vertigo and gravity. It also involved avoiding Mr Hay, who found it hard to differentiate between rats and boys; Bobby saw it as part of his janitorily duties to drive off the intruders with brush and shovel, causing many a budding pigeon fancier to leap to either death or safety from a great height.

Later in my career, when my son Scott was about age five, I happened to park outside the Club as four boys leapt at least fifteen feet from the steeple, and ran off holding birds. I chased them, forgetting about my infant son was left behind in the street

- a desertion which he has not forgotten. All I can offer, by way of apology, is that reflexes die hard for veteran Club leaders.

It is well worth mentioning that anyone who has never seen an East End of Glasgow 'dooket' has missed one of the wonders of the world. Given a patch of waste ground, the local youths will build there a tower made out of corrugated iron, bits of wood, tar, etc. These structures are architectural marvels well able to withstand the elements, even earthquakes. When our boys took the pigeons from the old Church House steeple, what Mr Hay failed to realise at the time was that they were simply rehousing them in some palatial, purpose-built 'dooket', where they could be educated in the mystic arts of homing, and racing each other for fun. I don't know if the Royal Society for the Protection of Birds is considering awarding Mr Hay a posthumous medal for his dedicated defence of the Church House pigeonry, but if they are, I trust they will also build a 'dooket' in his memory. He meant well. Steeples are for bats and pigeons, not boys, but let us not forget that even boys can mean well too.

To pigeon-hole one further note on this subject, I recall a family living near the Club who dined regularly on pigeons. A railway embankment behind the house made an ideal shooting gallery, and the family would 'enter the butts', so to speak, bring down a brace or two of plump birds, and hang these in the kitchen until they matured into a local delicacy. The children of the family seemed in excellent health and spirits, so I do not hesitate to recommend a nourishing daily diet of pigeon. It is, I'm told, an acquired taste but try it, anyway, and let me know how you get on. You will, of course, have to employ a ghillie if you do your own shooting, and, remember, to pot a pigeon, whether it is in flight or just strolling around, requires considerable skill with an airgun - so practise. You can't use our embankment, because the ack-ack rights there have already been taken.

If I learnt one thing very quickly from visiting, it is that cleanliness does not necessarily go with Godliness. God seems particularly uninterested in some of his most faithful servants washing a lot. I found it advisable to sit on a hard chair, for fleas love my blood (Monica Morris' blood was of inferior quality to mine, so she never got fleas). One night I was due to give a slide presentation to an audience of civic dignitaries gathered by Geoff Shaw, and I arrived late. After my apologising, the audience settled down for the magic lantern show. No sooner had I shown the first slide than an enormous member of the genus *pulex* bit my neck. To the bewilderment of the viewers, I immediately said, "Well, I hope you enjoyed the show", packed up and left hastily without explanation! There was never enough room for me and a flea in the same town - we had to shoot it out to the death without delay!

One of my very first parish visits was to an old woman who lay dying in her bed-recess. A nurse had changed the bed linen and provided clean, pure white sheets, but as I leant over the bed I recoiled in horror - the bed was alive with vermin! I had the doctor in double-quick. Ugghh!

One of the signs of progress these days is the retreat of the louse, a creature well described by none other than Robert Burns as "Ye ugly, creepin', blastit wonner, Detested, shunn'd by saunt an' sinner." Fleas seem to have retreated from the social scene, but in the old days, it was not a good idea to wrestle about playing with some of the Club's junior boys; the saying, "Toe the line" comes from teachers avoiding contact with their pupils by keeping them standing well back. Be that as it may, fleas would leap vast distances to get a hold on me, and when I married, Margaret and I spent many a night changing the sheets and hunting the fleas I brought home. While staying with the family at Crieff Hydro one time, when Scott was about six years old, we went into the swimming pool. His back had lots of spots, and an elderly gentleman grew suspicious that he was carrying some infectious disease into the water. Scott brightly informed him not to worry, the spots were 'only flea bites'. His mother's blushes were not spared!

My most deadly struggle with the fleas happened one night shortly after going to Bridgeton. I read that Turner, the famous artist, would not paint a raging storm until he had been in one and placed himself in the scene. Being equally keen and dedicated, I decided I needed to experience life in the raw by spending a night sleeping in a model lodging house. I chose a well-known doss house in the Calton called 'Rosie's Homes', paid my nine pence to an unshaven bloke behind a grill, found my way into a long dormitory lined with beds, and lay down to take my rest. After a while, a staggering, shadowy figure loomed out of the darkness, stripped off, threw my clothes off my chair, dropped into the next cot, fell asleep, and started snoring in stereo. This startled the fleas dwelling in my bedding and the whole horde of them flitted into my pyjamas: uncles, aunts, great-grandparents, every member of the extended family, including the toddlers learning to make their first jump. Naked as the day I was born, I lay on top of the bedclothes, trapping my tormentors between the sheets, and this seemed to help me to glide into a state of trance-cum-nightmare. At 6 a.m. I was on the streets, heading for Church House, scratching all the way. Well, I hear you say, what did you expect for nine pence - The Hilton?

I might add here, seeing I am into the business of making my readers itchy, that there are things which are worse than fleas: bluebottles. When I became the minister of St. Francis-in-the-East, my vestry was a very small room situated above the cellar. In the heat of one summer, the vestry became alarmingly infested with bluebottles, and pumped full of a most noxious, putrid stench. Investigations revealed no obvious source of this disgusting affliction, for though the sewers and drains lay directly below in the cellar, they were smelling no more badly than they normal did. In the end, after much inspection by experts in these matters, a dead rat was found under the vestry floorboards and the corpse was removed, thus closing the Ideal Homes' Exhibition for bluebottles. After that, signing the register in the vestry after a wedding became much more pleasant experience for happy couples.

There was not one house in our parish with a bath, and during my stay in Church House bathing was a problem. Geoff and I solved this by compressing the body into the big sink in the canteen. As this could only be done at the risk of being crippled for life, a better alternative was crossing the road to the Barrowfield Steamie and using the public baths.

On Friday nights, I would avail myself of a good soak in an immense tub, calling out from time to time for Mr Darling, the baths attendant, to come along with his key and provide more hot water from a tap outside the cubicle. I must say there was much splendid choir singing those Friday nights: "Just One Cornetto ..." and other favourites from Grand Opera filling the steamie with song - I gave my all in the tenor section. Entertainment, soap, and a towel for just a few paltry pence! Those were the days! The great baths of Diocletian in Ancient Rome are now but a ruin of fallen Corinthian columns and shattered soap-holders; likewise the great baths of Ancient Barrowfield are now no more than a fading echo of the past. Sad to say, things aren't what they used to be since people started getting baths into their houses. But times must change. By the way, I would like to mention that should the occupant of cubicle 10 on the Friday night of October 19th. 1957 read this, will he be good enough to return my wallet which he went off with without permission.

Chapter 11

"Brigton's a dump, aye - but it's a GOOD dump" - the tart reply of a Church House boy to an outsider visiting the Club and expressing criticisms of Bridgeton.

"Hello, hello, we are the Billy boys,
Hello, hello, you'll tell us by the noise,
We're up tae wer knees in Fenian blood,
Surrender or you'll die,
For we are the Brigton Billy boys."

(traditional medieval Glasgow folk song
sung while dancing round the maypole)

In the Sixties, a television personality (David Jessol) turned up wanting to make a programme about the Club. I was cagey, and asked if he had come to make one of those 'Glasgow Gang' spectaculars which are such a misrepresentation of the city. He listened, and promised to go along with my picture of the Club — no gangs, no life-threatening dangers, etc. As we walked up the lane to the Club, he remarked that the door looked very badly scorched. I explained that the previous night two local bobbies had dropped by to show community spirit, and taken tea with us in the canteen. This had not gone down too well with some of the boys, who set fire to the door so they couldn't get out! "No dangers here then, eh?" commented David Jessol drily, with more than a touch of irony. "Erh! yes and no", I chimed. Inside, the gym wall was running with water; this I explained nonchalantly was caused by the theft of lead from our roof. He grew thoughtful: this was my opportunity ... "It's hard to explain," said I, "but this sort of thing doesn't happen *all* the time. It's really a very quiet life here, nothing to be upset about." He grew more thoughtful; then aimed in my direction an unspoken "Oh yeh?"

Another time, when the Church of Scotland decided to make a film called "Frontiers" featuring its involvement in various areas of society (e.g. Industrial Mission, Prisons, etc.), Church House was visited by a film crew from London. With camera and tripod fixed high on the roof of their van, they took shots of the surrounding streets, while some of the trailing crowd of curious weans were taking shots *at them*! As I sat beside the driver, a small boy threw a brick through the windscreen. The driver muttered something about regretting having "come up here". Filming continued, but at ground level.

The thing is that it is almost impossible to explain to outsiders is how one could wander the streets, or even The Green, late at night without fear. Street battles, and break-ins at the Club, were part of the curriculum, but life was only dangerous if you were a teenage youth who happened to be in the wrong place at the wrong time. In those days, muggings of old ladies were unheard of; the gangs fought amongst themselves. Driving through the neighbouring Calton district, our senior boys would crouch down on the floor of the Club van lest they be seen by the Tongs!

Our Club in-house gang was the 'Spur'. This was a non-religious, non-sectarian organisation even though they based themselves in Church House. A leading member of the clan wanted me to be quite clear on that point, and he stressed it. It seems that jeering members of the 'Torch', an enemy gang, were calling Church House youths "Christians" because they went to the Club, and our youths preferred being called "agnostics". To help sort of this unfortunate misunderstanding, I promised to approach the 'Torch', under a white flag, and put them right on this contentious issue, while at the same time taking the opportunity to remind them that, though non-religious, the members of the 'Spur' were not pacifists either!

Old photographs of Bridgeton in the late 19th century show how little it had changed well into the 'Fifties and late 'Sixties. London Road was then, pre-motorway, the main road south, a canyon filled with traffic and trams, and lined with every kind of shop. Cinemas abounded: from the 'Gegi' (named after shows at the old Glasgow Fair in Saltmarket) all the way upmarket to the stylish 'Olympia' at Bridgeton Cross. I possess a 1935 programme from the 'Arcadia' cinema which begins with a personal letter from the manager to the patrons, all very gentlemanly and ever so polite! But, at that time, Bridgeton was populated by a mixture of professional people and good working-class Scots folk, many highly skilled. John Street Secondary was noted for its output of University undergraduates. Bridgeton was, until recently, a community, like Govan and other areas of Glasgow. There is much use of the word 'community' these days, but communities cannot be politically decreed or arranged - they take generations to grow, and a very short time to destroy. The State is not a community, nor is it a church, though it likes to see itself as both.

For all the wonderful community life of Bridgeton, the housing was the worst in the city. As I've said, there was not a single bath in my densely populated parish. The poorest tenements were in what were called 'backlands', tenements in the middle of a square of tenements. One was called 'The Hairy Ham'. Instead of three doors on a landing there were six. In the oldest tenements, each apartment had a number plate on the door setting a limit to the permitted number of occupants. Not one new house was built in our densely populated parish for a hundred years. A very old lady told me she had gone as a child to live in one of the old tenements when it was newly built, and had stayed there throughout her very long life.

I once visited a single-end late at night with an urgent message, and knocked until the man of the house sleepily asked me through the closed door what I wanted. I told him to open up, but he explained he couldn't because the family were all asleep and the entire floor was covered with fold-down beds. To open the door, he had to get everyone up, and move the beds and furniture. It was a real life repetition of Our Lord's parable about the man who went to a friend at midnight asking to be lent some loaves, only to be told "the door is shut and my children are with me in bed; I cannot get up and give you anything." (Luke II: 7).

How poor folk were in those days, yet it was unusual to find a dirty house; folk used to admire the 'braw windaes' of the tenements across the street from Church House, and many a home was a 'wee palace'. I had a boy in Sunday School who was always smartly turned out, and if ever absent, his mother always sent me a beautifully hand-written note of apology. In those days, if a child was missing from Sunday School for a while, you went to find out what was wrong, so I went round to his house. It was up a dilapidated close, in a crumbling tenement, and I arrived to find the door open. Peeping in, I saw it was spotlessly clean and tidy, but very, very poor. I just couldn't bring myself to go in. How could I embarrass the mother, the fine lady who lived there? I tiptoed away. To this day I still wonder if I did the right thing by not going in.

The good thing about our community was that we had no class barriers. Some lived in better tenements, others in very poor ones, but there was no distinction of people because of that. True, every

Old Bernard Street, opposite the church, around 1964

London Road, the main road south before the Motorway

community, no matter how small and rural, has its 'lower tenth' of difficult, anti-social, and even criminal elements, and Bridgeton was no exception. True, the police were called 'The Busies' by the Club boys, and animosity between the two was mutual. True, I once saw a Co-op shop window smashed and a crowd of looters helping themselves to the windfall - and yet, the same old London Road had a milliner's shop which sold fancy ladies' hats.

How things have changed! Men raised their hats to ladies in the street, and referred respectfully to a married woman as 'Mistress So-and-So'. As a boy, I was told off by a bewhiskered old bloke for whistling on a Sunday! A man would never be seen pushing a pram. My old Session Clerk, Bob McEwan, would never deliver church flowers - heaven forbid! Much of old Scotland lingered on into the mid-20th century. If men swore at work, it was not done at home. Ironic that in what was a socially harsh world, good manners mattered, whereas today, with its soft living, vulgarity and coarseness prevail.

I was old Dr. Greenhill's patient, and his surgery was a shop front in London Road. He was a most interesting person: he was the doctor at Maryhill Barracks who examined Rudolph Hess after he parachuted near Busby in May, 1941. Dr Greenhill found Hess neurotic, and in possession of a great amount of morphine. Various Hess conspiracy theories keep appearing, but none mention Dr. Greenhill. Why is the doctor's vital report being avoided? I met a soldier who had guarded Hess in Spandau, and he told me the old Nazi was a rotter - he would ask for cigarettes from some kindly young guard, and then get him into trouble by reporting him for breaking the strict rules. He had no doubt it was the real Hess in Spandau. But I do doubt it.

In London Road was one of those extremely old, two storey buildings which had been, over the years, a pawnshop, a pub, and then a fruit shop. While being demolished, there was a gruesome find: a skeleton stuck up the chimney, and it wasn't Santa Claus! It was dated to 1916 by the brand of a packet of cigarettes found in the victim's pocket. Was it a thief trying to get in? or trapped trying to get out? The demolisher got a terrible fright; and the owner of the skeleton got a pretty grim death.

Looking back I feel sure that the worst thing to happen to Glasgow was the passing of The Rent Act in the early Sixties which led to the selling-off of tenement apartments. Properties were on their last legs

The years of demolition; the church is visible in the distance.
1970s

New housing, 1970s

and off-loaded. Factors no longer visited to see the close was kept clean, the windows washed, and anti-social behaviour stamped out. For a pittance, a flat could be bought and the new owners paid scant attention to the welfare of their neighbours. What had been a proud area rapidly became a slum, and folk who lived in poor conditions, but had made respectable homes, were abandoned to their fate. This was particularly hard on the old folk as the young people moved away to the new housing schemes. Fortunately, the Glasgow Eastern Area Renewal project seriously tackled the housing problem, and between 1971 and 1981, the population of 28,500 fell to 15,049. However, the impact on the community was drastic in terms of facilities, employment, and loss of human resources - problems still unsolved.

The most notorious of gangs in the 'Thirties was the 'Brigton Billy Boys' whose praises are still sung at Ibrox in moments of enthusiasm, though few who sing nowadays come from 'Brigton'. In contrast to Irish Catholic Gorbals, Bridgeton was for the Union, and Loyal - even now pavements at the Cross are painted red, white and blue, and the 'Proddie' pubs show the flag. To explain, Glasgow has Protestant and R. C. pubs and betting-shops. I once entered one of the latter, not to bet, but to seek out a gentleman; he was very polite, and assured me that though an atheist, he was a 'Prodesant atheist' The pub nearest the Club (we had three within forty yards) was an I. R. A. pub, but the proprietor kindly allowed me to put a collecting tin on his bar! No hard feelings - well, most of the time! When the Pope described Protestants as "our separated brethren", the Celtic crowd at Old Firm matches would shout - "Get intae these so-and-so separated brethren!.

Other gangs were the 'Nunny' (from Nuneaton Street), the 'Dickie' (East Main Street territory), the 'Norman Conks' (the South Main Street badlands), the 'Baltic Fleet' (Baltic Street), and the Calton 'Tongs'. The Norman Conks were of the Roman persuasion, and a boy told me his father painted him, and his wee brother, from head to toe in green paint when the Orange Walk was on! Calton was another R. C. stronghold. Glasgow's reputation for gangs is so misleadingly presented on television and in books that one can be pretty sure that those doing the presenting have never seen a gang! The same is true of those who fulminate about Rangers and Celtic matches - they've never been! The image of Glasgow put across in many plays, and even comedy shows, e.g. Billy Connelly, has done the city's reputation no good at all! Insufferable plays circulate a horrible picture of a city of endless slums, populated by foul-mouthed drunkards and drug addicts - does the West of Scotland need this rubbish? In Bridgeton, in the heart of the inner city, I could always find some spot from which I could see green fields. It is time outsiders were told that Glasgow is not the creation of the Industrial Revolution (like Birmingham), but an ancient city, with a cathedral founded earlier than Canterbury.

I met an old minister in Gourock who had been Assistant Minister in the old Fairbairn Church, Bridgeton, during the General Strike of 1926. He confirmed for me tales I had heard of street brawls with the police chasing strikers down Main Street with batons drawn. Rough days! And I had heard stories about the Billy Boys, and the famous police chief, Sillitoe, who cleaned up gang warfare. Such were the tales one heard of the old days in Bridgeton, but stories always toned down by assurances that folks never locked their doors when they went out because neighbours looked after each other.

The summer season was, as with the Apaches and Comanches, the time when the young braves went on the warpath. Hot summer nights were the ones I disliked most: street brawls outside pubs were nasty; and when I got married, it upset Margaret to see women and children hanging about to pub doors to collect drunken husbands and take them home. We had a pub on every corner. Of course, in those days women did not frequent such places - they were for men - but nowadays women fairly knock it back at weddings and funerals! What was "a wee refreshment" has become "a good bevvy". Men are rarely seen lighting a fag, while young women wander the streets smoking like lums! These days, women even attend funerals, going to the graveside or the crematorium instead of staying in the house to make sandwiches - dear, dear, what is the world coming to?

When I show old coloured slides which I took of my early days in Bridgeton, people are shocked at the conditions. But at the time, working-class folk's expectations were different than they are today - a two room and kitchen with an inside toilet and you were really happy! As an old Brigton lady said to me recently, "In those days we were poor and didn't know it. Then we were told we were poor. Then we were told we were deprived. And then, finally, they tell us we were 'multi-deprived'.

Much improved housing and social conditions are more than welcome, but they have come at a human cost. I once visited an old lady and her husband, living in a very nice flat, high up in a very well-kept multi-storey block, in a nice part of the city. They didn't go out much these days, didn't see the neighbours. When they saw some wee children playing outside their door on the landing, they both went out to watch them. Loneliness - they were living a modern, lonely existence. And worse: by the end of my time in Bridgeton, neighbours avoided each other. Everyone had a peep hole in the door; there was the fear of mugging. One of my elderly members was mugged by some scumbags who didn't even get out of their car to take his wallet - they ordered him to bring it to them! Much gained, certainly - but much lost.

Visiting a crippled lady, I found her all dressed up, handbag and all. As she never left the house, I was surprised when she told me she was going to a wedding - "Len and Rita are getting married," she explained. I panicked! The blood drained! Had I forgotten a wedding? - the minister's nightmare! Immense was the relief to find out that Len and Rita were characters in Coronation Street, and the wedding was on the telly. For her it was all real, and she was going, and she was dressed for it. For living people, we now have television characters to fill the gap in our glossy, brave new world.

Chapter 12

"If you think it is hard finding God, then try finding a plumber on a Sunday."

(Woody Allan).

For me, to find myself in a Club with four football teams was a dream come true. Not that I got to play much myself, but I had my own special team: the Juniors (12-14).

We were supposed to meet on Saturdays at 9.30 a.m., but the Junior boys turned up at 8 a.m. in eager anticipation, perching themselves on the wall a few feet from my bedroom window, a dawn chorus of "He's no up yet" and other embarrassing shouts shaking me into consciousness. One morning the game was cancelled. I had passed the word round to notify the juniors, but one of them turned up, David Whiteside, boots polished, strip neatly folded. When I told him the tragic news that the game was "aff", he said, "Oh, naw!", and the memory of the misery which filled his uplifted wee face brings a pang to my heart to this day. We were keen.

Off we would go on the tram to Glasgow Green where we would strip off in an earthen-floored tin shed, and take the field in sunshine or in falling snow. It would be but a slight exaggeration to say that for the next several years, taking my cherubs from success to success was my major interest in life, though, of course, I had to pretend to be interested in the ministry as well.

From the above, it might appear that as the Minister's Assistant, I spent 90% of my time taking football - in fact, it was only 80%. The rest of the time I preached unmemorable sermons, ran the Sunday School and Youth Fellowship, and visited folk. Visiting hospitals in those days took ages (no car), but visiting homes was easy because everybody stayed up the next close! The drawback was that all our members seemed to stay three stairs up, and in some closes four up, which was all right coming down, but not going up! It reminds me of the rent-collector who climbed up the four stairs every week but never got the rent. Finally, determined to succeed, he knocked, and the lady of the house told him she had good news. "Paying at last?", he gasped from the climb. "Naw," said, she, "the good news is I'm flitting to two up!"

My main job was to link the older Church House youth and the church by running the Sunday night youth fellowship. I took them for weekends - my first being to a castle in Lochgilphead owned by the Girl Guides. All went well until the first night when, to my dismay, I was the only one interested in sleep. I moved my bed beside the exit door, but my efforts to get them to stay under the blankets were in vain. At one point I thought exhaustion had stilled their enthusiasm for prowling about the castle (the boys heading for the girls dorm), but, in the stillness of the hot night, I heard the voice of Willie Queen, as he crept past the end of my bed on all fours, whispering to his companions, "Foaly me ... "

In spite of such setbacks, I took the older and more responsible elements to Switzerland aboard a wartime Dakota. This was regarded as a most daring thing to do, air travel and the tourist industry being novelties. We had a great time at Lake Lucerne. In the party was a newly-wed couple who were given their own bedroom, but after the first night they asked for a move. A picture of His Holiness the Pope hung over the bed and was apparently doing their love-life no good because they were they both of the Orange persuasion. Perhaps if youth fellowships are hard to find these days, it is because ministers do not realise that it is no good unless you go with your young people - and don't have an ulterior motive like preaching at them. Youth fellowships are essentially ephemeral things as the young people grow up and move on, but to create good and shared memories brings great blessing to you as much as to them. Mind you, in my old age, allowing a Y. F. to have an 'all-night disco' to raise funds did not seem much of a blessing when it was my turn to take the dance-floor at 4.30 a.m.

One of my first Assistorial challenges was to address the Women's Guild, and face an audience of some eighty matronly ladies seated on benches in a packed hall, wearing coats and hats. They were full of good cheer and affection for their new, young, unmarried minister who was evidently in need of a good mothering. Unfortunately, I failed to capitalise on all this goodwill by taking as my subject the proposition: "That the mothers of today are better mothers than the mothers of yesterday". The thrust of my argument was that modern education, facilities, etc. had improved mothering no end - a reasonable position to take, I should have thought, but they seemed to miss the point. Faces flushed, voices were raised, fists shaken in my direction as eighty women informed me that their dear old mums were not to be maligned and their honour impugned. It went something along the lines of "*My* mother was ... etc." I only escaped tarring and feathering thanks to unavailablity of these commodities. I got the impression that I would have been hanged, had they not considered hanging too good for such a louse. However, good came out of these regrettable events. Through time they forgave me, and I learnt the most important lesson a minister can ever learn, namely, make sure the Woman's Guild is on your side. It was the Guild ladies Our Lord had in mind when he said that the gates of hell cannot prevail against them.

In 1955, Bridgeton had no less than fifteen churches, including 'The Methodist Central Halls' which was built as a music hall, in which celebrities like Harry Lauder had once performed. It was there that a small, Iona-minded group of local ministers met for an 8 a.m. breakfast: Geoff Shaw, Walter Fyfe, Jesse Parkins - the Methodist minister, John Sim, David Redwood - the 'piskie', myself, and the irrepressible Jack McLennan, minister of Rockcliffe church. I was very fortunate to find myself in the stimulating company of such men of outstanding education, intelligence, and ability.

Our dedication was exemplified by our time of meeting (*sic*), and our zeal by our efforts to take political and social action. Around that period, the Iona Community was thundering against the evils of Sir Roy Welenski's Federation of Rhodesia and Nyasaland (Sir Roy was a friend of one of our Club's voluntary leaders, Tony Rennie), and Hastings Banda was being feted as a heroic democratic leader for an independent Nyasaland (Malawi). When the Suez crisis arose, we got very hot under the collar about that as well, and our breakfasting group hastened to 'chalk the streets', and stand outside factories distributing anti-war leaflets. Walter Fyfe, the only ideologue amongst us, took his soap box to Bridgeton Cross. In Glasgow Presbytery, we staged a walk out, led by wee Jack McLennan. Looking back, I now see how wrong we were on both these issues of the day: we meant well but brought in the dictators Banda and Mugabe. However, we did some things right: we gave out leaflets at the 'Buroo' inviting the unemployed to a meeting to see what could be done for them. This made a good impression, and better still, got some men a job. Out of our efforts emerged, in the long run, the Community Council, and the tremendously important local T. B. screening campaign.

The central figure in our group was Jack McLennan. Short, portly, balding, Jack chain-smoked and was so permanently covered with ash in his upper body that he looked like a miniature volcano. He was one of those people who never get tired. At our breakfast meetings, he would bounce in, fizzing with ideas and good sense. He was one of the most remarkable men I have ever met. Jack, a pre-war lecturer in educational psychology, had been chaplain to the prestigious Scots Greys during the Western Desert campaigns, and he would speak quite unemotionally about "scraping the bodies out of burnt-out tanks" and burying them. After the war he had wound up in a back street kirk in Bridgeton, and when his lovely wife told him they could not live on his meagre stipend, Jack started selling morning newspapers at Gorbals Cross. Prospering, he opened a newsagents in Caledonia Road, and then a fruit shop to provide a job for Jimmy Bennet, the Bridgeton M.P. who had suffered ill health.

Jack's fellow spirit was Jesse Parkins, the Methodist minister, a John Bull-looking Englishman. Jesse could buy and sell you anything from jam to Bibles! His father had been a horse trader and Jesse was keeping up the good name of that dubious profession. Jesse's manse was three stairs up in the close next to our own manse overlooking the Green; when it went on fire he bravely ran to the top of the stairs and into the flat to throw a tea-chest full of his old sermons out of the window to safety. As an afterthought, he went back to save the family. A minister must keep his priorities right!

In the fifties, T. B. was a scourge in the city, and the campaign to scan the whole population led to my being given the job of helping Jack organise this locally from an office in Jesse's Methodist Halls. Without the church folk, this campaign could never have been done, and those quick to deride the churches need reminding of that fact. Our folk went round the doors day after day. When it was over, I accompanied Jack to the City Chambers to meet a white coated gentleman I took to be the Chief Medical Officer, and he greeted Jack like a long lost wallet. The meeting of these two old chums was like a meeting between two Toby jugs, for they were exactly the same size and shape, belly to belly. "We must settle up your expenses, Jack," said the whiter of the two stomachs, and without batting an eye, Jack asked him for £300! I was astonished - my wee electric fire for one month? The medic blanched too - though ever so slightly. £300 fifty years ago was ... well, a lot of money. It set up Jesse's church finances for a couple of years, and Jack moved on to his next good deed.

Jack was highly regarded in education circles and invited to lecture. He told me one time he had double-booked and asked if I would go in his place - absolutely assuring me that *all* I had to do was chair a small discussion group on Sunday School teaching which was to meet in Iona Community House, Clyde Street. I fell for it: a large audience awaited my arrival, and I was introduced as the speaker in Jack's absence, owing to illness. I do not wish to relate what happened that night, it being a most embarrassing and painful memory, so suffice it to say I found myself a lion in a den of Daniels. The audience soon left, and I departed in search of the Rev. Jack McLennan, who I found making toffee apples and hanging them on a string in his kitchen for sale through his commercial outlets.

In this age of 'company men' (ministerial 'I.B.M' types), we will not see Jack's like again. He left Bridgeton for St. Katherine's Club in Aberdeen where I visited him. He expressed satisfaction at getting - quote - "£20 a week for doing nothing"; and a strong desire to walk down one of those douce Aberdeen streets kicking over all those neatly lined up half-pint-sized ashcans.

When Geoff departed for Gorbals, Jack pointed out to him that it was the biggest Irish R. C. stronghold in Britain - news to Geoff who had not given it any thought. Old Gorbals was also approaching its final days, and Jack said to Geoff and Walter, "Go, if you want - you won't do Gorbals much good, but it will do you a lot of good!" Mindful of those wise words, I decided not to join the Gorbals Group and stayed where I was.

One good thing Geoff did before going was to replace himself as Boys' Leader with George Buchanan-Smith. It was the perfect choice, and I welcomed an old friend warmly.

Chapter 13

A haughty Roman officer stopped the giant Androcles as he was being led past in chains, and said to him, "Christian, does not your religion tell you that if a man is struck on the right cheek, he must turn the left also?" Androcles agreed this was the case. "Then shall I test your Faith," said the Roman, striking Androcles on the right cheek and then, as Androcles turned it, on the left cheek also. These blows struck, Androcles addressed the Roman saying "You will agree, Sir, that your religion tells you that if a man is struck on the one cheek, he must not turn the other, but at once strike back. So, as you have just tested my Faith, now let me test yours." So saying Androcles showed the Roman officer his mighty arm and rolled up his sleeve!

'Big George' was not really all that big in height, but he was a hefty rugby player of sturdy, powerful build. When he arrived at the Club, he tried to be a Geoff Shaw, all theological psychology, until I advised him to forget Geoff and be himself. He did, and there was no more of the 'Mr Nice Guy' at Church House. Though an affable, well-mannered man, the sobriquet 'Big' was soon added to George's name by our members, who quickly noticed that, when angered, their new leader's face resembled the mouth of Mons Meg, primed and aimed in their direction.

George came from even further up the social scale than Geoff. His father was Lord Balerno, and his brother Alick was a very highly regarded Tory M.P. His uncle was Rab Butler, holder of several cabinet posts, and when George moved into Geoff's vacated room and kitchen, letters arrived bearing the Home Office seal. I often wondered if Uncle Rab had any idea where his posh letters were ending up! The Balerno estate was, I was told, the largest farm in Scotland, and the house entertained many leading statesmen. From time to time, groups of Club boys visited the place and viewed it with wondering eyes. George's father was eminent in his field of genetics, and a charming person. George was unusual for people from his background, in that he not only wanted to know how the other half live, but was ready to live it with them. This he did without any hang-ups about being rich, which was healthy and refreshing.

With George came money - he once told me he had no idea how much money he had to spend. He bought a minibus - our first. And a television set - another first. Where his predecessors had to scrimp and scrape, George bought whatever he required. A great man of the outdoors, he organised camps on a lavish scale, using his widespread social contacts to good effect. He took me to places I would never have been otherwise. No more baths in the Club sink, or the Steamie. It was the Arlington Baths (where we met Lord Hailsham floating about one day) for me, and on Saturday nights a dip in the tub at one of the city's poshest hotels. Dressed in a battered hat and wellies, George simply walked in and ordered two baths (just the baths, mind you!), and we were provided with towels, no questions asked - ten shillings each. It must have been obvious that we were both members of the nobility, and given due deference.

Friday night was my night off, and I spent it in George's flat watching *Hancock's Half-hour*, and writing scripts for Club shows. When George came in after the Club closed, we watched a TV programme and phoned up one of the performers at the ITV or BBC studios to invite them over for a drink (programmes were live in those days). We often ended up after an all-night session with one of these celebrities, having breakfast at the old St. Enoch's Hotel, after which we would rush back to the Club to take the boys to their football matches.

One Friday we invited a famous actress, a complete stranger to us, and she arrived festooned with diamonds and furs. Being well-oiled, she was in sociable mood, and two-up left, 983 London Road, rang with laughter and good will. Seeing an expensive limousine parked outside the close, Jimmy Little, our local policeman, came up to check that all was well, and I have rarely seen anyone so astounded as he was at the scene which met his eyes! This great lady in a room and kitchen in Bridgeton at 2 a.m! As he stood there gaping and swinging his helmet, this Empress of the Silver Screen waved a languid wrist and said, "Ah! constable, have you come to tell me that you have found my stolen jewels?" We drove her limo to the St. Enoch's Hotel, leaving her to sleep it off. We breakfasted heartily while she recovered, and P. C. Little spread his tale of the strange goings-on in Brigton after dark!

On another occasion, George returned from the Club to find me

"Big George" Buchanan-Smith and 'prohibition' at dances
- no bottles!

Monica Morris, Geoff Shaw and senior boys, around 1955

settled down watching the television as usual, and also find his door into the flat lying open with the locks burst. Two cameras were gone from his front room, and to this day I cannot understand how I sat a few feet away in the kitchen and heard nothing. The neighbours across the landing heard nothing either. Whoever did it was a skilled operator, and we had no shortage of such local experts. Happily, the cameras were recovered, thanks to Billy Beattie making what may be described euphemistically as 'discreet enquiries'.

Billy was George's 'minder-cum-butler', an appointment in which he took considerable pride. I first met Billy at a Club dance, when he drew attention to his presence by spilling a bottle of juice over the suit of Big Willie Wilson. Billy and Willie were in their early twenties, but there the resemblance ended. Willie was a whale-sized, quiet soul; Billy was only half his stature but a million times more talkative - a right 'patter-merchant'. As the bigger of the two, Willie was about to strike this stranger dead for tainting his new suit, so Billy was ushered to the safety of the canteen and eventually a meeting was arranged in the hope of reconciliation. Billy opened with a speech worthy of Pericles. "These good Christian people have come here to help the poor, giving their time to provide needy young persons like ourselves with, etc, etc ..." He went on to catalogue all the virtues of the leaders, together with all the wonderful facilities of Church House. It was deeply moving address, aimed at William Wilson. "Willie," appealed Billy, "let us not make trouble for these fine people; they care about the likes of us, and have given us table-tennis, indoor football, baking, craftswork, billiards, and boxing exhibitions." At the mention of boxing exhibitions, Willie, in emulation of Androcles, raised a clenched fist, placed it under Billy's nose and said grimly, "Aye, boxing exhibitions!" I could see that Billy would be with us for some time to come, talking his way out of trouble. He bore a strong resemblance to Rab C. Nesbitt, physically and philosophically.

Before going to the Club, I had never met anyone who had been in prison. I was still living in 'Toy Town', with 'Larry the Lamb', and 'Mr Policeman'. I soon learnt that when a guy shook your hand and told you he was going for his 'cocoa', you wouldn't be seeing him at Christmas. I began to see going to jail as a sort of 'holiday'. Bill was often imprisoned for petty crimes, but the experience did not daunt his spirit, or stop him getting a job when he came out. He was, by all accounts, a hard worker, though unfortunately one inclined to help himself to the goods.

During one of the interludes between his incarcerations, Billy got a job in the docks, and was arrested for stealing cigarettes, typically opting to defend himself in court. The chief witness for the defence was a Chinaman who spoke no English, only Mandarin with a Liverpool accent. Cross-examining this tiny oriental took up much time but produced little information, and greatly exasperated learned counsel. The Sheriff, a busy man not unacquainted with the accused, threw up his hands and dismissed the case, with dire warnings to Billy as to the consequences of their meeting again, as they surely would, on some future occasion. We drove Billy home. Next day he got himself another job - no slouch, our Billy.

I don't suppose you could call Billy a 'hard man' in the Glasgow usage of that term. But like all the hard men I met he was characteristically very deferential towards ministers. He was not long in the Club before he was giving out the hymn books at the chapel door, and deploring the behaviour of juvenile delinquents. The big time crooks, the hard men, looked down on the lesser criminals as lacking respect and conveniently saw their own criminal activities as harmless - after all, the insurance paid for it, didn't it? Billy took it upon himself to guard George's flat, and George became a favourite with Billy's pleasant family - a law-abiding clan, including an amiable brother who, nonetheless, when in his cups, needed the Keystone cops to overpower and arrest him!

A party, to many of the under-privileged elements in the parish, meant a drinking spree. When I asked a single parent young mother why she didn't have her baby baptised, she explained that she couldn't afford to pay £100 for the drink at the party. I remember Billy coming to a Christmas party in the Club and he was, like many others, as delighted as a three-year-old by the games we played. He was essentially a simple soul. He came to the vestry one night to consult me about a problem he was having with the police: he used some waste ground beside Celtic Park for the fans to park their cars for the price of a protection fee. The 'Busies' told him he was being charged with not paying income tax on these illegal earnings! I assured him his enterprise was tax-free, but what I hadn't the heart to tell him was that the local cops were winding him up and he was falling for it. I should add that boys offer to watch cars at Celtic Park for a fee - a wise precaution worth taking seeing that Alex Mair and I one night counted a dozen cars outside the Club with broken windscreens for not utilising this protection racket. I once saw a boy wearing an Irish tricolour round this shoulders offering this service, and was surprised because I knew he was a true blue Rangers fan. His answer to my questioning was a shrug followed by "Well, business is business".

Very recently a former Club girl, now a Grannie, telephoned from down South to ask for Billy's address. I pointed out I hadn't seen him for forty years, adding that the last I heard of Billy was an unconfirmed report that he had died in Govan of a drug overdose. I know he was a bit of a rascal, and a plausible one at that, but I liked him enough to be sad to hear of his death. It takes all kinds.

Dances were very popular in the Glasgow of those pre-Rock & Roll days. A church lady told me that she had joined the church through attending one at which she watched John and Jean Sim dancing, noting how happy they were together in comparison to herself at that low point in her married life. Francis of Assisi said "We preach as we walk", and he might have added, "We preach as we dance too!" It seemed strange at first for me to hear Club boys talking about "you Christians" (I thought everybody was a Christian!) but I was learning another vital lesson: that folk may not read the Bible but they read *you*, and it is when you are least aware of it, that your conduct is noted and judged.

By Geoff's time, dances were for young people only - rowdy, packed out. You paid a shilling to get in, and got a receipt for the bottles taken off you at the entrance. This did not stop the boozing, because the girls smuggled it in anyway. The band sat on a high platform and was solemnly warned not to play 'party tunes', but as the night wore on, enthusiasm grew and 'The Sash' and 'Hello, hello, we are the Billy boys' (to the stirring melody 'Marching through Georgia') received full orchestration. Our dances did not involve drugs: they were ecstatic enough without such stimulants!

No one was admitted after the 9 p.m. deadline. One Saturday night, I found myself at the door denying admission to a gang of undesirables. They simply could not, or would not, understand why they couldn't get in, and the pros and cons of the case were argued at length until finally one of them declared himself enlightened, stating firmly, "You'll no let us in because we don't go to your f******g church!" This explanation seemed satisfactory to his companions, except for one of them who did something I had never seen before, and have never witnessed since: he began foaming at the mouth, big bubbles flowing out! I previously thought 'foaming at the mouth' was a figure of speech, until I actually saw it happening. I was learning another lesson: that reasonableness has its boundaries, and violence is never far away. They went away but came back later, somebody let them in, and they marched into the hall in a scene like the shootout in a Wild West saloon. Geoff was a very lucky man that night, because he happened to be standing on the band's high platform when they went for him. A 'rammy' broke out, our own boys set about the intruders, and I was hit over the head by a flying chair. Our security arrangements were strengthened later, but things became so stroppy that when George came, he stopped the dances.

Our last dance night ended with boys lying around the Club drunk, and George going round collecting the bodies two at a time, and throwing them like sacks into the back of the van. We then drove round their places of residence, dumping each body on the pavement. The last delivery was to an address in Ruchazie and we opened up the van and laid the prostrate youth outside his close. To our consternation, he sprang to his feet and ran off at high speed. Instinctively I ran after him. What I did not know was that a police car was chasing after me, and I was pinned to the wall by two big cops! Having to explain to the sceptical officers of the law what I was doing running after a boy in Ruchazie at 1.30 a.m. took some doing.

Chapter 14

The reproduction of mankind is a great marvel and a mystery. Had God consulted me in the matter, I should have advised him to continue the generation of the species by fashioning them out of clay.
Martin Luther

"Crime and How to make it pay" - as recommended by the Barlinnie Bookman's Club.

Credit rating was a problem which went with the Bridgeton manse address - if I missed paying the milkman on a Saturday, he got me up on a Sunday at dawn. In vain did I plead that I was hardly likely to run away for a couple of quid - NO credit, that's that, minister or no minister. It was the address which counted. Little wonder then that folk going for a job claim their address is in a better area.

Getting a delivery van to call is also a problem in certain areas - and taxis will not pick up passengers. One Christmas, I parked a van full of food parcels outside the church, intending to deliver them round the poor and needy. I came out to find the van empty, but knew the goods could not have gone far in the time I was away. An informant directed me across the street to an apartment harbouring our parcels. A lot had already gone, presumably to the poor and needy, so I left the guy with the rest as he seemed quicker than I could be at making deliveries.

The first indication of drug-taking was a rash of glue-sniffing, boys looking as if they were suffering from a heavy cold. Drugs followed; Alex Mair had to deal with the problem at the Club, by which time heroin had got a real grip. Young people staggering around the streets has become a familiar sight, and even shootings are not considered uncommon. Alex used to track the dealers' cars cruising round selling the drugs - a dangerous thing to do though Alex could always look after himself

At times Alex ran risks which I considered inadvisable After one break-in at the Club, we walked up to a group of ne'er-do-wells at the street comer, Alex picked out the one he thought was to blame, and felled him on the spot! That took guts, as did the time Alex took a sword from a drugged up youth standing on the billiard table waving it about. Alex must have often been scared, but I never knew him to be intimidated.

Full time Girls' Leaders need to be wary too; Joyce Campbell was mugged; Lismay Dougal was very lucky somebody happened to turn up one time she was alone in the Club with a dangerous bloke. On the whole, the atmosphere was very rarely menacing, but you just had to watch it.

My finest hour in the war against crime came while I was helping Mr Sim with the class for First Communicants. In those far off days, these classes consisted of couples marrying, teenagers told by caring parents to join the kirk, newcomers, etc. Amongst these was a chap I had got to know through visiting called Davie McClure, a young-to-middle-aged, respectable but tough chap. One afternoon, I was strolling along the busy London Road when he came running towards me, followed hot-foot by a group of men. At first I thought he was being chased by these guys, but he stopped and breathlessly asked me if I had seen anybody running past me. I said I had not. When the others caught up, Davie explained to me that he was part of a posse in pursuit of a thief who had been breaking into people's houses and gas meters - in those days, a heinous crime. My First Communicant swore me in, deputised me, and I joined in the hunt.

We spread out along Queen Mary Street, each taking a close; mine was number 5. I cautiously ascended the well-worn stone stairs, timidly pushing open every stairhead toilet door until, on the top landing, the toilet revealed a huge, unsavoury looking individual who was hiding within. To my indescribable relief, he offered no resistance. When I informed him he was 'nicked' (as the coppers say) and instructed him to 'come quietly', like a lamb, he followed me down to the entrance of the close, where I delivered him into the hands of Davie and his assembling vigilantes. Then I went round to the police box and called the boys in blue.

Davie left Bridgeton but some twenty years later, I met him on a social occasion. We got to reminiscing about the time I caught the burglar, mentioning that when I looked back, it puzzled me that he came with me so readily, indeed almost happily. Davie smiled: "He was glad to see you," he explained, "if we had got him we would have kicked his head in!" It seems I had, unwittingly, by my beneficent clerical presence, restrained the dispensers of rough justice, and simultaneously saved the criminal from his fate. As he had been dropping shillings as he fled, in a sort of paper chase, little gas-meter money was recovered at the time, but that did not take the shine off my reputation as a hero!

I was not a regular customer of the public houses at Bridgeton Cross, as the sight of me inevitably led to my being plied with 'wee refreshments' I did not desire. But I did call in from time to time, if only to uphold my proletarian credentials, and receive cut-price offers of three-piece suits, sets of tyres etc. As these goods were to be delivered at 2.30 a.m. (no questions asked, by the way), I expressed appreciative gratitude but regretfully declined.

I suppose one good turn deserves another, and the fathers of weans I had shriven at the font were very favourably disposed towards repaying me for my ministrations. There were times, however, when I feared the Law would show an interest in these dubious transactions. In particular I recall the time a former club member, who worked in the docks, arrived at the manse with two large bags of bone meal for my garden. It was a most generous offer, but fearful of Inspector Knacker, and also of contracting anthrax from untreated bone meal, I buried the pile in the garden where it still lies. If the unsolved crime files are ever reopened on the case, the spot where I buried the fertilising stuff will be easy to find: there will be a tree the size of a Californian Redwood growing there!

That there is an underworld of crime in any big city comes into public notice every now and again, but you can live in a place with a bad reputation for a lifetime and never be affected by it. It never occurred to me there was any (well, much) danger in walking around Glasgow Green with the dog at 1 a.m. when all I saw was rabbits. I fearlessly wandered around unsavoury closes in the dark, relying upon my clerical collar, and popularity, for protection from the inhabitants. Benefit of Clergy did not extend, however, to their dangerous pet Alsatians, Rotweilers, and Bull Terriers with which I had life-threatening encounters on the stairs - all named 'Rebel', by the way! I banked heavily upon two things: firstly, naiveté; and secondly, being hell of a quick on my feet!

Bartenders are a valuable source of information, and one in particular, a very dapper fellow, always immaculately turned out, did a lot of intelligence gathering about the underworld of crime. Some of this he passed on to me, in confidence, of course. I still don't know whether or not to believe the half of it, but the the half I did believe scared me. It is, I now understand, better not to know what goes on - just read about it in the newspapers.

I have never found out who telephoned the manse one day and threatened to kill me, and have often wondered if I had been told more than I should have been about someone or something. Anyway, at first I thought it was a joke, but soon realised the caller was very serious, and I got quite a fright. A few nights later, after the vestry hour, it being late, I decided not to take Margaret in the car down to friends in Troon but to drive home instead, and I soon realised there was something wrong with the car. Somebody had taken off, or loosened, all the nuts on the wheels and they would have fallen off had I driven fast to Troon. The police could do nothing, of course, but I could, and did, take the warning I had been given not to meddle in certain matters.

I sometimes ran into familiar criminals I was trying to avoid: one Friday night vestry hour, a young lady came in and asked me to visit her. I called at her very clean single-end, with her three wee ones asleep in bed. She led me over to the window and said, "See that windae, three-up across the London Road, well, the 'Big Man' is up there. These are his weans and he's moved in with the lassie o'er there." "Really?" I responded, trying to look sympathetic, "What do you want me to do about it?" This reply surprised her. "Why, go and bring him back here," said she. Being familiar with the name and reputation of the man concerned - he had done time for a violent murder, and was just out - I declined, politely, leaving her the name and address of a marriage counsellor I particularly disliked.

The 'Big Man' is now a prominent guest of Her Majesty, but during the Seventies he stayed for a time in the new houses being built beside our church. I went round some of these and despatched my new, very young and somewhat timid Assistant to visit the others. The windows in the entrance to one of the new blocks were all broken, but Allan started knocking doors and introducing himself until he came to one opened by a gorilla of a man who asked him in. A large picture of King Billy adorned the wall and Alan ventured to ask if his host was a member of the Orange Order. "Why?" growled the orang-outang, "have ye goat something against it?" This query was met with a hasty assurance that Allan was not against it one teeny, weenie bit, and that he was, indeed, more than enthusiastic over the admirable qualities of the said King Billy. Changing the subject, Allan asked about the state of the entrance to the building. "What a shame about the place, a new building and already the windows are all broken; you must have a lot of vandals doing damage". "Naw," was the reply, "I broke them aw myself - they'd just have goat broke onywey!" When my Assistant returned to report on his visitations I couldn't help laughing - he had entered the lion's den, and paid a pastoral visit to the 'Big Man's' hoose!

One time I knocked a door with no name on it and asked the man who appeared if he was a certain Mr So-and-so. The man replied he was not, but added that the name was familiar to him, because it was the name of the flat's previous occupant. How long had his predecessor been gone? - Six weeks. Had he met the man? - No. Did he know where he had gone? - No, but there was mail waiting to be collected and the chances were that somebody would come to collect it.

So far so good, thought I, going on to say, "If the guy turns up, would you find out where he is staying and phone to let me know?" "Sure, no problem, glad to help," answered the agreeable fellow. After thanking the guy, I walked away, little realising that the bloke I had been talking to was the very same man I was looking for! He must have mistaken me for a debt collector - you meet some shrewd operators, and Our Lord himself commended to us their intelligence, though not their practices.

A debt collector of my acquaintance couldn't find a man who kept flitting from one nameless house to another, until one day he saw the guy's dog wandering the streets of Bridgeton, and followed the hound all the way to its new home in the Gorbals, where he found his quarry and apprehended him. However, such captures were rare.

When Fred and Rosemary West were arrested for their appalling crimes, I read that he had lived at one time in Bridgeton (Soho Street), and operated an ice-cream van called 'Mr Whippy'. The name of the van struck a chord with me, and I realised that, on my way home on Friday nights, after the vestry hour, I may well have bought cones for my three children from Fred West! I can picture summer nights - a crowd of weans round the van - a friendly vendor giving priority to my order, and bidding me, in an English voice, "Good evening, vicar!"

There was a baker's shop at the corner of Queen Mary Street, one of a chain of bakeries belonging to the Mr Watt who was arrested for the murder of his family in Burnside. As our kirk was across the street, he came into my vestry several times to talk and talk about his terrible problems, a bit drunk and stressed out, poor man. The case became sensational, and he was falsely accused on circumstantial evidence. The real murderer was the evil house-breaker Peter Manuel. I was really sorry for Mr Watt.

You get some idea of how naïve I was in those days when I recount the tale of how, in righteous indignation, I went to see the police in order to protest at a false arrest. I explained to a very nice Superintendent that I had seen two young men of my Club acquaintance walking along London Road when a pair of bobbies arrested them for breach of the peace. One was certainly singing, I admitted, but *sotta voce*, and causing no disturbance. The other was behaving like a model citizen. I recounted with horror how they had been forced into a nearby police box, and how a crowd had gathered demanding their release. I swore on an invisible Bible, that with mine own eyes I had seen them thrown out of the police box and into the street by the policemen concerned, and that they had not, as was being alleged, 'escaped' and gone on the run.

The Super was an intelligent man, a churchman to boot, and he heard me out patiently. Then he explained matters to me in a most delicate fashion. What it amounted to was this: the two officers concerned were not psychologists touring the streets in white overalls; nor were they school teachers with a mission in life to educate - they were soldiers in the front line in the war between the Law and the Neds, and these two officers had the best anti-crime record of any East End beat. This line of argument had not occurred to me before, but I stiffly replied that justice could not be trifled with, etc, etc, and I would take the matter further when the case came to court.

It never did come to court. When I offered to gather witnesses to their innocence, the accused did not receive the news with the enthusiasm I had anticipated. They were going to plead guilty. I expressed astonishment, but they put me in the picture by saying that if they got off with this, the polis would only get them for something else. They, and the arresting officers, were playing the same game; each side understood the rules; that's how it went. The phrase *'pour encourager les autres'* came to mind, and it dawned on me that I was in a moral no-man's land, and about to leave my childhood Toytown world forever.

One of my young men in the church and the Regnal Circle was Joe Park, a small, swarthy bachelor with a limp, and a sharp wit. Joe worked as a lift-operator in Lewis's store in Argyle Street. He stayed in a single-end at 5 Queen Mary Street opposite the church, one of the poorest closes in the parish. Joe was taken into hospital one time, and I was surprised to notice that, every evening, the light was on in his window. Visiting him in the Royal Infirmary, I asked who it was that was staying in his house, and Joe's gast was flabbered by my news! I promised to investigate and report back.

Joe's window was directly over a shop which had a ledge wide enough for someone to stand upon, and as I made my way to the close, the window opened and a man came out and stood on the ledge screaming blue murder! "Help!" he cried, "They've got a gun and are trying to kill me!" This unexpected turn of events sent me hastening to the nearby police box, and telephoning to H.Q. for assistance pronto. In no time at all, police cars arrived and I told my tale. But by then the mysterious figure on the ledge had vanished. Extensive inquiries amongst the neighbours met the usual 'omerta'. Nobody had seen or heard anything, nobody knew that somebody had been living in Joe's house, and so on. Joe never found out who had been occupying his house for a fortnight and what all this alarming business of a shooting was all about!

Collecting scrap metal was another hobby in Bridgeton - collecting it and taking it to a local scrappy who was none too scrupulous about where it came from. As some of the local bobbies received hospitality from these merchants, the trade in what was advertised as "non-ferrous metals" (lead and copper) flourished. A wary eye was kept on the Church House roof, but the lead kept disappearing just the same. I recall a bitterly cold, dark winter night on the roof with Alex shovelling off snow and laying felt in the valley gutters - all part of the job in those days! To combat the thieves when I designed the rebuilt Club in 1970, I made sure all the copper pipes were buried under the concrete floor, and that there was no lead on the roof. It was quite a job convincing the Scottish Education Department not to favour putting on a fancy flat roof. Give them every credit, for they did what the people at the Board of National Mission used to do in the days of Horace Walker and Ian Doyle: they listened to the people on the spot.

St. Francis-in-the-East Church roof was always a joy to me - it is as steep as the South face of the Eiger, inaccessible to thieves. Just thinking about it always sent me off into a deep, pleasant, undisturbed sleep at Presbytery meetings. However, the building is not entirely invulnerable to an enemy at the gates. I came along once to see an aged, scruffy old ragamuffin with a pony and cart, breaking up our iron church gates with a sledge-hammer. Some of our rone pipes were already broken up and piled on his cart, so I politely asked him what the heck he thought he was doing! He informed me the church was an abandoned building and he was helping to demolish it! I told him his information was incorrect, read him his rights and put him and his nag under citizen's arrest before sending someone to call the cops. I held on to the nag to prevent him riding off and escaping. If the Queen had given me a medal for this brave act, I suppose somebody would sooner or later have pinched it for scrap.

George B-Smith's losses were fairly considerable over his period as Boys' Leader, his flat being a target. One Christmas he lost a lot of stuff, including a carton of cigarettes. I was able to return his cigs as they were given to me as a Christmas present by a boy who had fallen out with George. George then gave me the fags back because he had bought them in the first place as a Christmas present for me!

My own losses were slight, because although Mr Hay's flat in the Club was also broken into regularly, and he lost his suits, etc., my room was so small that either nobody knew it was there, or else the thieves couldn't find it. Sitting quietly one night after the Club closed, Mr Hay on one side of our kitchen fire and yours truly on the other, we heard a crashing noise and I ventured downstairs to investigate. At the back of the old Club ran a rubbish-choked, narrow lane with a side door into the Club which was never used and barricaded up. A youth wielding a sledge-hammer was pounding on this door and when I tartly asked what the blankety blank he was doing, he coolly replied that he had 'left his jaiket in the Club' and was attempting to retrieve it. An unlikely tale you may think, and you would be right. I suggested that in future he might try ringing the front door bell, and he slunk off facing a month's banishment from Church House.

In the Sixties, 'love-ins', and 'sit-ins' were popular, but at the Club we went in for 'break-ins'. All our windows were boarded up, so they came in through the roof. They even tunnelled in! I entered the old gymn one day to see a boy's head appear through the floor! Round the back they had taken out bricks and got under the floor boards. After Mr Hay died, and I married and left the flat, the Club was even more exposed to burglary. On many a night I had to get out of bed and start nailing up burst doors. Nobody would insure the Club, and it all cost good money getting joiners at the weekends.

I owned an old bicycle on which I rode around the flat plains of Brigton. It was insured. My hope was that somebody would swipe it so I could get a new one, but no matter how often I left it unprotected outside a close, it was always there when I came out. I even left it one whole night at Bridgeton Cross, only to find it still propped up outside the Clydesdale Bank. I left it in places where even the most myopic of thieves must have seen it, but I just couldn't get it stolen, and like the poor, it remained with me always.

I was very unlucky with bicycles. The same was true with my old blue Triumph 2000 - it had no locks, having been broken into so often I didn't bother fixing them, but nobody took it. I like to think it was because everybody knew it was mine, but I guess its battered appearance and venerable pedigree made it hardly worth the taking. It was the only car in the world with bricked-up windows!

Horace Walker, when he was running the Home Board (and doing it very well!), once said to me, "Bill, you are imperturbable". He was right, you got that way after a while ministering in old Brigton: if someone had told me the church had been stolen, and all that remained was a big hole in the ground, I would just have said, "What, again!" Life was never dull, that was the only thing you could be certain about.

Breaking into the old coin gas meters was a favourite solution to monetary problems: I was called once to an old property off the Gallowgate in answer to a telephone call from a man requesting urgent spiritual assistance - or so he said. He was an unkempt blighter and his house was a tip, Without further ado, he directed my attention to his gas meter. This had been broken open, and its contents removed. I expressed great indignation at the amount of thieving from gas meters going on, and then waited for the inevitable plea to come from him. Yes, as I feared, he wanted me to reimburse him for the missing amount. I explained that I was not insensitive to his plight, but he would have to proceed through life without the benefit of my monetary assistance. He displayed no dismay at my refusal, offered me tea, and looked very surprised when I asked him if he knew who had broken into his meter. "Why, I did it myself," he chirped with pride. 'Fair enough', was about all I could think to say, for I could see he was an honest man at heart.

One of the daftest thefts I came across was by a youth who took a taxi to Templetons' carpet factory, broke in, and loaded carpets into the waiting taxi. The driver immediately drove round to the nearby Eastern Police Station and handed him over. His mother worked in the factory and her nickname was 'The Flying Carpet' due to her reputation for nicking the carpets.

The finest crime I ever witnessed was a masterpiece in ingenuity. The distance ftom Celtic Park to Church House is only a few hundred yards, and London Road slopes slightly downhill all the way. Lorries ran down the slope until they came to a zebra crossing beside the Club. As I watched, a boy crossed the zebra and stopped a lorry which was carrying a long, rolled up carpet, the end of which was hanging out over the lorry's tail end. Two boys then darted out of a close, held on to the end of the carpet. As the lorry drove away, the carpet slid off. The three boys dragged it up a close and vanished! It was all done in seconds, and the lorry driver must be mystified to this day as to where his carpet went that afternoon!

Two other memorable thefts stick in my mind. A small garage under some railway arches up a narrow lane did repair work for me, but I didn't relish going there because the owner kept a ferocious Alsatian dog which didn't welcome company. Fortunately it was restrained by a long chain. One day I called for the car and no dog! Intruders had got in during the night, and stolen it! The only explanation for this extraordinarily brave act is that the thieves were some of these animal rights activists you read about, but that is unlikely.

The other theft was in a plumbers' merchant's warehouse next door to Church House. I knew the owner well, and he had lots of thieving to contend with. One day he told me he had installed a state-of-the-art burglar alarm system at great cost. Some weeks later, I asked him if he was benefitting from this, and he smiled grimly, saying, "You won't believe this, but they broke in and stole my alarm system!"

When I think back on the countless break-ins at the Club, I reckon we came out of them pretty well on the whole. The thieves left ladders and tools (all high quality and doubtless stolen from neighbouring businesses), and all we lost were lemonade and crisps. A fair trade from my point of view. I sometimes wondered if thieves deliberately broke in to leave me things, rather than take them away! Perhaps they were moved by gratitude for all the nice things I did for them - like burying dear old dad. I buried Lulu's grandfather, but I don't think Lulu ever broke into the Club to show appreciation.

H. L. Mencken, the brilliantly witty pre-war Baltimore journalist and atheist, once wrote: "The chief contribution of Protestantism to human thought is its massive proof that God is a bore". I find it difficult to disagree with this somewhat acid judgement when the proof is, indeed, pretty 'massive', but I believe Harold Louis Mencken would have reconsidered his criticism had he visited Church House before his death in 1956. The Club in those days was the least boring place on earth.

One night the Club was visited by a coach full of overseas students from Edinburgh University. Their visit was part of their studies into juvenile delinquency, so they looked round the place and then met for a lecture by one of their staff. Meantime, their swanky coach outside was being robbed, and when they returned to it, their belongings had gone. One huge, very black young man from the Sudan asked me if I knew who had done it, and, seeing some wee boys peeping round the corner, I said that I didn't know, but that these wee guys did. He called them over and offered a pound note to those who brought back the missing goods, especially his own briefcase. Immediately, dozens of weans began bringing stuff back from hiding places in the middens, until all was returned! A pound between them all worked out a few pennies apiece. I shall aways feel the utmost respect for that Sudanese gentleman: there was nothing anybody could teach *him* about juvenile delinquency. Incidentally, how did they get into the coach? The doors were locked, the windows shut (here was a mystery to rival Edgar Allan Poe's "The Murders in the Rue Morgue"). Well, in the floor of a bus is a small inspection trap door over the rear axle, and if you open it from beneath the bus ...

We all say that if some of the criminals turned their brains to honest living they would make a fortune, for some are extremely clever. But not always ... A friendly young thief by the name of Catchpole told me how he ran away to London to get away from the 'Busies', and thought he could hide away in the crowds swirling round Trafalgar Square. Feeling safe, far from Glasgow, totally anonymous, he was feeling relaxed and happy when two men in plain clothes came up beside him, one on each side. "Come along with us, Mr Catchpole," said one, as they took him by the arms, no questions asked, such as "Are you Andrew Catchpole from Glasgow?" "They just lifted me," Andrew told me with considerable astonishment, and ungrudging admiration for the London Bobby.

The nastiest experience I had of a car theft was when I saw some opportunistic neds of my acquaintance smashing the rear window of a hatchback and stealing a golf bag and its contents. As a golfer myself, this was the unforgivable sin, and I stopped and gave chase, leaving my two small daughters somewhat scared in my car. The bag and clubs were heavy, so I easily caught up with the youth carrying it and grabbed hold of the bag. As he knew me well, I expected him to let go, but to my surprise, this he did not do. His pals gathered round, pulled out the clubs and began threatening me with them. According to their own twisted mentality, they thought I was trying to steal from them! The thought that I might wish to restore the bag, and its contents, to the owner did not enter their heads. It was a sticky situation; I had the bag, they had the clubs. Cars were passing, so I leapt into the road and tried to stop one and get some help, but each driver sped past, plainly not wanting involved. I had to stand right in front of a car to force it to stop; it had three men in it but none of them got out. However, by that time the boys had started to retreat, hurling the clubs at me as they withdrew. Two big polis arrived and I reported to them. They wanted to know who were my witnesses. I offered them the names and addresses of some of the culprits, but explained I had not recruited witnesses during the emergency. Doubtless the police had their own methods for dealing with the thieves, as well known to them as to myself, so they departed to pursue their investigations.

I returned his property to its owner: a well-dressed young man I found doing business in a local office unaware of the theft. I wised him up on the folly of leaving valuables on view in a hatchback, especially in the East End. He took the bag from me, didn't ask how I had retrieved it, nor did he thank me - indeed, he glared at me as if I had stolen it! Hastening back to my own car, I found two wee girls in a state of considerable anxiety, and what with one thing and another, almost regretted stopping the thieves!

Unfortunately for me, however, the matter was not closed; that afternoon, a Saturday, we were holding a sale in the Club, and the gang came to the door threatening me. A few nights later, I left the

Club to find my car upside down in the street, all four wheels up in the air. It wasn't easy to turn it back over and the damage to the roof cost me quite a bit.

Intimidation is not a daily feature of life for many people so they find it hard to understand what it is like to live with it. A bad night at the Club could lead to our transit van being taken and burnt out a mile or so away. Little wonder people either keep to themselves, or move away. Nowadays, even the churches are fair game, and those in the East End not already burnt down are like fortresses festooned with barbed wire. Who would have thought it? I read that the Scottish Parliament has allocated a million pounds to protect the Glasgow and Edinburgh mosques, but it does not seem to be politically correct to recognise that kirks in 'deprived areas' are under siege and the folk unable to afford adequate insurance cover.

I was briefly arrested myself on two occasions; on the first of these I was chased for carrying a suspicious-looking bundle late at night. Jouking up a close, I was nabbed by two Bobbies who were new to Bridgeton and didn't know me. Pinned to the wall, I unwrapped the goods in my possession, and submitted them for forensic examination. These turned out to be posters for Christian Aid Week, and the outcome was an amicable settlement of the misunderstanding, followed by contributions from the constables to the good cause.

My second arrest occurred around midnight in Miller Lane, off Argyle Street. The lane, which was at that time home to *The Glasgow Herald*, is a very narrow, dark channel between high buildings. I was there to put an envelope through the door of a printing firm. Having done so, and hearing the rumble of the last tram approaching out of my view along Argyle Street, I made a run for it. Instantly bright lights shone about me, and the forces of law and order closed in. Apparently they were staking-out Miller Lane in anticipation of a robbery, and I had sprung the trap. Without pausing for introductory civilities, they seized the big brown paper parcel I was carrying under my arm, and demanded to know the contents. I remained silent - dumbfounded just about covers it! They opened it up, expecting to find 'the swag', but instead, to my delight, they peeled out smelly socks and football strips which I had ready for the bagwash. I was questioned, and released without charges. They then melted back into the darkness and resumed their ambush positions. I missed the tram and walked all the way back to the Club, a sliver peeved, but a free man.

Suffice it to say that arrest in those days was an unpredictable business - I once stood talking to a group of corner boys when along came two cops who joined in our cheerful, if edgy, conversation for some time and then booked everyone for loitering - I was spared this stab in the back, an act of clemency, I guess. Not nice! But all's fair in love and war, and some of the boys gained their revenge, I'm told, by shopping these same cops for sitting in a pub after closing time.

A policeman's lot is not, they say, "a happy one", and one must sympathise with the *gendarmes'* efforts to put the lid on crime. A certain feeling of "what's the use of it all" must affect their morale from time to time, and I saw this illustrated when visiting a lady who lived high up in the multi-storey flats. From her lofty perch, her eagle eye spotted some youths stealing the local school bell, a metal object so heavy they had to slowly drag it along the ground. As she looked down, she phoned the police saying: "Quick, you can catch them; they're taking the school bell." A weary voice answered, "Oh it's you again. You are always phoning here", and put the phone down. I think it is called 'community policing'.

The hazards of life as a policeman or a minister extend to other professions, as Bill Bunton's tale doth show: Billy was one of my elders, a solider citizen and a nicer man the world has never known. Very shy, grievously afflicted with a skin condition, he had given up his bus inspector's job due to stress, and gone back to driving a one-man bus around the city.

Everyone who knows Glasgow at all, knows the "Heilanman's Umbrella", the huge bridge over Argyle Street at Central Station. Amongst the shops lining the street beneath the bridge, was one called 'The Dido' which sold leather goods - handbags, briefcases, luggage, etc. Outside the shop was a bus stop. Late one dark night, Billy drove his omnibus under the bridge, and drew up at this leather goods shop. As he stopped, a man smashed the shop window, helped himself to an armful of the contents, and boarded the bus. To Billy's searching question, "Where do you think you're going?", he quietly answered, unperturbed, "Glasgow Cross".

Twittering with nerves, Billy made his position clear: "You're going nowhere on this bus - get off". At this, the guy pulled out a big knife, shedding his load in the process. Billy grabbed his wrist, and a 'Mexican Stand-off' ensued, followed by diplomatic negotiations (the guy was very nice about it, Billy reported later). It was finally agreed he would drop the knife, gather up his ill-gotten gains, and disembark - this done, Billy drove off, shaking like a leaf. A dear old soul who had witnessed the encounter addressed some words of comfort to her driver: "Ah'm awfy sorry, son, but Ah couldnae dae much tae help ye". "That's all right, Mrs," responded Billy, "thanks anyway." But she had more to say: "Och weel" she added, "it's an ill wind that blaws naebody ony good!". The meaning of this mysterious remark became plain when she held up a couple of shiny, expensive, brand-new handbags - while the confronatation with Billy had been going on, she had been robbing the thief! Only in Glasgow, only in dear auld Glesca' Toon, could you see such sight. Who would want to live anywhere else?

Chapter 15

CAMPS

" 'Tis the maddest, most merry
The saddest to bury,
The sunniest season of life. "
Anon

In the early days of Church House, Iona was the venue for camping in both the North End and Village camps. These were mixed, and during my time working on the Abbey rebuilding in 1955, I had my first encounters with many of the Church House young people. However, when I started as Minister's Assistant, and Geoff Shaw became Boys' Leader, all our camping on Iona and elsewhere was for boys only.

Geoff arranged for a camp to be held at Camus, a small bay across from Iona where there was a row of four stone houses once used by salmon fishers. It could be reached either by rowing boat, or by a long walk overland from Fionaphort, the clachan from which the wee ferry left Mull for Iona. A youth leader from the Community, Dave Windsor, and myself were sent on ahead from Iona to prepare their arrival in a couple of days time.

A lonelier place than Camus is hard to imagine, and it would have put the wind up Robinson Crusoe. Once the sun set behind the hill, the wee bay went very dark and spooky. The houses had been joined together to make one long, single building, without electricity, or running water. The furniture was very crude, but an upper room chapel with barrels for seating and fisherman's gear for decoration, gave an appearance of civilisation. Tales of grey ladies haunting the Abbey had long circulated, and, not to be outdone, Camus had a ghost of its own. It was therefore something of a shock to me to be told by my companion, at set of sun, that he was about to return to Iona, having been instructed that I was to be left alone for the next two nights with only the ghost for company! As he tramped off into the gloaming, I lit the lamp and, having nothing else to do, crept into my camp bed and under the covers. That I did not emerge from those two nights of terror white-haired and with the sort of expression of horror on my face, such as Poe specialised in describing, shows that we Shackletons are made of the right stuff. However, if asked to repeat those two days and nights at haunted Camus, I would have to tender my apologies, even at the risk of offending the ghost who lurks about that gloomy place.

A pleasanter place for camping was Glen Feochan, a few miles south of Oban. There, by a silvery pool, we pitched our bell tents under the trained eye of boy scout Geoff while the boys wailed that sheep and green acres did not appeal to them as a place for a holiday resort - "Why did we no go tae Blackpool, etc?" The energetic Geoffrey soon had them plunging into the ice pond, leading the way with squeals of feigned delight which did not fool any of us one bit.

We tramped the hills, played football in the thistles, and cooked and ate a great deal. The food was downed with grumblings: "At hame ma Maw gies us rice crispies and chips, no' this c--p." (I had a picture of Maw thrusting Mars bars and crisp packets through the school railings at playtime). But hunger and fresh air can work wonders, and second helpings were in demand. One of the interesting things was that while the boys so often grumbled at being away in the wilds, nobody ever wanted to go home again. We would pack up the tents in a telling silence.

Our Iona camps with the boys were more popular than Glen Feochan ones; there were girls about, fine beaches, football matches and, of course, all sorts of things going on at the Abbey. We would all troop along to some of the evening services, opening new horizons for boys who had never been outside the East End of the city.

One particular boy accompanied me every evening to the Abbey service, and I wondered what interested him so much. At the end of the week, as we were leaving, he asked me a question: "How does everybody know it is time to leave the church?" He couldn't understand why everybody stood up all of a sudden and left, so had spent the whole week puzzled by this. I explained to him there was a thing called "The Benediction" - the minister stood at the front, held up an arm, pronounced certain words of blessing, and the Service was over. He seemed less puzzled to be told this, and left it at that. I was left realising again just how much we take for granted in our churches, and how much we need to remember that not everyone is initiated into our mysteries. Mind you, we must not go with the popular misconception that young people find church services boring - when I asked two young guys, out of curiosity, why they came to church every Sunday for months, they looked surprised and said it was because they liked coming!

When Geoff's couple of years at Church House ended, George Buchanan-Smith brought new dimensions to our camping: he could get the use of Icelandic ponies for pony-trekking. Camps became large scale expeditions as we moved boys, ponies, and equipment over land and sea.

Our first camp with the Senior boys was far up the west coast in Glen Shiel, at the head of Loch Duich, on the way to the Five Sisters of Kintail. As was his wont, George dropped me off with the gang and went off to visit somebody - some old school friend from Glenalmond. There was no road up the glen to the bothy (which belonged to Edinburgh University Mountaineering Club), so we had to cross rough terrain for several miles, carrying all our equipment and stores. A very heavy calor-gas canister was the big problem, but sturdy Hector Riley picked it up. How he carried it so far and over the bad ground is something at which I still marvel! I offered him a cash bonus for this feat of strength, but he refused it. Of course, when we arrived the bothy was locked, and we had no keys - no problem to some of my experts in such matters. We were inside in no time! There wasn't much to occupy us there, but fortunately, somebody caught a fish in the burn as soon as we got there, and the rest of the week was spent trying, unsuccessfully, to emulate this success.

A friend of George was Stewart Macintosh, a pony-trekking specialist who had been frost-bitten in Iceland. With a lovely bay at the back of Bunessan for our future camps, we set off across the Sound of Mull, like Alexander the Great crossing the Hellespont with infantry and cavalry. The Junior camp came first, and we set up the tents amongst the sand dunes, digging a very neat, very deep hole for a wind-swept latrine which afforded a magnificent view of the ocean - ideal for meditating on the glories of nature while humming Mendelssohn's "Hebrides Overture". George took a special delight in digging deep, and square, latrine holes.

We were not there long before the juniors were happily jumping off the top of the dunes and landing in the sand below. Inevitably, (being Church House boys), one soon writhed in agony, arousing the morbid speculation that he had broken his back. The lady doctor had to be sent for from many miles away, and her diagnosis assuaged our alarm, but the boy was confined to bed. The following day she was back to remove a large fish hook which one of our charges had put through his hand. We were not popular with the doctor.

Nor, for that matter, were we popular with the local farmer. When George and I awakened one morning, there was an eerie silence, a deserted camp, and a missing van. The wee rascals had plotted to steal the van and go for run in it before we got up. They were only twelve year olds, and the only way one of them could put a foot on the clutch and brakes must have been by driving standing up! The interesting thing was that they had been watching us drive and knew what to do - up to a point! They drove half a mile and then hit a wall. Looking for them, we were met by an irate farmer who demanded to know what we were thinking about sending boys of that age out driving into the village for food - their story to him! It was a chastened group of boys who reassembled at the camp and were offered an unwelcome individual choice between sending home, or six of the best. They queued up for the latter, and George leathered their behinds one after another.

The camp for Intermediates (13-15) at Bunessan passed off relatively peacefully. My pal Tom Skinner came along, and when they were not jumping off sand dunes, they wrestled with him. Though on the short side, Tom was noted for his bodily strength, and beating him was a challenge for the bigger boys who took him on. Though undefeated, Tom did not emerge from these contests unscathed, breaking two ribs. The doctor made her third trip in as many weeks. When she heard the Seniors camp was next, she departed looking much older than when she had the misfortune to first enter our wigwams.

For our Seniors' camp, Stewart Macintosh brought a lot more ponies so that we had a grand herd of twenty. I remember sitting on a rock watching these grazing while Stewart cast his eye over each one, drawing comparisons between a particular pony's temperament and that of one of the boys; some easy-going, others hot-headed, and so on. The hot-heads seemed in the majority, and his analysis of human nature *vis-a-vis* the equine species was most instructive. We rode about a good deal once the 'tough' guys had overcome their fears of being bitten or falling off; fears expressed in language I will not repeat, lest some of my readers are former Sergeant Majors in the Scots Guards and easily offended by sweary words.

We trooped off for a concert in the Bunessan hall. This was billed to start at 9 p.m., but by 10 p.m. the hall remained shut. In true West Coast fashion, folk began to show up around 10.30 p.m. and the performance eventually began. All I remember of this was one act by a man from America who had brought along a pair of roller-skates. Objects as rarely seen on the roads of Mull as a violin being played by a one-armed fiddler, roller-skates had considerable curiosity value for the audience. His act consisted of skating from one side of the wooden stage to the other and bumping into the walls. The noise was what you will imagine it to be - considerable; but the audience loved it and gave him wild applause. Much singing in Gaelic topped and tailed the roller-skating. By 1 a.m. the show was well and truly on the road!

I had with me my Vespa scooter, and tootled off to Iona for a meeting. On my return journey, I approached Bunessan in the early morning light to see an agitated George standing on the jetty, hailing me with considerable alarm - "Bill, they've set fire to the van!" He disclosed that, he having been in dispute with some of the youths, they had decamped after putting our transport to the torch. Fortunately, the damage was repairable, and peace was restored, but that was our last Bunessan camp. Shortly afterwards, Stewart drowned in a tragic accident when, falling into a shallow stream, the cold water affected his frostbitten legs and he couldn't get up. His death saddened us all. His wife, Margaret, was to later become George's wife and I married them in Currie Kirk.

My own trips to Iona continued, of course, for the annual 'Community Week' get-togethers of the scattered members. When I started the Regnal Circle, there was also a Regnal Conference for members from all over Britain, and we were blessed with a week of magnificent weather.

On one of these trips to Iona, I took my Vespa scooter by train to Oban, took the boat to Tobermory, and jumped ship. A German tourist, landing one of those three-wheeled, one occupant, torpedo shaped Messerschmitt wee cars, had not done his home-work on Mull's roads, for as soon as he left town, his back wheel began crashing up and down on the central bump, and he couldn't drive beyond Tobermory's main street. It was most comical! My own misfortune on that occasion was to miss the Fionaphort ferry to Iona, and I rode back to Bunessan for bed and breakfast in the pub. I booked a room, and asked for a drink, only to be told the bar was closed. As considerable merriment was going on there, which continued far into the night, I gathered that a bar in those parts was open to locals, but not to potential police informers.

After my trip on the Vespa, George borrowed it for the same purpose, his van being out of action. This scooter was an unreliable machine, and it broke down half way across Mull, leaving George to sit by the roadside for long hours until a car came along the lonely road. After it broke down on me outside Central station, I pushed it about four miles to Bridgeton and bade it an unregretted farewell.

DALMALLY AND LOCH AWE

For some four years, our main camp site was a spot beside the main road to Oban, just beyond Dalmally. Somehow, George got the use of a single-storey brick building which had been used by the army to store butcher meat (the hooks still hung from the flat concrete ceiling), so it was cold, very cold, inside. Outside, there was plenty or space for games, and down the road was the junction of the river Orchy and Loch Awe, at the point where stand the ruins of Kilchurn Castle. With Dalmally kirk nearby, Inveraray, Oban, and beautiful, wild Glen Orchy not far off, we couldn't have picked a better place for boys.

Our first stay was, however, almost a disaster - George took ill and had to leave me with the Senior boys. This was not all that bad until one of them pushed me into the river! We had a great place for swimming beside the castle, and I was looking down on the boys from the high river bank when I got shoved in the back. This caused much hilarity, of course, until it was realised that though I had survived the plunge, my specs were lying somewhere in the muddy bottom ten feet down. The prospect of a fortnight 'eyeless in Dalmally' (to borrow from Aldous Huxley) was an alarming one for me. I had read that Mary Slessor faced a similar situation, when she lost her specs in an African river, but had been saved by prayer plus the retrieving efforts of a native, so I got a deep diving boy to search for mine. To my astonishment ('O ye of little faith') he came up with them first shot, and my eyesight was restored.

Travelling around with a band of exuberant youths from the city aroused suspicions in certain quarters. The snooty attitude of some people made me angry; but I had to admit that at times such suspicions were justified. In the bigger shops in Oban, I followed the boys around, and the manager followed me around! On our return to Dalmally camp, all sorts of goodies appeared for which payment had not been made.

We had a big tree behind our brick abattoir on which hung a rope swing. When the rope broke, we needed another, and in we went to Oban to buy one of suitable price and length. This I failed to do, and we returned empty-handed - or so I thought until later I saw a brand new rope hanging from the tree. I began investigations into the source of this asset, and was told it had been found 'lying on the beach'. Further enquiries disclosed that it had been 'lying on the beach' attached to somebody's boat which was doubtless drifting far out to sea, a thought which troubled not the 'finders'. I must say that I find such an enterprising, insouciant attitude to life appeals to my sense of adventure, though not, I hastily add, to my Christian conscience.

At Church House camps, it paid for leaders to expect the unexpected: like the time the football went missing. George bought a new ball, and after a couple of days kicking the thing, it disappeared, and nobody knew where it had gone - or so the boys said. A search was begun, but judging by the indolent way this was being carried out, George and I guessed its whereabouts were well known to the searchers. As darkness fell, we retired indoors, and lit the fire to cook the bully-beef hash. After awhile, back smoke came from the chimney, followed by an explosion and fall of soot! We now knew where the ball had been - stuck up the chimney! Some boy had either kicked it or shoved it down the lum, and the heat of the fire had expanded the air and blown it up. All denied knowledge of the crime, and it remains to this day on the 'unsolved crimes list' in a file labelled 'Church House Camps, Dalmally'.

The Junior boys loved Dalmally, but were none too keen on the dark nights, the sight of the meat hooks dangling overhead doing nothing to dispel their fears of being murdered in their beds. Ghost stories and camps go together, and once they were tucked up, I would tell them creepy tales such as 'I want my bone', and the even more chilling one about 'The Bashed Heids'. These horror stories were listened to in silence, and I concluded them with a terrifying shriek. The results from a leader's point of view were rewarding- the Juniors shivering themselves to sleep (and nightmares) - thus granting us a restful night.

It was during the telling of the ever-popular wan aboot 'The Bashed Heids' that a very strange thing happened; half way through my highly dramatic monologue there was a knock at the door *at the midnight hour!* I kid you not, the hairs on the head of every boy stood straight up! The knocking continued. We arose, took our candles and huddled in a tight knot at the door. "Who's there?" I asked in a trembling voice. The knocking grew louder and we guardedly opened up. The figure was hard to make out in the moonless night, but to the terror of the Juniors, there stood before us a gigantic black man! Why he was wandering about at such an hour in such a remote spot required an explanation; he said he was lost. This seemed a pretty far-fetched answer, but it briefly crossed my mind to invite him in to find shelter with us - until one look at the quaking boys put that idea out of my head. We drove him into Dalmally and left him to his own devices. How on earth an African came to knock at our door that fearful night I cannot explain, but my ghost stories from then on were heard with a dread of evil spirits putting in an appearance! It was the only time I ever saw all the junior boys silent. At the Club, there was a standing prize of £10 to any leader who could shut up *all thirty* of them for one just minute; it was a bet never won!

If you have travelled up the road through Glen Orchy, you will have stopped to see the Falls of Orchy. The falls are not high, but the torrent rushes between the rocks in a dangerous fashion, and it is wise to stand well back from the edge. Having heard of frequent drownings, when we visited the scene warnings were sternly issued to the Juniors not to go anywhere near the sides. Feeding into the falls ran many slippery rivulets, chutes to slide the unwary into the water. Needless to say, in spite of strict instructions to avoid these, one boy stood on a greasy, mossy streamlet, and shot into the foaming cataract, vanishing from sight. Aghast, I cannot describe the panic which seized me, but I can say that when I heard a faint voice calling "Help", my heart began working again. Investigation showed he had done something only a Church House boy could have done: he had miraculously landed down a chimney-shaped hole, some two-thirds full of water! The problem was that he had to be got out. How I did

Camp, Dalmally. Grace before meals, 1958

Senior Girls' Club; Margaret peeping at the back.

it I do not know, but fear drove me to achieve what I would normally never have done: I am told I went over the falls, into the chimney hole, and lifted him out to the safety of George's extended hands. I then escaped myself, like a submariner in distress, though how I did so I cannot remember at all. The boy was none the worse for his fright, and I was mighty relieved, and, indeed, astonished at my bravery. (I am a natural born coward which explains why I am such a happy person.)

AHOY THERE!

This escape from a watery grave did not put us off sailing, and George bought the Club a boat. This was lifeboat-sized and petrol-motored, and we collected it from its moorings in Eyemouth harbour. Dressed more like a Great White Hunter than a *matelot*, George took the wheel and off we went along the rocky coast and up the Firth of Forth. His knowledge of the workings, steering, and capabilities of our craft falling into the novice category, our crew of two youths soon exhibited signs of distress approaching panic - and I was not far behind them in that! However, Neptune was on our side, and we passed Edinburgh in safety. Seeing the city in the distance one of the youths asked me if it was London! I corrected his shaky geography - though not without a momentary thought that George might be going the wrong way. The entrance to the Forth-Clyde Canal came as a welcoming sight. It was dark by the time we emerged into the home waters of the Clyde, and we got stuck on a sandbank. Much muddy shoving and George blowing up the engine's exhaust pipe failed to free us, so we sat waiting in the cold until the tide rose to float us off. That George had immense pride in his vessel was obvious, but it was not entirely shared by the Club members.

Having a boat meant using it for conquering the deep and travelling to camp sites in places only accessible by sea. One such was as far west of the Scottish mainland as one can go - Sanna Bay at Ardnamurchan Point.

Accompanied by three unemployed young men he was assisting to live a nobler life, George sailed to North Connel in Benderloch (just north of Oban) where I met him with the van. The plan was to proceed to the head of Loch Linnhe and set up a base camp at

Corpach; then, our three companions would return to Glasgow in the van, collect their 'buroo' money, fill up with Senior boys and rejoin us. All was going well until George did something not unusual for him - he disappeared.

I later learnt that he had met up with some old school friends in Connel. We awaited his return for a day, then, the time scale for appearing at the 'buroo' tightening rapidly, we left him and drove up to Corpach. The next two days I passed in the pubs of Fort William, between times driving to Corran and the narrows at Ardgour, straining out to sea for a glimpse of George in the missing boat. Impatience characterised our attendance, and a cheer went up when finally George appeared over the horizon, hailing us from afar with "Hello, Bill, been held up". It was a scene not entirely dissimilar to that on Elephant Island when Sir Ernest Shackleton's stranded men welcomed the return of 'The Boss'.

After that, things went swimmingly - almost literally so, for once we gathered the boys and left the sheltered waters of Loch Linnhe, the waves rose, the spray fell, and the boat crashed up and down. Our passengers, unused to a life on the briny, clung to each other for dear life as we smashed our way up the Sound of Mull. Not surprisingly, one boy, Jamie, was very sick and it was decided I would land with him, walk across land to Loch Sunart, and meet up again with the party. He soon recovered and together we sat on a hill, looking down in pensive mood upon the magnificent panorama of mountain and sea. After a while, Jamie asked, ''Why dae they no build ony hooses here?'' I chose the words of my reply carefully - "Because this is far away from everybody and everything, and there's no work here." "They could build factories and picture hooses an a' that," Jamie suggested. We threw this proposition around for a bit, but the sunshine and balmy air soon overcame Jamie's interest in revitalising the economy of the West Highands, and we trekked on in silence.

'Das Boot' drew into a bay and Jamie and I caught up with it to pitch camp. Our stay there was extremely brief; armies of the most vicious midges assailed us, determined to drive us back into the sea. Ardnamurchan midges are the SAS of gnats, and we upped anchor and fled. The Vikings defeated the midges and conquered the Western Isles, but my guess is that they left Ardnamuchan well alone! Sanna Bay, with its wee crofts sitting on mild white sands is some sort of 'no-fly zone' for midges, and a good time was had by all, though the return sail aroused considerable misgivings amongst passengers and crew. George, enjoying every thrilling moment of sea-faring adventure, would have set sail for Newfoundland had we not indicated that mutiny was on everyone's mind.

When George took very ill with encephalitis, we sold the boat. I went with some of the boys to his sick bed in the luxurious surroundings of his Balerno home. A greater contrast to Church House and his wee flat cannot be imagined. His serious illness was, I feel sure, due to his exposure to an unhealthy, alien environment. Happily, when he left to become a House Master at Fettes, he recovered. But George was never fully cured, and in 1983, shortly after taking up a parish ministry in the Borders, he died suddenly, leaving his wife Margaret widowed for the second time, and depriving me of a very good friend. In a way, George's stay at Church House cost him his health and his life. Geoff's Convenorship of Strathclyde Region cost him his.

ARRAN

John Webster's camps were on his beloved Arran; he had been evacuated there during the war and knew it well. His camp was on an exposed site at High Corry on the foothills of Goat Fell. The first camp was a disaster: after a few nights of gales and downpours, all the bell tents were blown away, and the only tent left standing was the tiny bivouac occupied by my dog Sandy, and myself. A moat surrounded my tent, the camp-bed threatened to float away at any time, and the guy-ropes were worn to a thread. For the undiscourageable Webster, all this was good fun, and climbing Goat Fell in flood a rare treat. 'Carry On Camping' was his motto to the last.

Our next camp at High Corrie enjoyed good weather, but was not problem-free. Having set up a fine camp of bell tents, John led us up Goat Fell. His degree in agriculture, and dedication to running marathons - he has run sixty of them for charity! - will give you some idea of his love for the great outdoors and energetic pursuits. Unfortunately, one member of our safari was a youth with a weasel face, disagreeable nature, and intentions of his own which did not include climbing Goat Fell. He lagged behind as we climbed and made his way back to the camp.

Upon our return, weary from our exertions, we beheld this unpleasant individual standing amidst the smoking ruins of what had been the camp. Rings of burnt grass outlined where the tents had stood, and all we could salvage were scorched remains. Of most serious concern was the loss of our funds which John had left behind, no trace of charred bank-note or hot coinage showing up as we poked about in the ashes. The finger of suspicion pointed in one direction only: our resident thief. He had an unconvincing tale to offer - how he had returned to camp, been attacked by some men he could not describe, and these guys had set fire to the tents after swiping our valuables. The police had to be sent for, and he was questioned and thoroughly searched - but without result. We all knew he had taken the money, but where was it? He was searched again as we got on the boat from Brodick back to Ardrossan, but he was as clean as the proverbial whistle.

We were not long back before rumours circulated that he was spending freely at the carnival on Glasgow Green - a sure sign that he was squandering our financial resources. Proof lacking, he had got away with it. Many years later, I found out how he did it: a couple of middle-aged men came into the Club one night to talk over old times. They had been amongst the boys at that particular camp, and we rehearsed the story of the burnt-down tents. "You know," I said, "I still don't know how that wee fox got away with our money when he was searched twice and it certainly was not on him when he left Arran." They both grinned at my bourgeois *naïveté*, and enlightened me. "He posted it to himself. He bought a postal order, posted a letter to himself, and cashed the postal order when he got home." Blow me! why hadn't I thought of that? So simple, so obvious. You have to admit a certain amount of admiration for the criminal mind when it is fully operational - clever, eh?

Scripture warns, "Be sure your sins will find you out" (Numbers 32:23) so, in the long run, criminals get caught no matter how long a runner they do. For example, while camping with the junior boys at Dalmally, a tin of peaches went 'missing' and the forager who took it would not own up to the crime. The drive home was along Loch Lomond side, the van swaying and swerving its way round the innumerable bends. One boy grew pale and felt particularly travel sick so we stopped to let him out. He threw up ... and out came the contents of the tin of peaches! Justice was not only done, but seen to be done.

With John's and Jennifer's departure for Dr. Graham's Homes, Kalimpong (where John would run the farm and act as school chaplain) camping days ceased as one Boys' Leader followed another for the next seven lean years at Church House, However, I discovered that Church House had long owned a very fine big hut near Carluke called 'Hut Point', so the BB began using it (by coincidence, 'Hut Point' was the name of Shackleton's hut in Antarctica). Alas! the farmer pulled it down and that was the end of that,

LINDISFARNE

When Alex Mair became boys' leader in 1971, I hoped he would restart Church House using the Iona Camps, but after a couple of visits, Alex felt unwelcome. Alex, at heart a country boy, camped several times on Bute, courtesy of the Rev. Ronnie Samuel and the local farmers. However, there followed one of those happy coincidences which seem to queue up in my life, a big door swung open, and Church House entered a new era of happy camping.

My wife Margaret and I were driving north up the A1 approaching Berwick-on-Tweed, when we noticed a small signpost saying 'Holy Island'. This was quite exciting. We set off in that direction, hoping the causeway was not impassibly under water. It was dry, and we found ourselves captivated by this famous, ancient island associated with St. Aidan, and remarkably like the Iona from which the saint had come as a missionary in 635 A. D. at the request of King Oswald of Northumbria. Holy Island does not have the supreme beauty of remote Iona, and with its surprisingly big resident community, is very much a lived-in place, but it is still special, and one cannot tour the ruined Abbey without feeling Iona's influence. We went into Marygate House, an Anglican centre, and were made most welcome by Kate Tristran, a former lecturer at Durham University who had got the idea of starting a Lindisfarne Community while on a retreat to Iona.

I little thought at the time of the results which would flow from our unintended visit to Lindisfarne; these have been considerable. On returning home, I told Alex Mair about our discovery of Marygate House, and suggested he might like to go see for himself. He did, and ever since there has been a very close conection between Church

House and Lindisfarne. Kate, and the Warden, Ian Mills, provided facilities for groups of all ages, including our Pensioners' Club, to enjoy holidays there. Alex and Margaret loved the place, and some of the Franciscan brothers came to help in Bridgeton. All because God showed Margaret and myself the way to Holy Island while in the passing going elsewhere! A Regnal gathering of our own men and the men from Gateshead Circle was held on Holy Island. Following Alex's sudden death in 2002, his ashes were scattered on the beach there, showing his love for the place, and the gratitude he, and all at the Club, felt they owed to the Marygate folk. And it all began through a 'coincidence' - God was at it again!

Chapter 16

"I read in a book about a man who went about doing good; why then am I content to just go around?"
(Kagawa of Japan at his conversion to Christ).

VISITING

During all my years in the East End, I was never once kept at the door when I called on a visit. 'Minister' was a good word in Bridgeton, thanks to the good name of each of my predecessors. I always found a welcome, and often the unexpected!

After the old tenements were demolished, and the new houses built in the 'Seventies, I went round knocking doors to meet the incomers. At one flat, I was pulled inside by a large, anxious family and immediately beseeched to exorcise a ghost, and to do so without delay. Their story was that the alleged spectre haunted the bedrooms, and so they all slept downstairs with heads beneath the blankets. None of them had been upstairs for months! They wanted me to go up and tell the ghost to clear off! I sifted out of their excited conversation that somebody had told them that their block of flats had been built on the site of Barrowfield House, a mansion which once stood in present day Queen Mary Street. (Mary Queen of Scots stayed there while fleeing after the battle of Langside, giving the street its name. Bonnie Prince Charlie's fancy bit, Clementina Walkinshaw, came from Barrowfield House.) The family had been told that their flat stood directly over this potently haunted, long vanished pile. Although I tried to assure them that they were actually living nowhere near old Barrowfield House, I did not succeed. On subsequent visits I found them still living packed together downstairs. Desperate times call for desperate measures! So I uttered some words of Biblical sounding gibberish to chase the ghostie. Nevertheless, shortly afterwards, they flitted. On reflection, I think that their removal had more to do with my failure to exorcise the rent-man, rather than the ghost.

Calling unannounced could be hazardous; visiting a couple about a baptism, I walked into a fight between husband and wife. He had a black eye, and she was hurling objects and abuse at him as I attempted to restore order. When he exited the family home, vowing never to return, he turned out to be a very fine chap who had married this low-life harridan because he had made her pregnant and wanted to do the decent thing. I was a witness at the divorce, subsequently married him to the girl he ought to have married in the first place, and still possess (unused) a cigarette case he gave me in gratitude.

On another fraught baptismal visit, I knocked, found the door ajar, walked in, and beheld a young couple in the nude doing what comes naturally! The embarrassment of the situation was not improved by my discovering that I was in the wrong house!

Visits to strangers turned up the most impressive individuals: a cheerful ninety-year-old lady, who was blind and without relatives or visitors, explained to me that she was never lonely because the Lord was always with her. She sang 'Jesus loves me', and made me realise how important it is for the church to teach things which will be remembered from childhood. Far more important is that we all learn from real Christians like her.

One old lady had seen the funeral of Queen Victoria! Her father had been a gardener at Osborne House and, aged six, she had watched the black horses drawing the hearse through the grounds. Then there was an old boy who told me he remembered a great-aunt who had no fingers on one hand having lost them from frostbite while serving as a nurse with Florence Nightingale in the Crimean War! It is a pity the Church of Scotland has created such vast parishes that a minister cannot keep tabs on his parishioners - and they on him as their 'family minister' (the same has happened with 'family doctors'). By knowing everyone, whether churchgoers or not, you meet many very interesting people, especially amongst the elderly. Many ministers these days are very keen on holding meetings so that they never have to meet anybody.

I met an old bachelor once who had fought at Loos in 1915 and had a remarkably well informed knowledge of the battle, as well as his tale to tell. We were putting on a show at the time which included the old songs from 1914-18, and he joined in with me singing some through for fun! "My," he said, "I never thought I'd hear those songs again!"

Visiting a scruffy old guy one time, I was dying for a smoke and when he pulled out a packet of Woodbines he noticed my eyes watering with anticipation. The packet had only the one fag in it, so he rooted about in his pockets and took out a well worn 'dowt'. I thought he was going to offer me the one from the packet, but no! he handed me the 'dowt'. I managed to smoke this stained and withered object without it touching my lips! Although the Good Book says, 'The Lord will provide', it doesn't specify how.

When a dear old soul offered me a cup of tar, under the impression it was tea, it was in a dirty cup she had just used and emptied without washing. I did the usual in such circs, and took it in my left hand to drink from the least unpalatable side. "Ah!", she observed with pleasure, "I see you're like me, left-haunded Mr. Shackleton." As she had very mistakenly got the idea from somewhere that I liked my tea stewed to treacle, I had to go through this performance on a regular basis until her death delivered me from tannic acid poisoning.

Visiting a widow lady with flowers and a card for her 100th birthday, I asked where she had been married, and she replied, "Perth"; when I further asked in which church the wedding took place, she shook her head and said, "Och, ye cannae expect me tae mind that noo!" Folk of that generation spoke the Doric (now a dead language), using old Scots words - as did my father when he called his slippers his 'bauchles', and called stealing 'pauchling'. When I once asked an old lady, "Who's your doctor?" She replied, "She's keeping jist fine."

But not all visits of old people were so interesting and enjoyable. When the last of the old tenements were being emptied for demolition, a few folk were left in them till the very end. These were usually folk who had been there many years, and one such was a lady I was trying to help to be rehoused out of a shockingly rundown tenement. I found here standing on the stairs completely paralysed with fright. She was rigid, and had been standing there for hours unable to move. As all the other flats up the close were empty, nobody knew she was there. Everyone has heard of the term 'paralysed with fright', but I never expected to see it actually happening. Apparently, this lady had heard a noise, thought she was about to be attacked and seized up totally. The ambulance had to take her away. How little the 'authorities' consider the human cost of their plans - and the Kirk cannot complain; it has closed down congregations and sold off consecrated buildings to any buyer, showing an unforgivable insensitivity to the human factor. Illness and death even have attended such unfeeling closures - but the bureaucrats don't think or care a fig about that!

A fierce spirit of independence made it difficult to help many of these old Brigtonians. One such was an old widow woman of very strong Presbyterian convictions, who stayed in a room and kitchen in a close in a slum street. Kind but firm best describes her, and I was both fond and respectful of her. Her gas-meter was in the lobby, and high up, so she would ask me to put pennies in for her. I would always try to add a few extra of my own, but she would have none of that! She could 'hear the pennies dropping' (as the old children's hymn says) and count them one by one. I couldn't get away without taking my money back.

I used to visit a lady, who was a church member, in her single-end home. She was a person many found to be of a somewhat forbidding manner and appearance, but, for some reason I can only explain by alluding to my natural charm, she took to me most warmly. She had been a tough nut with a stall at 'The Barrows', but as often occurs with such folk, her gruff ways concealed a tender heart. On one visit I found a man lying in her bed: he was her upstairs neighbour who was dying of cancer. She took him in, cared for him till he died, and thought nothing of it. I wonder how many of those folk you see going about with a Bible under one arm, talking down to those they call 'unsaved', would have done that!

The worst house I saw, and there was stiff competition for the title, was the one in which Bobby Hardy stayed with his wife and weans. It was on the ground floor of a tenement with a broken window looking out into the street. The door opened into a lobby without floorboards, and to get into the living room necessitated striding from joist to joist! Some of the floor in the room had been used for firewood too, so moving around was tricky. Sparsely furnished with bunk beds, a table, some chairs, and a bed-recess shining like a jeweller's shop window with brightly lit tanks full of tropical fishes which drew the wondering eye!

I visited them one day bringing good news: I had found some panes of glass in the Club and offered them to Bobby; "Good," said he enthusiastically, "they'll dae my fishtanks," - a response which floored me, but not his house. "Ahem," says I, "actually Bobby, seeing you are such a great handyman, what I had in mind was using the aforesaid glass to fix the broken window of your domicile before your weans die of hypothermia." The thought of his wee ones lying stiff and cold did not seem to trouble him unduly, for Bobby was blest with that optimistic outlook on life which is so often denied to the rest of us.

This insouciant attitude has always appealed to me, and I found it to be prevalent amongst my parishioners. I recall with admiration the enterprise of one entrepreneur who turned his house into a make-shift shop, selling fish and chips through his ground floor bedroom window - how Mrs Thatcher would have approved! Then there were the members of the same family occupying houses on opposite sides of the same close who, to facilitate inter-communications and easier access, knocked down the walls either side of the close so that entrance from the street resembled the mouth of a cave. I had no need to knock their doors to get in when calling to enquire about their spiritual welfare.

I knew very well a lady who came to the Woman's Guild, and was a regular church attender. Maisie proudly wore her Guild badge, and was a weel kent face to the school weans, as she was a lollipop lady. She stayed in a top floor flat which had a big hole in the roof - you might call it a 'five-star' residence, because at night you could see the stars! Her husband, a plausible individual, claimed he was too old and frail for employment (being in his late thirties), but, in fairness to him, I must state that he did everything he could to encourage his wife to go out and work - he was an ardent feminist. They had several children in our Sunday School, one of whom, a son, being a slow learner. They were a family as happy as the day's long, and having a hole in the roof did nothing to dim their *joie de vivre*.

Calling one day, I found them all out; I was let in by a very old tramp smoking a pipe. Curious, I worked the conversation around to who he was and what he was doing in Maisie's house, and he told me he had met her and her husband as they sat together on a park bench on Glasgow Green. Upon hearing he was homeless, Maisie invited him to be their guest. So he had moved in, settled down, and was at peace with the world. An interesting old boy, he recounted for me his experiences in the Battle of the Somme, and subsequent decades of wandering the land. His views on life were of a philosophical cast, and most enlightening. He stayed for several years in Maisie's house, sitting by the fire, puffing his pipe, as indifferent to the hole in the roof as only a gentleman of the road can be. A happy ending ensued: the growing children won Duke of Edinburgh Gold medals, and the old boy passed away effortlessly to his heavenly hostel. I will always associate with Maisie the old stranger she met in a park, and took home. When she herself died, I think *he* said to her, "I was a stranger,

Maisie, and you took me in."

No Sunday newspaper these days is complete without its "Culture" magazine filled with articles by and about awfully good people possessed by lofty ideals, and a dread of being thought at all 'religious'. I notice that the only thing on which they solidly agree is that the Almighty is their intellectual and social inferior. Perhaps I am not sufficiently 'cultured' to know who these individuals are, or what attainments have brought them to such printed public prominence - their mugshots are included in the hope that somebody can identify them - but as far as Church House is concerned, I don't recall any of these people or their like volunteering to help. In the old French film comedy *Clochemerle*, the Duchess said she went to Mass because "God is my only social equal in the town". That may be just a start; but at least it is better than regarding The Almighty as an embarrassing poor relation. As Milton would have said had he thought of it: "New highbrow is old priest writ large".

Well, after that outburst, it's back to work: there were some pastoral visits which William here found particularly trying, occasions when the appalling smell of the house was positively nauseating, yet one had to sit through it. Why some folk allow their house to develop such a stench beats me, but they never seem to notice it or consider opening a window. There is a particularly offensive, corrupt sort of pong which cannot be described, only suffered. One day it will be bottled, loaded into ballistic missiles, and turned into a chemical weapon of mass destruction. That will mean the end for us all.

My two daughters were old enough to accompany me and our wee dog Rags on such a visit to deliver a parcel of fruit following our Harvest Thanksgiving Service. I knocked, the door opened, and Rags, wagging her tail, ran inside ... then she jammed on the brakes, sniffed the stink, turned tail and ran back out! No amount of tugging could get her back into the house, so the girls stayed outside while I took a deep breath and made the delivery to some old dear and her reeking son. The girls have never forgotten the 'pongy' house call that Sunday!

Another dreadful aroma arose from a certain young man I used to pick up in the car to take to the Regnal Circle on Monday nights. With all the windows wide open on the frostiest nights, I would convey him distances short and long, dropping strong hints about cheering up his depressed personality by taking a bath. I tried to get his doctor to cure his BO but to no avail. His lapsing from the Circle was the only solution, and, though it may not be a Christian thing to do, in the circumstances I guess the Lord understood why I prayed he would find other things to do on Monday evenings.

Having a van, folk often took it for granted that we were in the furniture removals business. Anyone replacing an old three-piece suite would offer it to us for our jumble sales, a pretext for getting rid of it. Some folk pushed their luck, one guy complaining to Webster and myself that we were an hour late coming to collect it! The guy did nothing to help us cart the stuff down the three stairs, but to be fair, he did stand holding the door open for us.

Some of these flittings were, we suspected, 'moonlights'. We removed one family from a multi-storey block into an abandoned building. This took many trips; we moved not only the contents of the house, but also many other items of furniture stored away in flats up and down the multistorey: tables, fridges, etc. To elude the Warrant Sales people, the contents of their home had been reduced to a minimum, the rest being holed up amongst friends and neighbours. Why they needed four wardrobes I know not; but what I do know is that lifting and moving their smelly carpets was a task I would not wish to repeat. Speaking of carpets, I remember a very nice, houseproud lady who got us to move her into another house, flitting because she was being plagued by mice. Rolling up and delivering her spotless carpets was no problem, but later she informed us that she had mice in her new home. Apparently, some of the mice had moved with her - we had rolled them up inside the carpet!

Pianos and billiard tables were also high on our removals list; folk in wealthy suburbs wanted rid of these and we took them off their hands for use in the Club. There was an endless supply of both these rejects. When the old Church House buildings were demolished and rebuilt, I had the remains of no less than twelve full-sized tables. Snooker later became a craze, but at the time nobody would take the valuable slates off my hands - even for nothing. In the Eighties, a thousand pounds would not buy an old table. Bad luck, eh! But this seems a good point to tell the tale of the billiard table cloth.

In the church we had a full-sized table which was precious in my eyes, attracting, as it did, men and youths into the Regnal Circle. The cloth was worn thin, and needed replaced. I was told that if one went to a billiard hall beside the old *Glasgow Herald* offices, in Mitchell

Street, you could buy an almost new cloth for ten pounds. It was the biggest such hall in Europe (17 tables), and they changed their cloths regularly. I bought one of these cloths from the lady proprietor, and as I went to leave, a chap standing in her office asked if knew how to put it on. I answered that I knew not, so he offered to do it for me for five pounds. Readily agreeing, 1 gave him the cloth and off he went with it. I then asked the lady what his name was, and when he would be coming to do the job - at which she astounded me by disclosing that she did not know the guy from Adam, and that he did not work for her. She had no idea why he was in her office, and did not explain why she had said nothing to correct my assumption that she knew him!

I carried out extensive inquiries amongst the regulars playing there and learnt that he was an alcoholic, and my chances of ever seeing him again were nil. Thus, left with a clothless table, I mourned my loss, and bewailed my foolishness. Months passed; then I got a 'phone call from the guy. He had lost my cloth (no surprises there!), but (big surprise!) he was going to put a *brand new* one on for me instead! (I'd better ease up on the exclamation marks, or I'll run out of them!) He not only put on the cloth for me, but he also replaced the cushes with new ones - all for free, too! My thinking evil of this person shamed me. I bitterly reproached myself for doubting my fellow man.

I already mentioned the primitive condition of 5 Queen Mary Street, where the doors to the flats were opened by the sort of latches you normally saw on a outside lavatory - the leaf type, thumb down. In one single end lived a young couple who came around the youth fellowship - he was a tall, emaciated looking guy who spoke very politely and considered himself quite a man of affairs. She was of very low intelligence, a poor wee soul. They formed a devoted couple. Their apartment had no fireplace, just a big hole in the wall. When they were rehoused, they discovered that, not being on the housing list, they were not entitled to a new house, and the last I saw of them they had been dumped in Possilpark - many like them finished up there, or in the Barrowfield Scheme. The same sort of thing happened in more recent years to those given what is euphemistically called 'care in the community'.

I married a couple of low mentality, who were manifestly unlikely to cope with life outside the Lennox Castle Institution, and were housed in an unsavoury tenement amongst unsuitable neighbours.

No doubt the staff who attended the somewhat macabre wedding meant more than well towards them, but they must have harboured unspoken doubts about what was going on. A lady doctor played the music on our grand piano - like Iona Abbey, we had no organ in St. Francis-in-the-East - and her playing was so bad the somewhat bizarre occasion became even more ludicrous. It was all politically correct, I suppose, but the marriage did not last long before they disappeared from the district. He was a timid wee man, and she would have made an excellent guard in a Japanese P. o. W. camp.

I got Sandy, my brown Cairn terrier, from a farm in Rob Roy country, and the first thing I did was give him a bath. Bathing was such a new experience for Sandy, that my temerity at introducing him to soap and water at such an early stage in our relationship so shocked him that he forgot to bite me. Cairns are one-man dogs, and his wee heart would be filled with joy at my homecomings, but there are limits to a terrier's devotion, and his dignity required that I never risk bathing him again.

Like the Royals going about with their Corgies, I took Sandy with me on my visits, and soon discovered that he loved budgerigars - in those days, just about everybody had a budgie. One lady had a splendid bird called Billy which was an accomplished conversationalist. Billy flew freely about the room, and if Sandy could have flown, he would have followed his feathered friend, for he loved Billy deeply, a high regard which was reciprocated in full. When Billy's cage was placed on the floor, Sandy would sit, nose to the bars, transfixed in admiration, while Billy hopped up close cooing, "Oh! here's poor wee Sandy"; I treasure a photograph of this touching scene.

Alas! the lady inadvertently trod on Billy while wallpapering and Sandy's heart was broken - although, brave wee dog that he was, he never showed his grief in public. There are drawbacks to owning a budgie-loving canine; Sandy had a habit of entering any and every open door up a close to follow his hobby of bird-watching. On one occasion, he climbed on somebody's sideboard to view a budgie in its cage on top of a wardrobe - not the best way of being introduced to prospective church members. If a cage hung in a window, he would perch himself on the window-sill. This fondness for budgies did not, however, extend to Alsatian dogs. These he sought to exterminate, and would attack them ferociously without declaration of war. In these encounters Sandy invariably came off the worst, but this no way discouraged his *kamikaze* assaults. It occurred to me that short-sightedness was his problem, impairing his ability to choose his targets wisely. One thing is certain though, he was a Prodesant dug! On my evening strolls, I would meet a nice old priest walking his waddling spaniel, an inoffensive creature which bore a remarkable physical resemblance to its master. To the embarrassment of the entire Ecumenical Movement, Sandy would launch himself at this poor beast, and to sightseers look good it did not. Sectarianism is an unfortunate feature of life in Bridgeton, and I am sorry to say that it is entirely the fault of my dear departed Cairn terrier.

My first Assistant was the Rev. Bill Miller, a Californian. Bill found himself in a most unusual (for him) place: St. Francis-in-the-East had a congregation without motor cars or even telephones. Back home, a vast car park was the norm, but here even the parish minister had no private transport. This astonished Bill. I recall him asking me if the local tenements were built to withstand earthquakes - a question which astonished me - but maybe he wasn't so far wrong after all, when you look back on the great hurricane which hit the city in 1969, and tore the place apart. Bill was in local digs and went down well with everyone. Our cold climate did not entirely suit him and, of course, nobody here had heard of central heating, so he slept wearing a balaclava. When Bill left after his two years with me, he went on holiday to Russia, so after Scotland in winter, he was well prepared for the winds sweeping down from the frozen steppes!

Bill visited a couple of old spinster ladies, one of whom had taken a heart attack in our church the Sunday war was declared and been bed-ridden ever since. They had at one time owned a fruit shop, and were reputed to be worth a few bob. Their flat over a shop was on a busy corner of London Road and a side street, and a visit there was a time-trip back into Victorian days - their house was a veritable museum. Bill was a soft touch, and when they accused him of stealing half-a-crown from them, he gave them the money, although I warned him about their miserly leanings. The bed-ridden sister died, and several years later, in the early hours of the morning, a huge lorry hurtled down the London Road and rammed into the shop, causing their flat above to collapse. I was informed of this disaster, and sped to the scene, only to learn from the crowd that the old woman was nowhere to be found in the rubble. She had disappeared.

That evening she returned to what was left of her home, dressed in her nightie and an old coat. She was soon rehoused, and I arranged for her to get compensation for her furniture, etc. Shortly after, she was knocked down and had just about every bone in her frail body broken, but she was an tough old bird, and after some months in plaster and bandages, was doing fine again. By then I had got her a large sum in compensation for her destroyed flat. A further sum was given her by the Insurance for her car accident; she was not entitled to anything, but a gratuity of £300 (a lot then) was awarded to the badly damaged 'poor old dear' and I took the cheque to the hospital. She was asleep, so I asked the ward sister what I should do with the money. "Oh, put it in the office safe with the rest of the money," she advised. "Rest of the money? What money?" I gasped. "All the money she had sown into her coat when she was knocked down," said sister, "£1,500 in banknotes!" The scales fell from my eyes! I focused the scene: the old dame is lying in bed; suddenly there is an almighty crash, the apartment collapses around her; what is happening? Oh, calamity! It is Auld Nick come to steal the coat! She grabs it and flees for safety, returning once it is safe to view the rubble of her home!

I must admit to a sneaking admiration for this paranoid maiden lady: she was not happy with the money I added to her crock of gold, and had the nerve to ask me to get her some more from the insurers! When leaving hospital, she collected another cash injection from the almoner's office - her back pension - but she left with a problem: I knew about the coat, and I also knew she had been defrauding the Social Security for years. Every story needs a happy ending, but I thought this one would not, because a niece of hers in Liverpool wrote to accuse me of exploiting her poor aunt's simple mind, and stealing her money! I straightened things out for the niece, finding out in the process that she had been told by her aged relative that she had given me all her money! Furthermore, the niece had been ripped off for years, travelling to Glasgow in the belief that her flesh and blood was on the bread line, and taking her out for meals, etc. The more I heard, the more, I must admit, my admiration for the old dame grew! The last I heard of her was a phone call from a nephew she had conned into taking her into his home. I was informed she was leaving the country and asked to forward her 'lines'. Anxious but discreet enquiries were made about any contacts existing between myself, the Social, and the police, but I let it be know that I was sworn to the confidentiality of the Confessional and we parted amicably. If she did go abroad, I can picture her amassing a fortune posing as a bagwoman in Las Vegas.

Another time, I was asked by a Deaconess to go and see a young mother living with her baby daughter in digs in Bothwell Street in the centre of the city. The flat was up three stairs, and it housed a colony of prostitutes of both sexes (I was not anxious to sign the visitor's book, by the way). It was my first experience of a bordello, but I was warmly welcomed, and the story was that the girl had been placed there due to a social worker's mistake. Having a van, I was to drive her, the baby, and her few belongings to new digs in the Haghill district in the East End. The mincing, painted males in the establishment helped me load up. At least, I think they were males, for it was not easy to tell the difference. In the van, *en route*, the girl filled me in with the details of her past, and how she had had the misfortune to land up in the bawdy house. Then, she added sombrely "I'm jinxed!" Theologically challenged by this remark, and seeking to console her in her time of need, I tut-tutted, told her that no-one is ever jinxed, and gave her my personal assurance that jinxed she was not. She remained unconvinced, despite my cheerful predictions as to her enjoying a rosy future in new surroundings.

We stopped in the dark at a fairly new slum tenement, and, with rapidly dimming hopes for her happiness, I knocked the door. An old man in vest and slippers opened up and I requested admittance for my charges. At this he looked blank! No, he hadn't a clue who we were or why we were there, and bade us depart. I checked the name and address, and insisted it was him all right. This information seemed to jog his memory, so I told him the hour was late, to honour his commitments, and take them in. He then raised a startling objection: he was, he said, leaving the next day for Canada, and was not coming back! What had begun for me as simple task, was beginning to look increasingly complicated. I asked him to take them in for the night, and promised to return for them next morning and sort things out to his satisfaction. At this, he agreed that they stay the night.

A police car and ambulance stood outside the close when I came next day to collect mother and child. She was standing in the street, and straight off said to me, "I told you I'm jinxed". What next, I wondered? What was going on? She explained as we drove away. It seems that during the night the old boy had died of a heart-attack and she had found him dead in bed! "I told you I'm jinxed," she kept saying, repeating her gloomy refrain. I made no comment or argument this time round; events had plunged me into deep thought. I conveyed her into the care of a Deaconess, who was, I hoped, jinx-proof and unlikely to die during the night. As for myself, I was only too happy to escape unscathed. "Yes," I admitted to her as we parted, "as you say, you really are jinxed!"

Being paid a pittance as the Minister's Assistant, once I had bought the week's rations of Ambrosia Cream Rice, Scotch pies, and fags, I was left short of enough disposable income to pay to have a tooth extracted by a dentist. So, out of dire necessity, I visited a local old woman who had a reputation for pulling teeth with great skill and for a fee of sixpence. Whether health and safety regulations were enforced in those days, I know not, but at a shrewd guess, in spite of her impressive display of tools of the trade, I figured that she was not registered as a dental surgeon - witchcraft, yes, but dentistry? no. A prevailing pong blew where it listeth, and it was not the smell of disinfectant, but of a horde of cats prowling about the house. This added to my suspicion that she was a practitioner of the black arts in whose hands I was unlikely to survive a minor operation. I declined a cup of what I suspected to be hemlock, brightly declared my toothache gone, and did likewise. To make sure she did not follow me on her broomstick, I headed for sanctuary in a holy place and there clung to the horns of the altar for several days.

One house visit I made is forever embedded in my memory: Agnes always turned up drunk at the Christmas Eve Service and nobbled me afterwards. No matter how busy I was clearing up, or anxious to get home before dawn, she would monopolise my attention. To free myself from Agnes' clutches, I promised to visit her house, where she could tell me her troubles, and discuss her requests to become a church member.

She stayed two up in a poor-looking close, and there was no need for me to knock the door as it was open when I arrived. Inside, I found Agnes sprawled on the bed, lying on top of her old mother - both unconciously drunk though it was only about 4.30 in the afternoon. On the couch a long, thin guy was stretched out in a stupor, looking like a decaying Egyptian mummy. It was the sort of scene which, taken in at a glance, inclines the beholder to depart without delay. Before the Rev. William could tiptoe offski, a barrel-sized-and-shaped man rolled in at my back. He wore working clothes, carried a knapsack, and looked, and was, an immensely strong individual. Without ado, he lifted Agnes and threw her out onto the landing! Next to go was Granny - he flung her outside too, where she lay, apparently either dead or indifferent to her predicament. Lastly, the guy on the couch was sent hurtling out the door. It was, I reckoned, my turn next, but to my relief this Brigton Samson completely ignored my presence. He began frying ham and eggs for tea as if I were the Invisible Man, and tossing Granny and Co. out of the the house was a normal daily event. Under the circumstances, I thought it best to leave the religious instruction of Agnes to another, more suitable occasion - though such an occasion has not, so far, presented itself, and I am not getting any younger.

Chapter 17

"God created the world so the boys could have somewhere to play football"
(Wm Descartes Shackleton, putting Descartes before Deshorse).

"God is always on the side which has the best football coach"
(Heywood Brall).

FOOTBALL -
YOU KNEW I'D GET ROUND TO IT EVENTUALLY!

Highlight of the soccer season was the annual Seniors v. Leaders football match. This was played on the ash parks of those days which made for lethal surfaces; a sliding tackle on the razor sharp clinkers 'smote hip and thigh' (Judges 15:8), and led to a lifetime of plastic surgery. The old leather ball 'stotted' from the iron hard surface into orbit, and heading it on its descent to earth brought instant death. These conditions were ideal for the leaders to avenge themselves for a year's suffering and torment at the hands of the Church House boys. Our opponents never came to terms with the ferocity of these engagements, being under the false impression that we leaders were gentlemen; bitter complaints would go up each time one of their number was felled by a tackle from one of our side. "Hey, you, watch it!" went up the cry as some startled youth writhed in agony under the gloating gaze of a leader old enough to his father. People often ask if there are any rewards for working with young people, and most certainly rich rewards are to be had, even if they only come once per annum.

My first experience of a Club football match was in Polmadie, where our Seniors played in a cup final on one of the foulest, blackest evenings in history - wanna see a photie? If we were not much good at anything else, we were good at football and that night we won a sort of mini-Battle of the Somme, and in the darkness of falling night were presented with the Cup. Alas! our moment of triumph soon turned into a Pyrrhic victory: of a sudden, a hot-headed member of our side 'gubbed' the referee for reasons best known to himself. We were relieved of the trophy, and expelled from the Churches League which drew the line at assaulting referees. We were thrown out several times: in George Buchanan-Smith's time twice. The second time he vowed never to let them play again. I knew better and said to him "George, come next season, they will all stand on the street corner and rot, and you will go up to them and restart the team," which is exactly what happened.

One of the hazards to taking the Seniors to play some mob of burly opponents was that you might finish up having to referee yourself, not an attractive proposition. The games were 'rough', the sort of football matches in which you played ten minutes before anybody noticed there was no ball! One such fateful Saturday on Glasgow Green, the 'game' had been going a few minutes when the referee stopped play, came over to inform me that his leg was too badly injured to carry on and that, as secretary of the home team, I would have to take the whistle. I paled, my entire life passed swiftly before eyes, and committing my soul to God, took the field. As I blew for my first foul, I noticed, in the far distance, the referee legging it at high speed, his injury miraculously cured. I forget which side was winning, or, indeed, how many were stretchered off, but I survived, which was all I cared about. I think there were six penalties.

The horror stories about playing in Lanarkshire mining villages, which I had thought exaggerated, I discovered at first-hand to be only too true after all! George and I took the Seniors to one of these places, and we were nearly lynched! The pitch was surrounded by two-storey cottages, with balconies which formed a sort of primitive stadium. It was a Celtic stronghold, and, though we tactfully wore red, the fact that we were from Brigton sent out danger signals. We kicked off and dared not cross the halfway line! Missiles showered upon our lads who, though no innocents themselves, were disconcerted by this reception, so I stopped the game, and displaying my clerical collar like a white flag of truce, informed the crowd that I was off to see the local priest who would sort them out. I had no need to go far because at that moment their spiritual head turned up in person, a big, bluff Irishman to whose Christian feelings for fairplay I confidently appealed. He listened and said genially, "Ah, sure, it's just human nature". At that moment I knew hope was lost! Angels and ministers of grace defend

9 a.m. Saturday morning, below my window in the lane
outside the Club door, 1957

"Whit ye da'en', Mister?" A young friend approaches.

us! We fled to the van, abandoning boots, clothing, belongings. One regrets having to say so, but it is incidents such as these which reduce one's confidence in the innate goodness of human nature, and, indeed, in the usefulness of the Ecumenical Movement.

The Pope was not universally popular in Bridgeton, and green was not a colour co-ordinate in the dress of many. My Orkney grannie objected to my wearing a green tie, but that was because she was a Sinclair, and her clansmen had worn green at Flodden, so she said green was bad luck. My first car (a Morris Minor van - £300), was green, which also drew disapproving comments, not from Sinclairs, but from those of an Orange persuasion.

One bitterly cold winter's day, we travelled all the way to Kirkintilloch to play a football match and, when the boys stripped, found we had come without a goalie's jersey. I borrowed one from the home team and offered it to Willie Woodburn, the agile youth who stood for us between the sticks. It was a green goalkeeper's jersey and he refused point blank to wear it! I tried to persuade him that hypothermia would end his young life should he not wrap up his torso against the arctic blast, but to no avail. With what some might regard as the courage of his convictions, Willie kept goal in his bare chest for ninety minutes - plus extra time - by which time his body had turned blue with the cold! That he is alive today tells you something of the high principles, and physical endurance of the youth of Brigton in those days.

I was born into a footballing family; football is in my blood, and my earliest recollection of a football match is being passed hand over hand from the top of the terracing at Hampden down to the trackside - as boys were by the men in those days. One game, while playing in the cinders, what had been nothing more to me than men chasing a ball, suddenly focused into a ballet, into football. It was a moment of revelation! Geoff Shaw, and George Buchanan-Smith were rugby men, and John Webster was cricket daft (still is), and all took Church House football teams round and about, but none of them shared my passion for the game, or became so involved as I did.

My boyhood hero was Tom Finney. On my way to church one Sunday morning, I saw him riding his bicycle with a roll of lead piping round his shoulder, off to do some plumbing. He had played for England the previous day at Hampden and, he told me, had received £50 for his efforts. I explained that my father had a nervous breakdown whenever he went to Hampden to see Scotland play England, because he wanted Scotland to win but Finney to score three goals! Knowing Finney, I was able to get him to bring players to Church House the evening before a Scotland/England game at Hampden - a big thrill for the boys! Tom, like Archie Robertson, a 'gentleman footballer' if ever there was one, would bring Scottish players, such as Willie Thornton, to tell stories and answer questions.

Is such a thing imaginable these days of 'star' players on fabulous wages? When the Club was rebuilt and re-opened in 1974, I invited two well-known players to do the opening and their agents asked for a fee. I indignantly refused. The agents mellowed somewhat; then said they would come if we provided their wives and children with presents - you can guess my response to that! I might add that (Sir) Alex Ferguson, a product of Harmony Row Boys' Club, Govan, was never like that, and he readily came to speak at our Regnal Circle when invited, making a good impression too.

If I might relate one of the stories Willie Thornton told: asked by a Club boy if he ever heard the crowd during a game, he answered in the negative - then qualified that by saying that he had, in fact, at one point in his career been very aware of one particular bloke's voice out of the thousands. This guy stood in the paddock at Ibrox and concentrated his vocal powers entirely upon Willie Thornton, to the exclusion of all other players. "Och, Willie, that wis terrible", "Gie yersel a shake, Willie", or "Willie, you couldnae cross a postal-order", or "Willie, ye couldnae tackle a steak pie".

This happened every game, said Willie Thornton, so that he started to actually listen for this guy's voice! One European evening game, for the whole of the first-half this went on, and continued in the second-half, until Willie heard this guy's voice shouting out, "Willie, I'll need to go. I'm on night shift. You'll need tae finish the game yersel!"

Church House produced several good football players, and scouts would turn up at our games looking for talent. Willie Miller is the best known name, but there were others. The best boy I ever saw was David Johnstone, a veritable George Best. He had everything, fast as a deer, two-footed, could head a ball. He was the only youngster I ever saw who received the ultimate accolade in the world of football - no, not the World Cup, but applause from another boys' team. To my everlasting regret, and total mystification, some of the most talented boys did not want to play, and had to be persuaded to turn up and turn out. How any boy with so much talent did not want to use it is beyond me. When I happened to find myself sitting next to Jim Baxter at a lunch the day before he entered hospital for the last time, I put that to him, but he simply replied, "When I was that age, football was nothing more than a game to me." Maybe, therein lies the answer. Scouts followed our boys, and Archie Robertson, the manager of the Clyde pleaded with them to kick-start a great future at Shawfield, but, like Baxter, some wouldn't train. How they feel now, looking back, I do not know, but I do know men who had similar offers as boys, and because of home-sickness or whatever, missed their chance and now regret it. With his father, I took one boy, Junior Hoy, for a trial at Preston; they were keen to sign him, but he was too shy to leave home. Willie Miller, spotted by the famous scout Bobby Calder, took his chance.

Old boys, now fathers and even grandfathers, drop into the Club, or stop me in the street these days to express surprise that I am still alive, and reminisce about football matches played long ago - they recall every detail, by the way. Recently, two turned up from Irvine and told me something I did not know: the day we won a cup playing St. Luke's Boys' Club in their Celtic strips, one of the staff at Celtic Park was so annoyed that he threw down the cup and broke off the handle. In my victory photograph, these two from Irvine are shown holding the handle against the cup. This news explained something which had long puzzled me: Jock Stein had come into the Club shortly after the game and handed in a £50 note. I thought it was a donation - there was some talk at the time of Celtic players using the Club for training seeing we are so near. What I did not realise was that the money was to pay to put the handle back on the cup. And all those years I never knew about the broken handle.

When John Webster became Club Leader, he became particularly friendly with a certain Gordon Goodwin, leader of Saracen Boys' Club, Possilpark. Gordies' father was a Glasgow worthy who played the fiddle in Buchanan Street for many a day and whose portrait embellishes the Peoples' Palace. However, friendship did not extend to unbiased refereeing, and with two minutes to go in a drawn match, Gordie could be relied upon to award his own side a penalty kick. Our teams rarely did well in Possilpark under such circumstances.

Due to play there one Saturday, Alex Mair arranged for the Seniors

Juniors, with my son Scott making an appearance, centre front, 1970s.

Fitba' daft: Senior team, with a young Alex Mair, 1970s

to meet outside the Club to travel to Possilpark. Everyone turned up - all present and correct. But when we stripped off, we found ourselves with only ten men - we were one short! This was a puzzle; Alex had counted eleven before setting off. The mystery was, however, soon solved: what had happened was that while everyone was boarding the van, two cops had come round the street corner and lifted our centre-forward and taken him away without Alex or myself noticing. We lost - but we would have lost anyway - so what, life's sometimes unpredictable, and sometimes it is only too predictable!

The second problem the younger boys presented to me was a tendency to steal the ball after a game. However, close questioning usually indicated who had it and where it had gone, and I was able to pay a call at the house and retrieve the ball from the coal bunker - it was always hidden in the bunker away from mother's eyes. It was to her I left the chastisement due.

Today there are no football teams at Church House; the old Glasgow Union of Boys' Clubs Leagues no longer exists - what has gone wrong with Scottish football? Well, once we stripped at the side of the park, or in a shed if it rained. We refereed our own games for free. A park, if you could get one, cost next to nothing. The strips were washed by the boys' mothers. Then things changed. They built a pavilion on the Green and you had to pay sixpence to get in. A referee had to be hired. New strips, laundry, expensive travel - end result: empty playing fields on a Green which was once a mass of games and spectators. There is a new football centre now, well patronised I'm told, but it all costs money. Money did not only 'ruin' the professional game, it did something less obvious but much more damaging, it did something I once thought impossible - it stopped boys playing football.

Church House is very close to 'Paradise', by which I mean Celtic Park, home for the Bhoys. To diverge for a moment; in Turkey I saw an English-speaking Turk wearing a football shirt of green and white hoops. When I asked why he supported Glasgow Celtic he vigorously denied it, saying he was a Bursaspor fan. "But your shirt is Celtic colours," said I, "green and white hoops," said I. "No way!" he retorted, "It's not green and white hoops, it is white and green hoops!"

Talking of Celtic, I was travelling from the city centre out east towards the Parkhead ground one day when the tram picked up two male students, tourists. They were very obviously German from their speech, dress, and physique. They sat in front of me, and unfolded a big map. A few stops further on, a crowd of Celtic fans came on board and started passing the cans of lager around. After a wee while, they spotted the Germans, and began making rude remarks about 'Huns'. One reminded the upper deck that he had had an uncle or two in the Highland Light Infantry in both Wars, and that he hated the 'Gerries' and all their works. Alarmed passengers like myself began to fear another war was about to begin, but the two Germans remained oblivious to the danger. Indeed, one of them turned to the opposition party and showed them the map saying, "Excuse, please, you show us this place?". This unexpected turn of events caused noses to be pushed into what was an outspread Glasgow Street Plan. "This place" was? could it be? yes, it was! - the 'Gerries' were looking for Celtic Park! Smiles blossomed. The young innocents abroad explained, "Zis place is famous. Ve vish to see vhere ze Celtic football plays, jah?" If only the conflicts of nations and races could be so easily and speedily ended! "Come on, Fritz, we'll show ye!" cried every voice - and so they did, one and all alighting at the ground, arm in arm, goodwill burning in every eye. What an uplifting story this is, and all true! It explains why 'The Huns' (as Rangers Supporters are known at Parkhead) are so popular with Celtic supporters from that day to this.

One mid-week game at Hampden, I took along my son and heir. It was a Glasgow Cup Final between the two members of the Old Firm before the demise of that competition. The evening was dark, dismal, dank, depressing, and the park was sodden. Through the gloom, in the far distance, each set of supporters could just about make out a few drooping opposition banners, but nothing relieved the dreary scene, especially the football of the first half, which was dire. To encourage the multi-culturalism so dear to the hearts of our political masters, a troop of Asian dancers appeared at half-time, and in their soaking wet garments, these unfortunates began to prance about waving coloured scarves, and playing strange instruments. This continued for some time under the silent surveillance of a dull terracing.

Ken Dodd pointed out that Sigmund Freud, never having attended the Glasgow Empire on a Saturday night, knew nothing about human psychology. Freud never went to an Old Firm game either. Had he done so he would have left pondering the mysterious spiritual forces which govern these occasions. With that inexplicable spontaneity which occurs only at football matches, as the multi-cultural spectacle proceeded in the pouring rain a deep groan arose at both ends of the ground. Green and blue were united in suffering; they could take no more 'culture'. From thousands of throats came an anthem - "Go home, ya Huns, go home, ya Huns, go home!" It would be regarded as racist these days, and the singers pilloried by worthy MSPs and the Quality Press. But there was no malice on the part of the vocalists, just a heart-rending infinite sadness, born of despair. The second half was no better than the first; the darkness deepened; Rangers and Celtic supporters splashed their way home like weary walking wounded.

Chapter 18

W.C. Fields never asked anyone into his Hollywood home, so Groucho was surprised to be invited inside one day when he was passing the mansion. Seeing the place was stacked high with cases of whisky he asked W. C. Fields why and got the reply, "Because of Prohibition".

"But Prohibition ended years ago", objected Groucho. "Yes, I know" said Bill Fields, "but it might come back!"

"I'm living so far beyond my income that we may almost be said to be living apart."
(Saki)

"Put all you eggs in one basket, and watch the basket."
(Mark Twain)

To complete the story of Sandy's brief criminal career and subsequent execution, I should add that he very naughtily bit his way through my Kirk Session, and then got to work on the members of the Congregational Board. But our strengths are our weaknesses and our weaknesses our strengths, and the little chap was a great help when it came to dealing with the beggars who called at the manse in search of donations. As one of these silver-tongued individuals, well practised in the art of cadging, was delivering some heart-wrenching appeal for funds to take them on a long journey, Sandy would sneak up on him from the rear, creeping silently towards an unprotected ankle. He had a way of just nipping an ankle which invariably resulted in the rapid retreat of the most persistent panhandler - for which I am forever in Sandy's debt, and even my dear wife Margaret, in her more tender moments admits the doggie had his good points, though few in number.

The Prince of Beggars was Danny McLaughlan, a shrimp of a man with a weasel face and the hide of a rhinoceros. Danny paid regular visits to the clergy of all denominations, showing a tenacity of purpose fit to rival the importunate widow, and an undiscourageable optimism worthy of Mr Micawber. Whenever he called, late or early, he would rehearse the same woeful story about needing his train fare to go somewhere; I won't repeat it here, because he might turn up at your door, and nobody can deliver the yarn like Danny himself - it is an emotionally charged tale worthy of Balzac, or even Dumas, and I wouldn't be surprised if some day it isn't turned into an opera with music by Andrew Lloyd Webber.

My best line of defence during my doorstep encounters with Danny was the afore-mentioned Sandy. With perfect timing, Sandy would nip Daniel's ankle at the very point when his sales pitch was reaching its zenith. This made his approaches as cautious as those of his famous namesake in the lion's den. News of Sandy's death reached Danny via his many itinerant colleagues in the business, and when it did I needed fresh ideas for a defence strategy.

My old mate Tom Skinner one day offered me a pair of brand new, Italian-made shoes - my size too! He lamented the huge sum he had paid for them, but the fact was that they did not fit him, and, indeed, were crippling him (in appearance Tom is not unlike Monsieur Poirot, and he walked like the great Belgian detective while wearing those shoes). He was glad to see them go, and wished me joy with them as I accepted the gift, most gratified by his generosity. They nearly crippled me as well. I put them away, and forgot about them until one day, there was a knock at the door, and with a groan, I beheld the snivelling Danny. Once he had furtively confirmed the absence of Sandy, he was about to swing into his well-rehearsed speech, when I remembered the shoes, looked them out, and offered them for free. Danny's eyes lit up! They were his size; he bore them off in triumph, a good day's work well rewarded.

It was not until several months later that I met Danny again; he was walking along one side of London Road as I walked along the other. With unwonted alacrity, he crossed and confronted me, a pained expression on his pinched face. "See they blastit shoes ye gied me," he hissed, "they damned near crippl't me, so they did!" One up to me on that occasion. Cheers and trebles all round!

George Buchanan-Smith was one of Danny's principal victims, but after several months George realised that despite all the benefits and prayers he had bestowed upon Daniel, no signs of improvement in his 'alternative life-style' were becoming evident. Now George, when roused, could command an extensive vocabulary of invective delivered at a blistering speed, and, as I was sitting in his kitchen one day, Danny called at the door. Out of sight, but within earshot, I listened as George addressed his visitor, and he was not issuing compliments. In fact, for a minimum of 15 minutes, George called Danny everything under the sun, moon, planets, and stars. Finally, unable to think of any more heavenly bodies, George's towering rage subsided, he summed up the indictment, and a chilling silence ensued. I pictured George gripping the wretch by the throat, and waited to hearing the death rattle, but instead I heard Danny's whining voice saying, "But Mr Buchanan-Smith, you don't understand!"

The aim of a fully trained beggar is not to obtain money, but to score; it is a matter of professional honour. I recall one of these 'gentlemen of the road' apprehending one of our voluntary leaders, Alan Bell, to whom he related the state of his economic affairs at great length. Alan, a Hielan' gentleman, listened, took notes, and after some two hours of careful sifting of all the evidence presented, took out his purse and awarded the suppliant a sixpence. After expending all his arts for such a small return, one unversed in these matters would think that a hard-working beggar would be disappointed - far from it! He went on his way rejoicing - he had won, *scored*, leaving Alan to wonder, for his part, whether or not he had been over-generous. The game has winners and losers, and that is what it is all about.

A very hairy and, I regret to report, rather smelly tramp came into the church one evening while the youth fellowship was on and we invited him to join us for refreshments and to tell us his business. He was of Irish origins, and he told us that he occupied his days travelling about doing good. Doing good consisted of getting people to help him through life, because he was a poor soul without fixed abode or income. Giving him money was good for people, he reckoned, and he had come amongst us so we could hand over our cash. He wasted no time before explaining his philosophy and eating all the biscuits.

He had to be asked: "How do you think it does us good to give you money?" "Well," he explained, "giving money to me is an act of merit on your part, and the more merits you accumulate in this world, the better chance you have of avoiding a lengthy, and unpleasant period of incarceration in purgatory in the next." This satisfactorily answered the question in full, so we purchased some merit, and he toddled off to do good for somebody else. In this particular case, I could see that though we were the winners, this 'ragged philanthropist' was anything but a sore loser.

Another 'gentleman of the road' was Toby, a sturdy waif who lived an intinerant existence based on various East End 'models'. He was a familiar sight either in the public library at Bridgeton Cross, studying the great philosophers, or wandering along Argyle Street picking through the bins. He came on Mondays to the Regnal Circle, appeared in some of my theatrical productions, and dutifully attended church on Sundays. Francis of Assisi had nothing on Toby when it came to withdrawing from the world into a life of poverty and piety.

Toby would call in to see me on Friday vestry nights to discuss theological issues raised by his extensive daytime reading of Dostoyevsky, Jean Paul Sartre, and other literary luminaries. We got on very well, as such intellectual discussions did not occur frequently in my daily work. The only time I fell out with Toby was when he ruined one of my finer plays: he was to go on stage with a picture to sell to another performer, but he forgot to take it with him. I laid it flat, and pushed it towards his feet using a long pole, but to my chagrin, he stood on it. The picture was ruined, and so was the script. The plot made no sense and the play ended abruptly. I pointed out to Toby that turning a comedy into a tragedy is no small matter in the eyes of a playwright and, taking the huff, he departed, vowing he would never again assist in one of my productions.

Our monthly parish magazine, "Challenge", was a splendid publication which won awards from 'Life & Work' of which I am justifiably proud. It was stapled together on the Friday evening prior to issue, and Toby never missed that Friday. He would come along, make himself comfortable, select a smoke from his tin of assorted rollups, and read the first copy off the production line. It will be seen from this that his presence was not essential, and his input nil.

One Friday night he turned up to take up his position, only for me to tell him that for some reason or other the magazine would be issued a week later than usual. He was furious! "Why was I not informed?" he fumed imperiously, "I've walked all the way from Glasgow Cross to be here, and now there is no magazine!" He continued in this vein for some time, adding in his best 'Herald' voice, "I don't know what the world is coming to these days. Why, only this morning I was making my way along the Gallowgate when this complete stranger stopped me and said, 'Excuse me, Sir, but you look as if you are a man who is down on his luck and could use some help'. 'Would you believe that!' I said to him. 'It's a bad day when an auld dosser like me cannae walk doon the Gallowgate withoot being accosted by some stranger and telt he needs help!'" I could see that Toby's dignity had been impugned by this incident, but sneaked a smile. 1 think he saw the funny side of it too, for he eventually smiled himself; but he never forgave me for not telling him that the magazine was not coming out that night. I think it made him feel his contribution to it was unappreciated.

I might add that the magazine took a lot of my time, but having been in the printing trade 1 enjoyed writing and printing it: on a Gestetner duplicator at first, then later on an ancient, heavy, offset litho somebody gave me to get rid of it. As there was no local newspaper, the parish magazine fulfilled my dream of including and reaching many outwith the congregation. It covered, not just church items, but general aspects of local life, and it circulated through the schools, etc.

Perhaps the *proudest* moment of my entire ministry came the day I went to get my haircut at the 'Maison de Paul', and the owner of that grandiloquently name joint said to me with some heat, "Where are my copies of the magazine? The customers are complaining that they don't have one to read while they're waiting for a haircut." 1 have never got so close to the Kingdom of God as 1 did that moment! When the local barber's customers complain they aren't getting the church magazine, you feel that the gates of hell have not prevailed against the Church after all!

Chapter 19

When W. C. Fields was dying a friend was astonished to find him lying in bed reading the Bible. "Just looking for loopholes, looking for loopholes", drawled the old trouper.

Asked where he wished to be buried, the dying Groucho replied, "On top of Marilyn Munro."

"His was the sort of career that made the Recording Angel think seriously about taking up shorthand."
(Nicholas Bentley)

"By all means marry; if you get a good wife, you'll become happy; if you get a bad one, you will become a philosopher."
(Socrates)

FOUR (THOUSAND) WEDDINGS AND A (MILLION) FUNERAL(S)

Funerals go with the job, and these are usually arranged to take place the day and hour the minister is looking forward to his game of golf. I have become convinced that, on more than one occasion, the main character in the proceedings has inquired when I was planning to play, and deliberately delayed his departure from this world in order to frustrate my plans. An entire week may be available for the obsequies, but betcher life the funeral will be at tee-off time.

The same is true of weddings, which fall on Cup Final days with unfailing regularity. In the good old days at St. Francis-in-the-East, everyone knew that the Rev. Arthur Gray spent his Saturdays following the Rangers, and no one would have dreamed of disrupting his arrangements for a mere wedding - you got married on a Friday night like all sensible people. But things had deteriorated by my time, and respect for the clergy much reduced. I knew of a minister of long experience who was haunted by a couple who kept turning up at his manse wanting to be married while he was out fishing. When they finally caught up with him he learnt they were both in their Seventies, so he told them to go off and co-habit, shocked that at their age they should be so inconsiderate as to interrupt a man fishing. I might add that another minister in the glory days forgot a wedding, and being found fishing in the river, retrieved his mistake by some very quick thinking and explaining he had a fine fish on the line for the bride, and would be along once it was in the bag. It is no surprise to me that the Kirk is not what it was, seeing we no longer have ministers such as these, men of strong character and high principles.

I only forgot a funeral on two occasions: the first was badly timed to coincide one Saturday morning with the junior boys' team playing a vitally important football match. It is most vexing when this sort of thing happens: you go into intensive training, give serious consideration to playing four at the back and two up front, lose sleep over your team selection, and then along comes some total stranger who lacks the common decency to get himself cremated on a Monday or a Friday. Really! Some people push their luck! However, by the chivalrous code of the clergy, duty must prevail. I decided to take along with me Bill Miller, the father of the famous Willie Miller of Aberdeen F. C., and arranged with him to replace me at half-time and take the boys back to the Club after the game.

All was going well with a few minutes to go before the final whistle when I realised that not only had I forgotten about the funeral, but so had Bill, the guy I had brought along to remind me! If you have ever lost your wife's engagement ring you will have some small inkling of the distress I felt. I rushed off, jumped on my bicycle, and knocked a pile of boot laces off the seat into the chain, jamming it solid. Desperately plucking at the oily mess failed to free the mechanism, so I pushed the bike into the Gallowgate, which mercifully sloped in the right direction, and free-wheeled down-hill into Barrowfield Scheme a half-hour late. At that point, the Lord did me a good turn: the cortège arrived at the same time as myself! I approached with those plodding steps police constables use to great effect prior to saying gravely, "Now then, what's all this then?" The undertaker was so impressed by my demeanour that I took out my watch and tapped it impatiently. At this he humbly apologised for the delay, and so I loftily forgave him. I guess that's how it goes in life (in death as well, come to think of it): we all have to learn to take the rough with the smooth, unless you can find a way to smooth over the rough.

Of course, the best thing about being a minister is that you always get the last word: "ashes to ashes, dust to dust" - a pleasing thought when planting an argumentative elder who has been a pain in the neck. By the way, the juniors won that Saturday.

I once attended the funeral of a man who had died alone in his tenement flat and lain there undiscovered for several weeks. There were no mourners. As the coffin was taken out of the house, carried down the close stairs, and placed in the hearse, the undertaker (a trusted confidant who teamed up with the doctors and myself in the carry-out side of the business) whispered to me that the coffin was empty! Nothing in it - no body, nothing! This was an unusual situation: the story was that the man had been a cat lover, and turned his room and kitchen into a sort of cattery. When he died, his dozen or so cats were marooned, their distressed miaows for help unheard and unheeded. The days passed and then the weeks; water was available from a dripping tap, but food, what could they eat? I began to see why the coffin was unoccupied. I was not entirely sure that conveying an empty coffin to the cemetery and bedding it down was theologically kosher, so I hesitated to make the suggestion, but there was only one thing to do and that was to er ... . well, coffin and bury the cats! I felt sure that was the way he would have wanted to go - amongst friends. The undertaker, a busy man, said it was too late to go hunting for cats, but he would bear my suggestion in mind should the occasion arise in future.

Funerals in the old days were often late due either to the traffic, or to our local undertaker, Matt Bones (no kidding!) having to go round to the 'buroo' to find drivers for his ancient vehicles. Mr Bones was famous in Bridgeton for his appearances on the Twelfth of July, as a stand-in for King Billy, riding a white horse in the Orange parade. In the light of the above information, you will understand that my funerals tended to be carried out at the gallop, so to speak. Tearing out the London Road to Daldowie Crematorium one day, Mr Bones' line of cars was stopped by the police for speeding, and the driver of the hearse sitting beside me made no complaint lest it be noticed that several parts of the vehicle, including the speedometer, were not working. However, I could not contain my indignation, and spoke up on behalf of the deceased, pointing out that being fined on the way to one's funeral was a breach of human rights, possibly the Geneva Convention, and not a nice thing for the *gendarmes* to be doing in any case. Such mutterings on my part made no impression upon the heartless guardians of the law. Booked for speeding on the way to one's funeral - that's a bit much, intit!

One of the most enlightening experiences I had was when a lady in whose flat we held a "House Church" (they were all the go in those days) asked me to take the funeral of an old man living above her. She didn't know much about him for he seemed to keep to himself and be a loner. His name was Billy Fullerton. I had never heard of him.

As I walked up the street to take the funeral, the nearer I got to the Fullerton residence the more choked the street became with people. I didn't know what to make of it. Outside the close stood two flute bands in assorted colourful uniforms, a hearse, and a long line of black cars. I had to elbow my way up the stairs to get into the packed room where lay the coffin containing Mr Fullerton. As usual at such funerals, the introductions were dispensed with, and I got down to the obsequies. Having expressed regrets that I had not known the deceased personally, and offered my sympathies for his relatives, should any be around, we then, with cries of "Clear the way", formed up outside in the street and moved off behind the two bands playing "Onward Christian Soldiers". The route was much longer than I expected: round Bridgeton Cross and slowly along London Road. The pavements were lined all the way with mourners, and I reckon some four thousand people must have been there. After passing through a guard of honour formed by prettily sashed ladies and bowler hatted dignitaries of the Orange Order, we headed for Daldowie crematorium, where another huge crowd awaited us. By this time, it had begun to dawn on me that Mr Fullerton was a local hero.

Billy was at one time the leader of the famous or infamous (according to one's preferences) Brigton Billy Boys. After that day's funeral, I never underestimated the strength of the Orange Order - though it is very much less strong these days, of course. The irony is that Billy was just a lonely, sick old man when I buried him; yet somehow he had become a legend ... "Dang ma hide and I'll be durned, Sheriff, if Ah didn't bury the last outlaw in the Old West (or Old East End) in Boothill. Yessiree, I sure got me Billy the Kid." (Seen Clint Eastwood as The Preacher in "Pale Rider"? What a ministerial role model for all you Bible slingers out on the range.) One can only suppose that outlaws are popular with poor people because they represent defiance of the powerful hypocrites who constantly despise them for doing what they do themselves under the concealing agenda of political correctness.

For a minister, duty comes before pleasure, and I never gave way to the temptation to let a football match take precedence over a wedding. Of course, one's heart bled for the groom who, poor soul, had to sacrifice a Saturday afternoon, but there was nothing I could do to save him, and all I could bring to the occasion was myself and loads of sympathy.

At one wedding, I calculated that I could go to Hampden for a big Scotland game, and by leaving five minutes before the end, get back to the kirk in time for a wedding. It was cutting it fine, but with a quick getaway I could make it. To facilitate this, I parked in a small garage near the ground, and bribed an employee there to make sure my car was not obstructed by other parked vehicles when I turned up to make a rapid exit. Needless to say, the inevitable happened: when I arrived, my car was completely blocked in, and the garage man who had sworn to see that did not happen had gone home! Calamity! Desperation! Panic! I rushed into the middle of the road and stopped the first car coming along, pleading with the driver to get me to the church on time. The motorist, appreciating the crisis, kindly delivered me in my highly distraught condition at the speed of light, and I arrived on the dot. Needless to say (so why do I keep saying it?), *yes!* the bride was late, a half-hour late - *women*! And there was I forfeiting the last five minutes of an important game for nothing.

A similar case occurred while I was playing golf in Troon. Carefully notifying Willie and Archie, my companions, that I had a wedding, I begged them to ensure I did not forget it - a forlorn hope, with these two, by the way, but the best I could do. Standing on the tenth tee, which is as far away from the club house as possible, I happened, by pure chance, to ask the time. 3 p.m. they casually informed me. In that awful moment, I realised that not only had I forgotten about the wedding, but so had they. The blood drained into my feet, and would have drained into the ground below had I not been wearing shoes! *Doom!* The wedding was in Bridgeton at 4 p.m. I took off like a rocket. It took me longer to tow my caddycar back to the distant car park than it did to drive back to the city and the church. My seventeen-year-old Triumph 2000 barely touched the ground, and I arrived five minutes before the ceremony was due to begin. I made it, amazingly, from the tenth tee in Troon to Bridgeton in fifty-five minutes - a world record! Trying to appear nonchalant and composed (and hoping my golfing attire would not draw comment in the crowds), I strolled into the church with nerves shattered.

Yes, you've guessed it - the bride was late! She turned up in all her glory about three quarters of an hour after I did, all sweet smiles. I am not a bitter man, but I still hold her responsible for the death of my dear old car. Like the poor wee horse in "True Grit", ridden to death by John Wayne to save the life of a snake-bitten lassie, so it was with my trusty Triumph 2000: it died of emphysema brought on by exhaustion, sacrificing its life making that desperate last ride to save my professional reputation. I was very fond of that car. I christened it "Micah", for it was my My Cah for many years, and we were very close. Why are brides always late? Why are they so heartless? Don't they care? Does golf mean nothing to them at all?

I occasionally attended wedding receptions in posh hotels, which made a change from steak pie in the Pensioners' Hall in the Gallowgate. It was disappointing, therefore, when a couple from families worth a few bob did not invite me to their upmarket wedding reception. What they did want from me was to marry them in Glasgow Cathedral, with all the trimmings, instead of in undesirable St. Francis-in-the-East, Bridgeton.

A few days after the wedding, I met the snobby mother of the bride, a lady of forceful opinions and haughty manner. "How did the reception go?" I enquired (having managed to avoid attending it). She looked at me as if I were burning brown paper under her nose. "It was absolutely wonderful. We had over a hundred guests. Jimmy and I promised our daughter she would have only the very best, and she got it." "Fine, where was the reception, by the way?" said I. "It was," she announced, as if showing me round Buckingham Palace, "held in the Tontine Hotel!" I stifled a guffaw! The Tontine was a model lodging-house near Glasgow Cross; what she meant to say was The Tinto Firs, a prestigious hotel in Giffnock! "You made the right choice there," I pronounced with a very straight face!

I was acquainted with the Tontine because the 18th century St. Andrew's Church used the halls next door to it, and when attending an induction, Presbytery members changed there into all their finery before walking along the street into the kirk. I recall, on a sunny evening, taking part in one of these ecclesiastical processions, the robed fathers and brethren snaking silently and solemnly past the astonished lodging house fraternity, some of whom were wondering if they had had a drop too much of the Buckfast!

These days, thanks to glossy T.V. programmes, weddings in hotels are increasingly common - I never did a single one. It was highly unusual to have a wedding outwith the church (although in the old days, as with my own parents, couples were often married in the house, or in the manse). We had 'big weddings', and 'wee weddings', the only difference being the number of guests and that hymns were sung at the 'big weddings'. The girls always began by asking for a 'wee wedding', but it was not long before they reconsidered and had themselves promoted into the Premier League of 'big weddings'. Prospective bridegrooms took news of this increase in expenditure stoically.

The only wedding I conducted in a house was for a middle-aged couple; the bridegroom being an Italian gentleman named Amato (not the former Rangers' player of the same name, by the way). Everyone knew that I was partial to a good cigar, so he offered me, as a gift for marrying them, a box of the best Havanas called 'El Capitane'. My delight was curtailed somewhat when, despite my protestations, he absolutely insisted I smoke one on the spot, immediately before the ceremony. I explained that I only smoked after meals, having suffered tobacco sickness in the past by smoking a cigar on an empty stomach, but he brushed my objections aside. To please him, I lit up and puffed away until we began the ceremony: what happened after that is, for me, but a hazy memory! I remember two anxious faces swimming around before me, and a distant, ethereal voice (my own) speaking words. But whether or not I got as far as pronouncing the Benediction I know not; indeed, whether or not I actually married them is conjectural; all I know for certain is that I collapsed at some point, green and sick as a parrot. Eventually, I recovered sufficiently to sign the papers in a shaky script. They seemed pleased by my overall performance, and I returned home realising that the words 'in sickness and in health' apply, not just to the bride and groom, but also to the celebrant.

Being uncertain whether or not you married somebody leaves room for reasonable doubt, but in the case of my dear friend Winston, there was no doubt at all. A most obliging fellow, Win married a couple in Edinburgh during his time there as assistant to a minister who had left him in charge while away on holiday. The niceties of legal protocol did not deter Win from taking the ceremony, and the happy couple left for their honeymoon under the mistaken impression that they were man and wife according to the law of the land and the rites of the National Kirk. Upon his "bishop's" return, Win's error of judgement came under the scrutiny and hot disapproval of the Registrar, but somehow, or so I believe, the matter was tidied up. I hope it was, or there is a couple living in Edinburgh today who have celebrated their Ruby Wedding, surrounded by scores of grandbairns, unaware that have been living in sin for many years.

PAUSE BUTTON:-

Jimmy 'Snozzle' Durante was asked where he wanted to be buried. "Bury me anywhere," he replied, "God will find me."

Finding one's way in or out of places has been a problem for me over the course of my ministry. One time I couldn't find my way out of a crematorium.

I took the last funeral of the day, changed in the vestry, gathered my things, and wandered around looking for the staff to say farewell. The place was strangely deserted; the staff had sped off home for a night far from their dispiriting duties, and left me locked in! I stemmed the rush of panic; I would calmly smash one of the huge plate-glass windows with a short pew, and escape the chamber of horrors. But first I would try the door into the boiler-house. It opened and I found myself in a place I had never seen before; it was the furnace room in which the coffins are kept awaiting cremation. As I stood in the creepy silence amongst the corpses, the boilerman came in at the other end of the room, took one look at me, and went sheet white! I hastened to correct his impression that he was seeing a ghost by saying reassuringly, "It's all right, I'm only trying to find my way out of here!" At this he recovered and said, somewhat gravely, "There's no mony finds their way oot of here!"

I used to think that 'ministerial burnout' had to do with overwork, but, obviously, it means clerical cremation. The alternative to getting roasted is, I suppose, getting drowned.

I had a funeral one summer when the weather had been hot and dry for weeks on end, so much so that the golf-course bushes were combusting, and the very fairway turf was set on fire (amazing how many lost balls could be found melted in the rough!). Under blue skies, the funeral arrived at the cemetery in sunshine, and we all got out of the cars. At that very moment, a squall hit the scene like a tornado! The heavens opened with a torrential downpour and hurricane-force winds. We struggled to the graveside, and managed to get the coffin into the pit, but that was it! The ladies were being blown off their feet and everyone was floundering about trying to stand up. I bellowed something about 'ashes to ashes, etc' and we retreated. There was no service, but nobody cared or even noticed. Safe, soaked, and winded, we sat in the cars and suddenly the gale stopped, the deluge ended, and out again came the sun. The undertaker beside me in the hearse said religiously, "The Lord didn't like that guy, whoever he was!" It was certainly a bit eerie.

So was the experience in another graveyard when, after the burial, I was being driven between the rows of gravestones. My driver suddenly slammed on the brakes and stared out of the window, saying "Look at that!" He indicated a stone with two names on it - a man and his wife, both well supplied with Christian names, and bearing an uncommon Surname. "That's my name," said the driver, "and that's my wife's name as well! Exactly the same names!" Uncanny seeing your own grave in advance.

In November, 1974, during the opening ceremony for the rebuilt Church House, Jim Herd collapsed due to an aneurism of the brain while giving a vote of thanks to George MacLeod, who had just dedicated the building. Jim died shortly after in hospital, his last words to me being, "How's the Club, Bill?"

Jim was the 'white blackbird' of Church House. Son of a local lamp-lighter, he grew up in the Club, entered the media, and became a prominent person in the B.B.C. (Jim began "Good Morning Scotland" on the radio). He was everything one hoped for in a Club boy; an elder, a voluntary leader, a fine man, a good father and husband, a successful and highly respected journalist. He stayed in Bearsden, a long way from the Bridgeton of his youth, so when he asked what he could do at the opening, all I could expect of him was to give the vote of thanks.

Jim's funeral was at Craigton crematorium, such a huge crowd attending that I couldn't get in. Afterwards, I looked around and was surprised to notice amongst the many celebrities present, a former Club boy called Joe, a big, hefty chap I hadn't seen for years. Joe told me he owned a pub in Coventry, a "Rangers Pub", and I remarked that it was very good of him to come so far for Jim's funeral. Joe had always been a rough diamond, and what he said in reply gave me much food for thought: said he, "I wouldn't have missed Jim's funeral for anything. He was the man I always wished I could be." Only such a highly emotional occasion could have opened Joe's soul to let out those revealing words. I had underestimated Joe, as we all do at times with people. Jim's life on earth was over, but his influence had been far more profound than I had imagined possible, and he lives on in who-knows-how-many men like Joe.

A note of advice to young ministers going to a funeral - travel in the hearse and not your own car. I once asked one of the funeral car drivers where a burial was to be, and he told me it was in Riddrie cemetery, so I drove myself there. After some twenty minutes, I realised something was wrong because nobody showed up! Anxious enquiries at the cemetery office disclosed the burial was in Rutherglen cemetery - the driver had told me the wrong place. Oh calamity! I belted from Riddrie to Rutherglen in what St. Paul called 'the twinkling of an eye', and arrived just as the hearse turned up. Unless you want to finish up with a heart attack and in a coffin of your own, go with the hearse!

On a tender note. I once conducted the funeral of an old maiden lady at the crematorium, went outside, met another funeral and immediately returned inside. The second funeral was for the life-long friend of the previous lady, another spinster. The two of them had been at primary school together. A double wedding is not unusual, but a double funeral like that left me with a very nice feeling. Death did not break their unity. Life can, indeed, be a lovely though mysterious thing.

On another occasion, I buried a lovely old lady, and her brother turned up. He had not been to see her for 25 years, and was only there to see what pickings he could get from her death. What little she possessed she had left to the neighbour who had cared for her most unselfishly for a long time, and when he heard that, he was much displeased. At the graveside, at the point in the service where earth is sprinkled into the grave, he lifted up a small boulder, bounced it off the coffin in a rage, and stalked off. As they say, "Where there's a Will, there's a relative" - and some pretty nasty ones at that!

Fortunately, you rarely see trouble at a funeral, but once a fight broke out amongst the family members at the graveside, and I had to stop the service until the undertaker restored order! Angry accusations flew around, and the emotional scene, fired by a few drams, aroused old family feuds. I shudder to think what will happen when euthanasia comes in. I see the family at each other's throats:

"You talked him/her into taking the pill." ...

"No, I didn't, we all agreed." ...

"No, we didn't all agree." ...

"Yes, we did ... etc." (to be continued).

On a recent conducted tour of the Gallipoli battlefields with my old pal Tom Skinner, we had as our guides two retired policemen (Len & Kieran) from Southend-on-Sea. We shared a common interest in the Royal Naval Division, who fought there as infantry, and we paid particular attention to those military cemeteries containing the R. N. D. dead. After a hot day's hiking in the sun over very rough ground, it was deliciously refreshing to go swimming about in the waters of the Dardanelles with Len and Kieran. As we relaxed, we began swapping yarns, and I happened to mention that at a funeral I always looked at the name on the coffin to make sure I was burying the person I thought I was burying and not somebody else (Mrs Smith sometimes turned out to be Miss Jones). To my surprise, this greatly amused my hearers, so I proceeded to tell the tale of the time I went to the wrong funeral.

I had gone one day to conduct a funeral in a very long street called Bernard Street. Seeing a hearse outside a close at one end of the street, I went into the house and, with a minimum of formalities, did the business. I was used to finding myself in a situation where the priest had refused to bury a lapsed Catholic, so the sight of rows of Mass cards on the coffin did not make me think there was anything amiss. What did hit me like a thunderbolt though was that, as we drove away, I saw *another* hearse sitting outside a close at the far end of the street! I should have checked the number of the close. I had gone to the wrong funeral!

We finished up in the far north of the city at the gates of St. Kentigern's R. C. cemetery. I wondered what to do if I was, like a colleague of mine, refused entry. However, all passed off without comment or embarrassment; the mourners were dropped off at the Celtic Social Club to drown their sorrows and, presumably, somebody buried the other corpse on my behalf, although I did not instigate enquiries.

This story threw my bathing companions into such fits of laughter than I feared they would drown. The anecdote took a big trick with the polis. If I am ever stopped for speeding or some other misdemeanour, I must remember to use it on the arresting officers and gain their goodwill. What's funny about it eludes me - and probably you too, unless, of course, you are a policeman.

I should have mentioned, *a propos* the above, that names were often missing from the doors in a tenement, which was why I was never exactly sure who I was burying until I read the brass plate on the coffin lid. The reason for being incognito was that the dear departed was probably living an adulterous life and the 'partner' left behind was not keen on a vengeful husband or wife turning up for the obsequies.

Mrs Sanderson was a weel-kent Brigton 'character'. Husband and sons owned a business and were considered well-off. Every congregation has a Mrs Sanderson, that is, a lady who takes things home which do not belong to them; biscuits ftom the Woman's Guild cupboard disappear into their handbags, and, in Mrs Sanderson's case, everybody kept an eye on her at Harvest Festival time because she would swipe the f & v. The women who do this sort of thing don't need it, they just take things on principle. When one of her sons died, Mrs Sanderson told me she found several sweetie jars under his bed full of half-crown coins; "I didn't bother putting them into the estate," she sweetly explained, "I just kept them." How many half-crowns can you get into a sweetie jar I wonder? -

Talking of collecting stuff reminds me of an occasion when one old lady died. I got involved in clearing her flat. In the kitchen was a black bin-bag full of packets of tea - must have been hundreds of them! Many of them I had sent her as harvest gifts, and so had my predecessors over many years by the looks of it. Some packets had 1/6d on them, but I suppose the tea was OK. I gave them to her old neighbour who was a 'tea jenny'. I had never considered tea bags to be collector's items.

Want to know the nicest funeral I had? Well, I'm going to tell you anyway: lovely crisp-sunny morning, and a Port Glasgow graveyard high on a hillside with a marvellous view overlooking the broad river Clyde - the place where Stephen Spender painted his famous 'Resurrection' scenes, now on sale at an art gallery near you for a king's ransom. Me, an old lady in a coffin, her son, and his dog. He was a shepherd from the Western Isles. We sang a duet (yes, we really did, at his request) - 'The Lord is my Shepherd' (Ps. 23) - he said "Thanks", the collie jumped into his Land Rover, and off they went. It was all so simple: no mobbed crematorium, no glowing eulogy of the kind which nowadays magically turns sinners into instant saints, no references to the prowess of the deceased as a bowler, no three curtain calls to the emotional strains of 'I Did It My Way' sung by Frank Sinatra, no two hour Service in Glasgow Cathedral with poems about the brotherhood of man, speeches by humanists, atheists, agnostics, secularists, and others desperate not to be thought 'religious'; no jokes, no laughs, not even a titter, no procession through crowded streets of mourners, no scattering of ashes in a fairy glen ... none of these mawkish fripperies - just the Lord, a shepherd, a dog, an old lady, an old Scots' metrical psalm, the ghost of Robert Burns and, yes, the faith of Stephen Spender,

After my Triumph 2000 passed away, I bought a second-hand Granada and had it promptly pinched outside the Royal Infirmary, It is a weird feeling having your car knocked! You stand there looking at the empty space and ask yourself - 'Did I come here on the bus?' You then see another guy asking himself the same question, and he tells you his car has been stolen, so you guess that is what has happened to yours as well. You inform the police, and are told it is probably on its way to Dublin, or heading down the M6 for Paris, and that recovery is highly unlikely. I mournfully told the nearby school janitor of my loss, especially emphasising that, grievous though the disappearance of the car was, what was worse was that the briefcase containing my diary was in the boot. He suggested phoning Radio Clyde, which I did,

At first the man said he was not interested in stolen vehicles, but on hearing of my diary, and the awful consequences of my forgetting weddings, his ears pricked up, It was broadcast; next day the newspapers rang me up, but they did not print the story, A week later, The *Sun* phoned. Then my brother in New Jersey, USA phoned to say "See you've had your diary stolen!" "How did you know that?" I asked in astonishment. "Read it in the *Sun* - it went with your car," quoth he. Via the *Sun*, the story of my missing diary had gone round the world, and concerned friends in the south of England phoned me to ask about it as well, In the end, I got the car back unscathed, It had lain for six weeks in Maryhill, and nobody had vandalised or used it. Happily, I got the diary back too, and weddings were resumed on time. Just shows how the interest shown in a minister having his car nicked is nil, whereas losing his diary with wedding dates commands universal attention! Marriage out of fashion? You must be joking!

COMMERCIAL BREAK:-

"Marriage is the union of two people, one of whom never remembers birthdays, and the other never forgets them," (Ogden Nash)"

I remember marrying a young couple who had met in Church House. Mary was an R. C.; Joe, the bridegroom, was one of my members. Mary was over an hour late, but nobody seemed to notice much, for everybody was having a good time - everybody, that is, except Joe who was in a state of nervous collapse. One set of guests sat at the 'Celtic End', the other at the 'Rangers End' of the Windsor Restaurant, but they united in singing heartily, with only the merest suggestion of competition. All went well until we reached the vows. Clutching his trouser legs in fright, the bridegroom froze solid, and was as dumb as Zechariah. The words 'I do' simply would not issue from Joe's lips. I tried again. Eventually he uttered a sort of low moan, which I hurriedly took to be a sign of agreement, and carried on. It was a small step for the Ecumenical Movement, but a big step for Joe.

Back to 'Paradise'. I rarely meet anyone who knows where the nickname for Celtic Park comes from, most guessing, wrongly, that it means that the ground is heaven for Celtic supporters. The real reason is that it is backed by a cemetery (Janefield) in the adjacent Gallowgate, only a narrow street and the cemetery wall separating Celtic Park from the graveyard and its occupants in 'Paradise'. I had several burials there.

One of these was the funeral of 'Irish Molly', a small, elderly lady who owned a shop in the London Road. She fell down the close stairs, and broke her neck. It was a dank, wintry Saturday morning as the few cars followed the hearse up the Gallowgate passed the pub which Irish Molly frequented. It was the custom, as a mark of respect for a deceased regular customer, to close the doors of a pub as the coffin passed, and a small knot of the regulars stood with doffed caps as we drove slowly by. The handful of mourners gathered round the graveside, and I conducted the service in the drizzly gloom, closing with the Benediction. That was the instant when it happened! Immediately I said 'Amen', the air was alive with the sound of music! Instinctively, as one man, we all looked up towards the sky - could this be the Second Coming? or was the heavenly choir giving the ould yin a great send off? The stirring tune, was it? could it be? yes, it was - 'Colonel Bogey ... Tah rah, and the same to you ..."

Like a scene from 'Bridge on the River Kwai', we formed up and marched back to the cars whistling the military tune, a spring in our step. This great volume of cheerful sound was not, as we had initially assumed, from the celestial regions, but from Celtic Park over the graveyard wall. The loud speakers there were being tested out prior to that Saturday afternoon's football match. But what, you may well ask, about the immaculate *timing* of the thing? Following the Benediction with a three-fold Amen is not unusual, but ending it with "Colonel Bogey" certainly is! Taking everything into consideration, I am convinced that Gabriel was watching over the old girl's funeral, time-piece in hand, poised to signal 'Benediction Over, Commence Playing'. No other explanation is possible. Anyway, the outcome was very pleasing, proving that, after all, it seems that every shroud has a silver lining.

Church funerals and weddings where nobody knows the Lord's Prayer or any of the hymns are more common now than they were then, but the organist and I often prayed and sang duets! However, on one occasion I got it all wrong: four members of a family wanted to sing hymns at their mother's funeral, and as they would be the only people present, I tried to put them off the idea. It turned out that they were all professional singers and gave a marvellous performance! See, you never know!

A minister meets with the prospective couple before a wedding to make arrangements and to impart to them his advice. My advice to them was 'Don't', but few - in fact none of them - took it. Some young women did not need any advice, they were very enterprising - like the one I married at a posh wedding, and whose new husband found her in bed with the best man on their wedding night (and that *is* true!). Speedily divorced, she married another guy (not with my assistance), and then a third. The last I heard of her was that she was running a close second to Zsa Zsa Gabor, Liz Taylor, and Joan Collins. The last I saw of her she was still an eyeful to look at, charming, well turned out, asking after the family, church and all that. Plausible type. I was, of course, curt and cold towards her, and made it plain I would not marry her, or even seriously consider our becoming engaged.

One wedding I had was particularly interesting because the bridesmaids wore 'see-through' tops to their dresses. The shapely young ladies were what is termed 'well-endowed', making it extremely difficult for me, facing them, to give my full attention to the proceedings, or close my eyes for the prayers. The unveiling of the bride disclosed that she was a girl with a big future in front of her.

Then there was the case of James, one of my many failures as an improver of morals. A small, cheerful young man, I took him with me one time to a weekend conference for elders (such was his rank). Shortly after our return his wife reported that he had formed an attachment to a young lady from England whom he had met at the conference. This began one of the longest of my stints as an amateur marriage guidance counsellor: it ran for years, countless hours spent trying to persuade James to keep to his vows of fidelity, and prevent his wife from killing him! Eventually, May gave up on her serial philandering hubby, and I lost touch with them for many years until, one Sunday I bought a tabloid newspaper and there, right across both centre pages, was a picture of a middle-aged man cuddling a Filipino maiden. I handed it to my wife. "Recognise anybody there?" I asked, helping her out with ... "Yes, dear, it's him right enough!" The article was about the charms and assets of Filipino brides, and there was James (yes! our James) advising on how to bring them over here to wed them and bed them. After all these years he was still at it, chasing the women!

A minister's wife tends to be unsympathetic to her husband's late night sessions sorting out pastoral marriage problems. One of these marathons left me with little bedtime over several years, and a marriage problem of my own.

The guy was a smoothie, the wife naive, plump, pleasant - they had been married for about ten years and had a son. The problem was that he had a 'fancy woman', and kept flitting between her and his wife.

For years he had been leaving home for a few days, then coming back - always promising to mend his ways, and always forgiven. This could not continue indefinitely, as even he reluctantly agreed, and I sternly told him to make up his mind one way or the other because I badly needed some sleep. At long last, he left Bridgeton and the wife for his *paramour* in Govan; that was it - he was gone permanently this time, or so I thought. A fortnight later he was back home again, but this time not by choice. Strange to say, after all the years of 'will he, won't he', no sooner had he moved in with his mistress (sorry, 'partner') than she died of a heart attack! Annie took him back, of course ... who can blame her? ... she wasn't daft ... Alex earned a very good wage.

One of life's mysteries is why some men leave home, when home consists of a gorgeous looking wife, a gorgeous house inside and out, and the gorgeous regulation one boy and one girl. These guys invariably take off with some brain dead bimbo half their age, or a dame twice their age with seven children and no income. If this is the Permissive Society, then they are welcome to it!

A mystery I never solved was who exactly were 'Uncle Eddie', 'Uncle Andy', and all the other 'Uncles'? A most likeable widow lady who came to the kirk seemed to attract 'uncles'. She always had one of these 'uncles' staying with her, gents who sat by her fireside and were called by her children 'Uncle'. A whole string of them, one after another, came and went with the passing years, and I buried them, replacement after replacement. As she grew older, naturally so did the succeeding 'uncles'. Where she got them I know not, but she was never long without a live-in 'Uncle', and had a seemingly endless supply of them. The moral aspects of this did not affect her attendance at worship or the Woman's Guild, or for that matter draw forth adverse comment. It crossed my mind to suggest marriage to one or more of these 'Uncles', but reckoned I had enough to do burying them without having to go to all the trouble of marrying them as well.

Not that I approve of 'living in sin' - it is true that, according to the Scriptures, in heaven there is no marriage or giving in marriage, but this does not mean that in heaven you can have a 'bidie-in' if you feel like having one - 'uncle' or no 'uncle'. I just wish to make that point quite clear! This 'sexual revolution' folk brag about these days is nothing new - it started long before anybody knew what sex was. The old girls could teach the young ones a thing or two.

In my early Bridgeton ministry, there were many holiday homes for the needy, and a crowd would sit around on Friday vestry nights waiting for me to arrange for them to have a free holiday in Millport, Largs, or some other resort (no Costa del Sol then!). One time I put forwards the name of a nice, very old lady I considered well worthy of such a holiday. A few days later, the matron of the home to which I had sent her phoned to notify me that she had expelled this old dear for bad conduct! I expressed surprise and dismay - shurely shum mishtake? Old Lizzie? Bad conduct? Never! Alas! It was all too true. She had smuggled into the Home a 'boyfriend' of lustful intentions, and the two of them had been found by matron amorously entangled *in puris naturalibus* and much the worse for drink. Old Lizzie, of all people, chucked out of a rest home for bonking, unbelievable yet true!

For years after I shook hands with Lizzie at the church door, gently caressing the tiny mit of this little old soul, this silver haired, sweet, loveable granny. As she toddled off, I used to think - well, well, life must begin at 80 right enough!

THOUGHT FOR THE DAY:-

"Adam and Eve held many advantages, but the principal one was that they escaped teething. "
(Mark Twain).

I have been called 'old fashioned' quite a number of times, once by a chap who phoned wanting a baby baptised. I pointed out to him that I had recently visited his distraught young wife, and discovered that he had done the dirty on her by sneaking off with another woman - the mother of the baby in question. I therefore declined on the grounds that not only was he a long lapsed member, but that I could not embarrass his wife on such a public occasion as a baptism. He said I was 'old fashioned'. "You're a hundred years behind the times," he snarled. I agreed about being old fashioned, but I am certainly not a hundred years behind the times - no way! I'm two thousand years behind the times! Ever wonder at how hard-necked some people can be?

Babies figure a lot in a minister's professional life - there's always somebody looking to 'get the wean done'. The rules of the Almighty Kirk laid various requirements upon the parents, and when one sought to apply these, however moderately, there began what I called 'The Battle of the Bulge'. Grannies would weigh in and blood would be drawn; I will say no more, as my memories of these contests of will are too painful to recollect. One of the most stupid things the General Assembly moguls have done in modern times is impose unrealistic conditions upon people to the point where, in some places, the Sacrament of Baptism has been abolished - and we only had two Sacraments to start with! Even Grannies have given up these days - but not all of them. At a recent 'Christening', an outspoken Granny present said within earshot, "Well, at least *one* of my grandchildren isn't a bastard!"

At a wedding in a very posh hotel, the bride's father said, "Do you remember, Bill, marrying Jean and myself?" I did, very well. "You know, after the steak pie and the jigging in the Pensioners' Hall in the Gallowgate, Jean and I pushed all we had in the world down the road in an old pram. Now, here I am, 25 years later, top hat and tails, paying a fortune for a posh hotel, arranging for young Jean's tons of wedding presents to be looked after!" The father of the bride passed these remarks to me as we stood outside amongst all the guests, the fire alarm having gone off during the dinner, leaving us with food for thought, if not for eating.

One wonders if marriages today are as happy as they were in the days when couples could not afford an engagement ring *and* furniture - so the furniture came first. Anyway, Ronnie's above-mentioned daughter was one of the handful of truly beautiful girls I have married - and how few stunningly beautiful girls there are. One sees plenty of really very bonny ones, but beauties are rare. Bearing this in mind, I once selected and arranged a gathering of the ten most lovely girls I married over the years - no husbands invited. They made a sight for sore eyes, and mine were very sore at the time.

I've had some unusual weddings: at one the bridegroom and best man were both named Richard Burton, and not related. Another was at the time that Fergie's wedding was on television, and my bride that day was an amazing red-haired 'Fergie' look alike! When I pointed this out, she was absolutely livid - fed up with the unwelcome comparison. She had a point.

Sometimes the couple did not turn up at all, leaving myself, the

Church officer, organist, and a stray guest or two at a loose end. On one of these spectacular non-events, I went round to the house of the groom concerned to find him watching the T.V. lying on the settee in his socks with his feet up. My enquiries as to his absence revealed that the girl was under-age and she had not told him! I expressed annoyance that he or she had not told *me* either! Another time, a few days after a couple failed to materialise, I met the groom in the street and he cheerfully informed me that they had decided to delay the happy day for two years for the sake of the weans - he seemed puzzled by my reaction!

John Webster married a couple once who were Church House members. Claire was a very intelligent, bonny, cheerful lassie; Henry a slim-built, rather good-looking young guy, with a ferocious temper. He turned nasty more than once on Club nights, and knocked out some of Phil Dibble's teeth - something Phil, a voluntary leader, took very well, considering he was in the heavyweight class compared to Henry the featherweight. When India called him away from Bridgeton, John asked me to keep an eye on them.

They stayed in a street in the East End which had a very bad name. I knocked the door, and it was opened, not by Henry but by Big Sam, an old adversary of mine in earlier Club wars. It is wrong to think evil of other people, but I admit to concluding that Henry had gone, and Big Sam had moved in. Happily this turned out not to be the case. Sam was in an amiable mood, and glad to see me, showing me a wound in his tummy which, he explained, had been caused by somebody knifing him, and leaving him in hospital, close to death, for many days. Claire made the tea, and bubbled with conversation. In a chair flopped out a weedy looking guy dead drunk and semi-conscious. I was not introduced to this friend of Sam. Having gathered that my fears were unfounded, and that Henry and Claire's marriage was secure, I wished all well and prepared to take my leave. At this, the tattered recumbent on the chair awoke, arose, and clasping me by the hand, insisted I take with me a £10 note as his personal contribution towards church funds. I expressed appreciation of his generosity, but declined the offer, pointing out that his needs were manifoldly and manifestly much greater than those of the Lord. He absolutely insisted I take the grubby 'tenner', so, with misgivings, I did. He and Big Sam then left, and Claire said, "You know, that's Glesca for you! When they're drunk they'll gie ye their last penny; when they're sober they wouldnae gie you a tosser!" Quite so! But I wasn't complaining - St. Francis-in-the-East was always self-supporting when I had it, and now you can see how it was done!

Turning up without the Marriage Schedule was another wedding hazard - one I tried my utmost to ensure did not happen by issuing dire warnings as to the consequences of coming without the documents. However, the message did not always get through, and at one wedding the worst happened.

There was a full church, and all was well until I found out from the bridegroom that they had no papers. To my enquiries as to the whereabouts of the Marriage Schedule, he blandly reported that the bride hadn't collected it. When she arrived at the church door, and had been diverted from proceeding up the aisle, I asked her why she had not gone for the papers, to which she replied - 'I had the cauld'. It was then that the full force of their sin of omission struck them. The wedding party held hurried consultations, resulting in them asking me to 'stretch a point'. I replied that stretching a point would bring me a stretch in Barlinnie. They held another confab and returned saying, "We have the hotel and the honeymoon booked up, what can we do?" "See the Registrar on Monday. Come back next week," said I. Off they went off again, coming back with - "Could ye no say a few words over us the noo, jist tae tide us ower the weekend?" Alas! I could not oblige. However, from subsequent reports, undismayed by the turn of events, everyone had a good time at the reception and, in the fullness of time, they tied the knot, this time signing the papers to the satisfaction of the law of the land, and with all due religious propriety.

The only time I had a bride failing to turn up, it left me comforting a disconsolate bridegroom, and trying to mollify his irate parents (later they privately confided in me their joy at their son not manying this particular girl). A couple of years later, the minister of a neighbouring parish asked me to cover for him during his holidays, and that included conducting a wedding on his behalf. I had never seen the couple, and all I knew about them was that the groom was an American sailor from the Holy Loch base. He was a very pleasant fellow when we met in the vestry before the ceremony. As I stood before the altar with the groom and best man, the bride arrived and processed up the aisle on her father's arm, dazzling in all her glory. As she drew closer to me her smile evaporated, she got a very, very big shock at seeing me - I was the last person in the world she wanted to meet! To avoid me, she had gone to this other minister and other church to be married, because she was the bride who had failed to turn up at the wedding in my church. Now, there was I, large as life, confronting her! Her Yankee matelot knew nothing about all this, of course, and I did not enlighten him, but I did give her a significant wink with the Benediction. It spoke volumes. "Be sure your sins will find you out," right enough!

During one wedding the couple insisted on kneeling for the Benediction. I took careful note and at the end of the service said, "Kneel down". They stood like statues, so I said louder, "Kneel down - still they stood. I shouted at them, "Kneel down" - whereupon the Best Man knelt down. "Not you, you blithering idiot!" I gasped, hauling him up, and pushing the bride and groom to the floor!

Some grooms are the bossy type. These pests reject all advice, and spout orations at the reception. The most obnoxious of all grooms was the moraliser with a sermon on the sanctity of marriage, and the need of the guests to pray more. Doctors seem prone to bossiness; nurses tend to scrutinise intently the papers after they have been signed - presumably to ensure that the guests are given the correct dosage of cake.

I had the police standing by at one wedding, as the bride's previous lover threatened to disrupt the proceedings. I wondered if I should ask them to exchange rings, or handcuffs!

A bride's father reproached me hotly after the Service for using the wrong name for his daughter. "You used the wrong name," he rudely insisted. "If you had objections, you should have voiced them at the appropriate time; anyway," I responded. "The name I used for her is the name on the Marriage Schedule." I had, of course, given out her Christian names, and he had thought her middle name was being offered as her surname. He did not know his own daughter had middle names! Dealing with the public - ugh!

What to do with a drunk bridegroom? I did not see the guy until I observed him swaying before me in the church, a half-bottle of whisky stuck in his pocket. Having had much training in dealing with unforeseen emergencies, I waited to see how the bride would take the situation. As she seemed serenely undisturbed, I carried on regardless, and she steered him safely through the vows, planting the rings, and up the aisle. Twenty years later, I was visiting an old lady when the aforesaid bridegroom turned up; he was, unknown to me, her nephew. The instant we met after so many years, Davie exclaimed - "You thought I was drunk the day you married me, didn't ye!" Twenty years he waited to say that to me! Twenty years ...

In the old days, we had the banns to call (now, thankfully, left to the Registrar). It had its pitfalls, particularly as sometimes folk gave you false information. I would find a girl coming into the 'surgery' on a Friday vestry night claiming her fiancé was abroad, or at sea, and unable to be present. One night I went out halfway through one of these interviews, leaving the girl in the vestry, and met a young guy standing outside who turned out to be the missing sailor! Why people gave false information, names and addresses, beats me, because they were bound to be found out. The usual excuse was that they didn't want anybody to know they were getting married - which was, of course, the whole idea of banns.

When it comes to marrying divorced couples, the minister is supposed to satisfy himself as to the background, and on one occasion I was told by a couple that they were both divorced. Their stories of desertion, abuse, etc seemed reasonable enough, and as they were both known by me to be active members of A. A., I thought a fresh start in life would be a good thing. However, as is often the case with humans, they omitted to tell me how *often* they had each been divorced (I assuming just once apiece), and after I hitched them it came out that each of them had been divorced four times! After that, I began asking "How often?", not a question which was always appreciated, but very necessary.

As if these hazards were not enough to make one a strong advocate of abolishing weddings completely, there was also the question of receptions. Having been told that one reception was in Eastwood Community Centre, I journeyed to Eastwood Toll, and searched for the place. Unable to find it, I entered a nearby hotel to ask directions, only to find a wedding reception in progress, and on the notice board a welcome to the happy couple. The names rang a bell as they were the names of the two I had just wed, so I assumed I was in the right place and had got the destination mixed up. After standing around having a drink and talking to the guests, none of whom were known to me, the couple came along and I realised something fishy was going on - I didn't recognise them! By a remarkable coincidence, my couple, and these other two, had exactly the same surnames - and none too common surnames at that! I withdrew surreptitiously to find the right reception in the right place.

There is a story about a 'wedding' taken by the Rev. Arthur Gray. As he arrived home for tea, his wife told him that she had received a phone call for him to go to a house in the Barrowfield Scheme at a certain time. A minister had lots of funerals in the East End, and the arrangements could be somewhat casual. Arthur turned up at the house, and pushed his way up the close and into the packed living-room. As usual, introductions were perfunctory, and he began the funeral service ftom the book. That done, he went down to the street outside the close and awaited the arrival of the hearse. No hearse. Anxious about the time, and the non-appearance of the deceased, he went back up to the house to make enquiries. "Hearse? what hearse?" said a voice. "The one with the coffin," said Arthur. Puzzled looks appeared on the faces of the assembled company. "It's a wedding," replied someone! The Rev. Mr Gray had gone through the whole of the funeral service, 23rd Psalm and all, without them noticing something was not quite right! The intended were, of course, 'awfy sorry', explaining that they had been under the impression that all you needed to do was phone a minister and get him round to marry you.

The 'Golden Rule', I discovered, is that there are no 'Golden Rules'. You never know how things will turn out, even with the worst-case scenarios. I had to intervene one day when I came across three fifteen-year-old boys holding down another boy; two were doing the holding down while the third (a boy called Stevie) pushed open their captive's eyelids and squirted ink from a fountain pen into his eyes. Stevie was not a nice boy. Yet, after I had married him to a very sensible girl, he changed dramatically becoming, of all things, a somewhat strict father to his sons, sending them all to the Boy's Brigade, and turning out to be a pleasant and polite individual himself. I said there are no 'Golden Rules', but I would like to nominate for all boys the rule: marry a good woman. 'Marry' is perhaps the wrong word, get yourself 'adopted' by a good woman is more like it, for males need somebody to give them their spending money, send them out to play, etc. Result? Married bliss.

Another 'worst case' redeemed by Miss Right was when a young 'ned' from the ranks of Club membership went off to sea and disappeared for four years. (I wasn't complaining.) His mother was a widow lady of exemplary character, a familiar figure in the street who, though paralysed, enjoyed a good 'hing oot the windae', on account of her bed being strategically placed for that good purpose. I knew her well, enjoyed her 'crack', and sympathised with her not hearing from her prodigal son for so long. At 8 a.m. one morning, he arrived home, unannounced, having travelled by taxi from Liverpool! He was drunk. His long absence was explained by his having gone to sea, and having done time in a prison in Australia. I will draw a veil of discretion over the reception he received from his bed-ridden Maw and move on to pleasanter things ... Six weeks later, he came to see me on vestry night seeking to enter the state of holy matrimony with a young lady, to whom he had only been recently introduced. The knot having been tied, they moved into a room and kitchen, and soon one and one made not two but three. They had a lovely wee family, came to the church, and lived happily ever after. End of story!

Chapter 20

SCHOOLS

A dreary place this world would be
Were there no children in it.
The song of life would lose its mirth,
Were there no children to begin it.
The dearest gifts God can bestow,
Do with the little children go,

As a parish minister, one of your pleasant, if at times demanding responsibilities is the conduct of school chaplaincy work. For me this included two primary schools, and a secondary. At the old Barrowfield Primary, the children sat on the floor and were as quiet as mice under the eagle eye of the head teacher, a lady who clothed most of her wards. The opening of the new, and present school, was a great occasion, it being the first new building in my parish for over a hundred years. I felt I was in East Kilbride seeing all those fancy murals and lights and open plan classrooms. It is difficult nowadays to appreciate what a change and a thrill it was.

Perhaps it is naughty of me, but let me tell of the time Mr Wyatt, the head teacher of Bernard Street Secondary, and Sheriff 'Wyatt Earp' to the pupils, called me into his office and handed me a letter saying, "What do you make of that?" I could see it was a letter of apology signed by a very well-known professor of theology in Glasgow, who was writing to say that his wife, a teacher in the school, was ill and would not be coming in. On close scrutiny with a scrute, I observed that, on this epistle, there was a greasy ring in the shape of a fried egg. I concluded that the author had been frying an egg at the time of composition, and had let the said egg fall on the document "That's what I thought," said Mr Wyatt, pensively, "a fried egg!" The name of the famous professor and preacher escapes me at the moment, but I seem to remember his name was ... erh ... it will come to me ... erh ... he was a very absent-minded chap ... anyway, you know who I mean, don't you?

One of the strange things about schools is that they each have their own ethos, and even when the head teacher changes, the school doesn't. My two primaries had a different 'feel' to them, and I guess that is due to them having been in distinct parts of the district in the old days, though today they seem very close to each other. Some heads were easier to get on with than others, of course, but over a long period, we got on very happily indeed. Dalmarnock Primary is one of those fine red sandstone schools Glasgow built to last forever, cool in summer, warm in winter. They do not leak or fall down within a few years of construction like many of the modern ones - that being so, I gather it is now going to be demolished and replaced by a new building.

I remember well the old Bernard Street Secondary, attended by many of our Club youngsters, because I took many a monthly school service. When the school opened in 1916, a young lady teacher went to teach science, and she was still in the same job when it closed some 60 years later. She taught generations of the same families. To get to Queen Mary Street Church, the pupils would leave Bernard Street School and crocodile some 500 yards through the streets, the number of pupils in the procession progressively diminishing as escapees slipped away up closes during the trek. The offering was taken at the church porch, worshippers putting their mites into the two big plates there as they entered. For years, when I counted the collection, the amount was always much the same, until after one Service the offering was double the normal. This warranted investigation, and there came to light a scam which had been going on undetected for an unknown but doubtless lengthy period of time (perhaps since 1916 when the school opened?).

The boys entrusted with gathering the collection at the door and carrying it up to the Communion Table had been skimming off a set sum every service, and leaving it with the lady who ran a nearby sweetie shop. This ensured that they would not have the money on them if they were found out. The shop lady knew nothing of the crime, and was distressed to hear of her part in it. What had gone wrong for the boys concerned was that before one of them had a chance to slip across to the shop, a teacher took the offering from them - in full. The clever thing was that the boys had always taken care to see their helping was kept the same, so as not to arouse suspicions. Corrective measures followed, and the Lord's work benefited by some £2 a month thereafter.

During my two years posing as a school teacher, I had a science class containing two big boys whose names are stamped on my memory: one was called Deadman, the other Grief. From my point of view, these two names could not have been more appropriate. In a short story which I wrote in 1984 to win the *Scots Magazine* 250th anniversary competition, I described my daily encounters with these two in the blackboard jungle, and how, many years later I met up with them again on a demolition site where I was picking up old slates for the Club. As others experienced in the teaching profession will testify, boys one has whipped within an inch of their lives never seem to carry over any resentments into adult life. Indeed, my former tormentors greeted me with the warmest affection, and not the hostility I had feared. I got loads of slates from them. Decent chaps, both of them. How bitterly I now regret having misjudged their innocent pranks.

Really 'bad' boys are more numerous than 'bad' girls, but one 'bad' girl is worse than a hundred bad boys in my experience. A 'shirakin' from one of these uncontrollable lassies is quite a sensation! Mind you, where there's life there's hope, and I remember having a particularly obnoxious female pupil in my class when I taught secondary. She led a pack of gangsters' molls, disrupting the lessons and giving me high blood pressure. During an English lesson (oh! the torture of the thing!) I asked for a volunteer to read a poem - nobody moved. After a while it became clear to me that the hefty, ferocious creature, who gave so much trouble, was regarded as the poetess of the classroom. So I asked her to read. She rose majestically and did so. She took a shine to me after that, and she and I got on famously thereafter! I ran her all the way through the 'Golden Treasury of Longer Poems', and the 'New Golden Treasury of Longer Poems' (twice).

Once you got used to expecting the totally unexpected, life became intelligible in Bridgeton. When Bernard Street School organised a trip abroad for a week, the older pupils saved up for it - the money being provided by their parents. When the day came for the group to set off, one boy did not go with the party for the simple reason that he had not signed up to go and had been spending his Mum's contributions! Afraid of the consequences if his duplicity became known at home, he hid in a cellar for the whole of the seven days, fed and watered there by some pals. When the trip returned he walked into the house, and nobody was any the wiser!

When Bernard Street school closed in the 1970s, I asked if the school lectern could be donated to the church as a memorial to a long-standing relationship, and it is still there. So also is a big plaster plaque of St. Andrew which had been made in the school, and carried to the church, where it still stands. It was very heavy, but a team of strong boys lugged it along the road, heeding my urgent pleas not to drop and break it. They got it the whole way without doing that, until it came to setting it down in the kirk, and then they dropped it, breaking off a corner. I considered making a slight reduction in their tip, but their distress softened my heart.

Bernard Street School was built around a playground and the classrooms were reached from an open surrounding balcony. Standing with a teacher and looking down on the pupils during one playtime, he said to me, 'You know, none of these youngsters is born to fail. I get so angry when I hear that said about children.' Having heard that said myself, and by people who should know better, I have not forgotten his words. He was one of those very fine teachers who see the potential in every child. Youngsters respond to this. Bridgeton produced many fine professional and trades people, and one boy from Dalmarnock Primary won the Gold Medal for Medicine at Glasgow University in my time there.

Chapter 21

CHILDHOOD

The heart of childhood is all mirth,
They frolic to and fro
As free as air, as if on earth,
Were no such thing as woe.

IN OUR YOUTH

We thought together we should hold the stars
We took the sun in heaven for a sign
We should together win the earth, and sit
In Honours Court, and drink the wine.

SUNDAY SERVICE & CHRISTMAS EVE

In St. Francis-in-the-East, the service was at 2 p.m., a ghastly time for keeping awake in my experience! I used to doze off while preaching my own sermons! I tried changing it to 11 a.m. (as is required in Scotland by the Law of Moses), but it didn't work. I then tried 11.30 a.m. - still no joy. Finally I upped it to 12.30 p.m and it has gone well at that time ever since.

The church building is quite small, with halls beneath the sanctuary, and this has been a great blessing, saving money on heating for one thing. I had the place painted by some friends with a small painting business, and this was done using 'sky hooks', in other words, by the sort of scaffolding used in the poorer parts of China. You could say I had "friends in high places". It was all done on the cheap. These days nobody could afford to do it at all without spending a fortune on scaffolding alone.

On the Iona pattern (which underpinned all I did), there was a monthly cycle covering healing, mission, politics, and liturgy. There was no 'Mission Praise' hymnbook in those days, and none of today's popular 'clap-a-clap-handies' stuff, but it was all there - something for all tastes and ages. Some snobby types have hinted to me that preaching in a place like St. Francis-in-the-East is easy, the folk uneducated. How wrong that is! Preaching to people who have often made a heroic gesture coming to church, and who have to return afterwards to most difficult problems is daunting. I used to see people actually cocking their ears to hear what I had to say, soaking it in. I felt an awesome responsibility lest 'the hungry sheep look up and are not fed'. Believe me, the folk in the pews were highly educated in the only place it matters: the University of Life!

To preach on suffering never goes wrong. One Sunday I preached on 'love thy neighbour' and an old Christian lady said to me, "Mr Shackleton, how can anybody love *my* neighbours?" - they were making her suffer, believe you me. But keeping it cheery is also essential - a lady in another congregation told me recently that her husband had stopped going because he was coming out more depressed than he went in! Alas! that's all too often the case these days.

Our services were enlivened at times by visits from men staying in models - local lodging houses. One thin, sprightly worshipper used to sit at the front, and if the singing was not enthusiastic enough, he would turn to the congregation and call for an increase of volume. He always seemed to place himself with two very twittery maiden lady sisters immediately behind him, and these two took the brunt of his calls to praise the Lord. I can picture them now, fluttering like two frightened canaries trying to get out of a cage! We also had a lady in the choir with a tremola voice, her warblings greatly entertaining the children - and myself who should know better at my age!

One Sunday I was preaching on music and its place in life, etc. At precisely the right moment, a band passed the church, and the folk were impressed, under the impression that I had arranged it. A similar event occurred when a neighbouring minister called Gordon Strachan did his usual Sunday morning thing in Dalmarnock Parish and led a band round the street before the Service. A young policeman was attending a domestic quarrel at the time, and as he stood in the street, various articles were being thrown out the window into the street below. The rookie cop got on his radio to HQ asking for backup, but the sergeant at the other end of the call heard Gordon's trumpets sounding round the corner and said, "Hold on, you've got the 7th Cavalry coming!"

My most memorable triumph in the pulpit was the Sunday Sandy came into the church. Before I married, I took the dog to church and

St. Francis-in-the-East Kirk Mural by the Glasgow School of
Art, 1955

A touch of class! -"Sunday Serenade" - biennial free
performances by professional musicians - Margaret and Irene

left him secure in the vestry, but this particular Sunday, a woman fainted, and she was taken to the vestry. Sandy escaped and went in search of his master. I had just given out my text, 'Behold, I stand at the door and knock', when there was a mysterious knocking at the door. The congregation went rigid; then an elder opened the door and in flew Sandy - right up the centre aisle and into the pulpit! Folk still remember that Sunday - probably all they remember of my preaching. My sermon that day was a howling success, especially at the point when I inadvertently stood on wee Sandy's tail.

One of the big events of the year was the Christmas Eve play. This was a fixture before I arrived, but I inherited the production together with the youth fellowship and club youngsters. Each year needed a new script, and when I left, Alex Mair and Margaret Beaton carried on the tradition until it was regrettably stopped.

In the early days, Geoff and I helped carry the stage all the long road from the Club to the church - a massive stage of wooden trestles with ton weight asbestos tops (when I became minister I had a permanent stage built into the chancel). Once erected, a crib was positioned on top which was big enough to contain Mary, Joseph, the Babe, and assorted cardboard animals. As the performers rarely knew their lines, despite much rehearsal, they walked about the stage while we sat in another room reading the script over microphones! As we had no means of seeing what was happening on stage, the chances of synchronising dialogue and movement were pretty remote. With the invention of the tape recorder (cost £36), I was able to stand beside the stage and get some better idea of what was going on, though curtains ensured I still couldn't see a thing.

The audiences liked these 'mystery plays' (a mystery to me how they ever worked!), and the scripts were inventively modern, though thinking up new plots was a strain every Christmas. True, spontaneity of appreciation amongst the audience sometimes spilled over into unwelcome enthusiasm, and I recall a lady from a posh church coming to our midnight service and saying that it was the only time she had seen a minister enter the pulpit and tell the congregation that if he had any trouble he would not hesitate to call the police! But on the whole it was OK. The grand finale was always the same: the opening of the crib, a flood-light on the interior, the singing of 'Silent Night' - not a dry eye in the house as I went on stage to deliver the Benediction. At Christmas I would watch some of our supposedly 'hard men' singing

'Away in a Manger', and life did not seem too bad after all!

One of the problems with the Christmas Eve play was choosing a suitable cast and persuading them to appear - fear of recognition by other members of their peer group figuring largely. To get round this, the performers were heavily disguised in dressing gowns, towels, and, above all, beards. Joseph was played every year by the same chap, but a lady in the congregation made a suggestion: she asked me if would tell Joseph not to wear a tartan bunnet. I had not realised he was doing this. I explained to him, as sensitively as I could so as not to offend his artistic susceptibilities, that Joseph was unlikely to have been wearing a tartan bunnet at the nativity, and I would appreciate it if he would perform without one. The following Christmas, the same lady approached me again - yes, Joseph was wearing a tartan bunnet when the crib was opened in all its brilliant splendour. Maybe there was a 'McJoseph' tartan? Or a 'Hunting Nazarene'? Making allowances for these improbabilities, I let it go at that, and Joseph remained secure in his anonymity in front of his cronies, bunneted to the last.

Apart from the cast failing to turn up, or falling off the stage inebriated (once only, I hasten to add), my biggest problem was the Rev. John Webster, when he took over from George Buchanan-Smith. John had studied agriculture, and retained a view of life which did not include hurry or decision. As the Irishman asked himself thoughtfully 'What does time mean to my pigs?' so time meant little to J. W.

Being a careful Shackleton, ready to meet any unforeseen disaster whether within or without the Antarctic Circle, I had arranged for a spare tape recorder to be available should my own break down just before the Christmas Eve play started. With relief, I congratulated myself upon my foresight when, at 11.00 p.m. my tape malfunctioned. I instantly despatched John across the street to get the replacement from a house there, and impatiently awaited his return. He vanished into the night; the audience grew restive; I was desperate with anxiety; then, when all hope seemed lost, he strolled in with the tape. To my hot enquiries as to his taking half an hour to do a two minutes trip, John looked pained: "The lady offered me a cup of tea. I could not refuse," he explained. This attitude carried Britain through two World Wars - "Time for another cup of tea, old boy?" - "I don't mind if do" - "And a fairy cake?' John, ever the old trouper, soothingly added, "It will be all right - not to worry." That's not what I said to him!

The making up and dressing up and excitement of the Christmas Eve plays left many folk with very happy memories of their youth and we had a great time with a good laugh. One lassie asked me if she could play the part of Mary Mandolin! The purpose of life is the creation of happy memories, and the more we do that with youngsters the better. The churches are far too serious these days, so no wonder folk stay away.

Amen to this:-

"A sparrow fluttering about the church is an antagonist which the most profound theologian in Europe is wholly unable to overcome."
The Rev. Sydney Smith)

The Rev. John Webster brought a style of preaching uniquely his own from his training under the Rev. Stewart McWilliam in Wellington Church in the West End. He was a firm believer that in order to get into heaven, conversion was an absolute necessity. He was an equally firm believer that if any sort of allowances could be made for anybody not being converted, then he ought to make them on their behalf. He talked tough, and was a big softie.

John had a sort of free-range approach to ministry, illustrated by the time he took a funeral in the street. It was the practice in the old days for a group of neighbours to gather round the close when a funeral service was being conducted in the house. This did not please John - he wanted everyone to be at the service, so he had the coffin lifted out into the street, and took the proceedings there, stopping the traffic! He was an outdoor type of guy, but I didn't expect him to extend that to funerals in the public highway.

Some of John's movements were mysterious - indeed, one in particular remains mysterious to this day: he took me to the old Buchanan Street railway station to catch the only train of the day to Oban - 8 a.m. I think it was. We arrived early, and he persuaded me to smoke a leisurely fag. All of a sudden he notified me of the time and I rushed off, only to see the train chuff-chuff into the distance. I then raced back to the van, only to see it ruff-ruff in the opposite direction. Stranded, I took the bus back to John's Bridgeton flat, and

Epilogue. John Webster and an unusually quiet congregation.

The Club's home-made Adventure Playground.

breakfasted with Jennifer. No signs of John. Couple of hours later, still no sign of the master of the house. Where anyone could go in the city at 8 a.m. still beats me. I have often asked him where he went that fateful morning, delaying my return to Iona by 24 hours, and have still to receive a reply. My guess is he went off, parked and slept. John could sleep anywhere at any time, a rare gift indicating an untroubled conscience, though when one is sitting beside him in church or at the cinema, his snoring can be distracting. He slept through the entire showing of *Monsieur Hulot's Holiday*, a silent film to which John added the sound track.

When a party of us saw John's family off at Central Station, for the long journey to India and the Himalayas, he might just as well been going to Largs for all the effect our sad farewells had on him. Indeed, so cheery was he, that he left their youngest son, Callum, in his basket on the platform, and we had to rush alongside shoving the abandoned infant through a carriage window. The British Empire was built by men like John Webster, a credit to the Raj - "Well played, Sir; damned fine fella and a cricketer as well, don't ya know!" John has run 60 marathons, raising money for Dr. Graham's Homes, Kalimpong; these have been stopped now, owing to his age, of course, but also because his feet have been wearing down the Himalayas to quite an alarming degree. On his return to Scotland after nine years abroad, I welcomed him back to the Club for a spell until he went to Troon Old Parish. His three sons spoke with pronounced Indian accents, and a church in Pollokshields or Woodlands was deemed inadvisable.

It was great to have John back, for my years with the Websters were my most pleasant in the Church and Church House. We caught up on things. I said, "You won't believe this, John, but while you were away I had a phone call from London - Bobby Hardy called at 2 a.m. to ask me the football results." "That's nothing," said John, "he called me in Calcutta! I waited anxiously for the operator to get a through line, and after nearly half an hour she said, 'That's Mr Hardy on the line for you now.' Having expected some desperate message from home, all I got was Bobby saying, 'How's it going, John?'" It was these little things which showed the affection in which we were held, even when we were far away.

By way of further explanation, I should add that Bobby was quite a handyman before he disappeared. His wife was a tall, very intelligent woman. He was a devoted father, and though his Mrs denied all knowledge of his whereabouts when he abruptly vamoosed to London, I knew she would soon follow him with the weans. After he left, a Pakistani shopkeeper visited me, demanding I repay him a sum of money, which he had paid to Bobby to do repairs to his shop and which had not been carried out. I could not persuade the man that Bobby was not my employee and I was innocent of any schemes to defraud him. It was with some wrath and ill feeling that we parted, I'm sorry to say.

Bobby's outlook on life was unusual: one day he asked me for a reference, stating it was his intention to go to college and become a school teacher. I approved of his ambition, but I had to point out something which could go against my reference and his application. 'Would it not be a good idea, Bobby, to first clear up this business of your being fined for not sending your kids to school?' He nodded - good suggestion. The last I heard he was working as a youth organiser in London, and, I hope, doing well there. No doubt one day he will come back to St.Francis-in-the-East Regnal Circle and expect us all to be sitting where he left us, and we probably will be.

I was the first minister of our kirk to own a vehicle - a Trojan Brooke Bond Tea van which I bought for £50. In it I passed my driving test without doing either a three-point turn or a reverse turn because it was without rear windows. To change gears in this great tank-sized vehicle involved double-declutching! Learning to drive it was challenging, and thereby hangs a tale ...

I knew a man who knew a man who knew where I could get hardwood flooring to replace the worn out church hall floor - which reminds me, I must pay him some day. The men of the newly formed Regnal Circle laid the floor and John Webster brought along a sander. The job done, it was time to return the sander, but John, lacking all sense of direction (which explains his fondness for marathon running in a crowd), could not remember the whereabouts of the suppliers "somewhere in Pollokshields". Cruising round in the hope of seeing such a place, we stopped at a garage to make enquiries, and an intoxicated, red-faced colonel-type gent came out to provide information. Seeing the dog-collars, his instincts to do good in the world were aroused and he insisted upon us accompanying him to his mansion wherein he operated as a radio buff. Following somewhat confused conversations with Buenos Aires and Tokyo, he insisted that we take the garage Trojan van for a mere £50. I hastened to raise the cash, and the following day went to collect - but by this time he had sobered up, and had no recollection of his generous offer. However, Webster stood witness and following veiled threats to ruin his reputation at the golf club, I got the van. So I became the first minister to have my own transport, and my days of travelling long hours by tram and bus were over.

The problem was - I couldn't drive, so Webster offered lessons in the quiet streets of Jordanhill. The second problem was that the passenger seat was hinged and any sudden stop turned it into an ejector-seat, hurling the occupant backwards. Approaching the nightmare maze of traffic lights at Anniesland Cross, my desperate pleas for instructions on how to stop the juggernaut went unheeded by my much amused tutor. That raised the third problem: my dog, Sandy. As I hurtled round the wall of death, jabbing frantically at the brake, the dog leapt in terror upon the steering-wheel just as the seat tipped Webster head over heels into the back of the van. As if by magic, every traffic light turned green as I shot towards it, and I passed safely through like Moses crossing the Red Sea! It was a much shaken and pale William who climbed out of the cockpit. Later, I was to have my revenge upon my grinning instructor, but I never matched the day he taught me the most important lesson about driving - don't take lessons from the Rev. John Webster. I think I could speak (or rather bark) for the dog as well. I reckon John went to India so he could give driving lessons - proceed 100 yards in a straight line and you've got the licence. Now he is in Arran, doubtless going around offering free tuition, so keep a lookout for him - he is tallish, rugged-looking, and dangerous.

Chapter 22

DEFINITION

"Archbishop: a Christian ecclesiastic of a rank superior to that attained by Christ."
(H. L. Mencken).

ECUMENICAL MATTERS

I heard many tales about the priests of a few years back driving people to mass, and not being loth to use fear and even violence! I was told how visiting priests did not scruple to call the children of a mixed marriage bastards; and I remember a school teacher I knew telling me that when he bought an old lady a Bible she requested, her priest threw it on her fire! Such tales I considered propaganda, until I asked a priest about them; he had no compunction about saying they were more than likely true! It isn't hard to see why so much bitterness resulted, and lingers on.

A bridge passed over the London Road outside Celtic Park, and after one game versus Rangers, I walked under it in a great throng of Rangers supporters (Celtic fans always used the Gallowgate, never London Road). It turned into one of the most terrifying experiences in my life: great chunks of concrete were dropped from the bridge onto the crowd below, while, at the same time, a mob of Celtic supporters ambushed us from a side street. I'll never forget the panic, and the little children with their mothers caught up in the battle and screaming with fear. How nobody was killed I'll never know! Nowadays, these games are tame in comparison.

I have been at the funeral of a Club boy stabbed to death after a game at Parkhead - "Sectarian Crime" screamed the newspapers, doing their hypocritical bit as usual to condemn what they do their utmost to inflame. There was nothing sectarian about this appalling crime - a Celtic fan himself, he was stabbed to death by Celtic fans from Greenock. When I see journalistic or political reports that Glasgow is a city of racist, sectarian thugs, I want to stop voting, and give up newspapers.

One of the odd things I had to contend with was a reputation for being anti-Orange lodge. Possibly this sprang from Mr Gray's time. Arthur put up a large cross beside the notice-board (a sure sign of Jesuitical leanings in the eyes of some locals), and furthermore he was noted for his Iona and I. L. P. sympathies in the days of the famous Jimmy Maxton. Labour in Bridgeton was not as identified with the R. C. church as it is today, but I horrified a lady from Ulster once when I told her I voted Labour. I was viewed by her with some suspicion thereafter. Glasgow, like Liverpool with its big Irish influx, is polarised.

The name, St. Francis-in-the-East, further confused this sensitive situation. I recall a drunk stopping to look up at the notice-board, read the name of the kirk, and ask me if it was an (expletive) chapel. I might add that I frequently had phone calls asking me what time mass was being said; callers mixed us up with St. Francis in the Gorbals.

An Irish priest wandered in at the end of the service one Sunday and asked me if we were celebrating the feast. I admitted total ignorance of the said feast, adding that St. Francis-in-the-East was Church of Scotland. He had never heard of the Kirk, or indeed of Scotland, and invited me to his rooms in the chapel presbytery. These were, like all the others I have seen, sparsely furnished, dreary places to live, but he had an enormous cocktail cabinet full of the choicest wines and spirits, so we got on fine.

He was, he explained, a White Father, and was fresh from a trip to Italy where he had fulfilled his life's ambition to celebrate mass (solo) in as many places of interest to his religion as possible. I was a wee bit sorry when he left, as he was a nice soul, unburdened by an education. Such associations perhaps made me seem tainted, like Mr Gray. Whatever the reason, in all my long years there I was never once asked to take an Orange Church Parade, presumably because it was assumed I would have turned down the request. In fact, I will preach the Gospel to anyone prepared to listen, to the Pope himself in the unlikely event that I will be offered the opportunity to do so. St. Francis went so far as to preach to the Sultan of Egypt, and that's good enough for me. I am not in the least bit prejudiced, and if the Pope wanted to marry my sister I would not object - if I had a sister.

I have met lots of very fine people, excellent church members, who were in the Orange Order, so I take people as I find them. A fine Christian lady whose family was Orange in background, once said to me, "Mr Shackleton, these folk need love like anybody else." So they do! I get annoyed when I hear of Pecksniffian ministers who turn such folk away when they wish to parade. Being largely working-class folk, they make easy targets for the cowardly press which carefully avoids attacking the real villains - the hierarchical bigots who protect their institutionalised vested interests by promoting sectarianism while pretending to deplore it. I would not wish to join the Orange Order, because it is exclusive, but so is the Green side of the same coin. The danger is that one can find oneself being sucked into all this, taking it too seriously. I found the Orange girls married Romans, and Catholic boys wed Prodesant girls with an ease and regularity which makes a mockery of all these divisions.

The son of one of my elders went for a job in a large department store in the centre of the city, and was asked which church he attended. 'St. Francis', he replied, and got the job. Wrong St Francis! He found himself the only Protestant in the place!

Bigotry is not confined to the West of Scotland, as popular myth has it. It exists in parts of England where there has been considerable Irish colonisation. I once went for a job myself to be told there was no job, and at night-school later met the boy who got the job because the priest got it for him - he didn't really want the job, by the way.

A friend of mine sold poultry feed. After visiting a farm in Lancashire for twenty years, he suddenly got the cold shoulder from the farmer who accused him of concealing the fact that he was a freemason. Bob had the same surname as a local Blessed Somebody or Other, and on the strength of this, the farmer had thought he was an R. C. and 'one of us'. After twenty years of sales, no more orders came Bob's way from that source.

Bigotry does not start and end with football supporters. But happily, 'the times they are a-changing'. I asked a Club boy draped in the Irish tricolour why he wore the Irish flag - 'This is not the Irish flag, it's the Celtic flag!' he corrected me. That could be progress - of a sort.

One of the remarkable things about Church House is the lack of bigotry there. Boys wearing both sets of colours have mixed for years. This is partly so because Celtic Park is next door, and some of the 'Prodesant' boys support them. All the youngsters are inseparably mingled, so you never thought of one being any different from another. In the early days, the parents of R. C. youngsters were always asked if they objected to their offspring attending, but none did. What they were prevented from doing at school - meeting and getting to know each other - they did in the Club without comment.

Not that the Club was anything but 'Prodesant' orientated when I first went to it. The battered piano could play 'The Sash' without the aid of human hands, so often was that sprightly tune played on it! Of course, the leaders frowned on all this, and before the start of a dance, strict instructions were issued to the band - 'No Party Tunes!' No dances these days, no party tunes. Better now? or just boringly politically correct? Phone me with the answer; calls cost £3 a second!

My mother was just about the least 'religious' person I ever knew. But there were times when even her 'Glesca Blood' came out. In pre-war Preston there was colourful Whit Saturday parade of all the churches round the town (Protestants in the morning, R. Cs in the afternoon). It was a gala occasion, bands playing, all the children dressed up, decorated floats, massive pictorial banners, etc. As Mam and I watched a parade passing, along came the Orange Lodge's contribution to the procession led by none other than King Billy on a white horse. As he passed, a hefty Irish woman began hurling at him an impressive outburst of curses and voluble abuse. This had the effect of causing my normally inoffensive mother's 'Glesca Blood' to rise to boiling point without delay and, to my astonishment - I was only about aged about ten at the time - she promptly laid into this Hibernian enemy of The Protestant Faith! When Mam's dear friend, Maggie Lyle, a formidable Edinburgh lady, joined in, the contest was speedily settled in King William's favour. I must say, I was much impressed by Mam's performance. As you yourself will know only too well, dear reader, all sorts of things can unexpectedly arouse a mother's wrath, and when that happens, we all know to take cover!

I was friendly with the Secretary of the local Communist Party, a nice man at heart, but unfortunately possessed of a somewhat bleakly doctrinaire Stalinist view of life. One sunny day, we were standing together at Bridgeton Cross, under the famous 'Umbrella', and he was explaining to me the finer points of Marxist dialectical materialism, when, from the far distance, there came the merry sound of an approaching flute band. At this musical overture, his ears pricked up like an elephant registering an alluring mating call, and the lecture froze on his lips. As the band bounced nearer, the music grew all the more entrancing, and I beheld an awesome sight: my Leninist companion's physog was transfigured with a strange beauty. He was a man transported into the Seventh Heaven, possibly even into the eighth! As the 'No Surrender Band' passed us by, he turned and said to me in loving tones: 'Oh! Ah do loo a baun, Ah loo a baun!' His heart may have been in Moscow, but at that moment his feet were in Brigton! Yes, 'Glesca Blood'!

The Sixties opened up ecumenical contacts, and I often visited the local priests, inviting some of them home. We held joint meetings, though the older priests, all Irish, did not like the idea much. One young priest in Easterhouse had said openly that confession was a boring waste of his time. Another said he did not believe in transubstantiation - adding he was by no means the only one. When the notorious Bull *Humanae Vitae* was issued, a large section of one R. C. congregation crossed the street into the kirk - only to be shepherded back by the minister keen on good relationships. They were stirring times, and I had one particularly talented young priest around the Youth Fellowship, Men's Regnal Circle, and Woman's Guild a good deal. He expressed great admiration for our Freewill Offering system, in contrast to his own church's money raising methods. But the new mood did not last long. As he feared, the young priest was moved by his old boss at three days' notice. And even the most liberal priests admitted, sadly and reluctantly, that we were not true Christians. However, there will be no going back, and I must say I like most of the priests I have known personally. Their bluff, open manner contrasts favourably with the wimpishness of some of the ministers I have known. The Father Teds are free of our Presbyterian hang-ups about drink and gambling. True, few had any worthwhile education, but they tend to be a pretty manly lot, and it must be added, to their credit, that some of them are low handicap golfers.

For 15 years I lectured on Philosophy and Comparative Religion in Langside College to students training to become House Parents. My job was to make them think, and experience the wider world. Only two subjects aroused any reactions from most students. The mildest biblical criticism drove the Protestant "Fundies" wild; any mention of The Pill drove some of the R. C.s berserk - particularly the old Irish nuns in the classes! The young nuns, for one afternoon let out of their cage, loved to see their starchy chaperones 'losing the heid' and getting all flustered.

I must confess to being rather naughty at times in my lectures in order to stir up some responses. When I hinted that the Bible might not have been dictated word for word by God, one young man got really stirred up and stormed out of the classroom in protest. The next lecture I was pleasantly surprised and relieved to see he had come back to his seat. Standing up in front of everyone, he apologised for walking out and went on to say something I shall never forget. "I went home," said he, "and opened my Bible, and read the passage in the Gospel where Peter cut off the ear of one of those who came to arrest Our Lord. Jesus rebuked Peter for what he had done. It dawned on. me, I was behaving like Peter, taking it on myself to be the Lord's bodyguard. I realised that He doesn't need bodyguards - He can look after Himself." Wonderful words many could do to learn.

Perhaps it was the mischievous streak in me which made me even naughtier one day while being shown round the Sacred Heart chapel. I popped in to welcome a new priest over from Ireland, and on his guided tour we passed a box at the door labelled *For the Souls in Purgatory*. I couldn't resist asking, tongue in cheek, "How do you send the money on?" This was a first time question for him, and he furrowed his brows, pondering the difficulties involved in forwarding postal orders to Purgatory. Under the circumstances, I did not press the point, and left him to think about it. However, before we parted with a handshake, he disclosed to me that his best attended congregations were on a Saturday after a home game at Parkhead - provided Celtic won, that is. If they lost, few turned up. Fortunately for his finances, the Celts rarely lost, so he was doing a roaring trade - with substantial additional fringe benefits for the 'To Whom It May Concern' souls in purgatory.

I first heard the term 'Glesca Blood' from Big Eddie. He was appearing as one of a trio of fairies in a pantomime I had written for the Club Christmas Show. Eddie was an R. C. and therefore The Celtic Fairy; another boy was The Shawfield fairy; a third The Ibrox Fairy. I was not a very imaginative writer! Alas, the Ibrox Fairy failed to turn up on the night, and I had to step in - step right into the Ibrox Fairy's costume. As we waited in the wings, Big Eddie, in shamrock green tutu, started to make rude comments about the demerits of the contemporary Rangers' football team, and went so far as to make mock of my frilly blue skirt, with matching red and white long-johns. I could not let this pass. Tempers flared. For an anxious moment, it seemed as if the members of the audience were about to witness, on stage, the unseemly sight of two fairies beating each other to death with their wands! Happily, however, the danger passed; the show went on, the panto was a great success, and the fairies were particularly singled out for favourable reviews. After the show, Big Eddie, in a gesture of reconciliation, magnanimously offered me his paw saying, "Och, don't worry, it's jist wur 'Glesca Blood'!" So, that's what can bring even fairies into disputes - 'Glesca Blood'. I decided to remember Eddie's genial diagnosis.

Some years later, Eddie became steward (chairman) of our Regnal Circle. During one meeting, a very surly church member of mine started behaving in his usual negative way, and Eddie astounded him by telling him that if that was his attitude, he did not belong in a Regnal Circle. Furious to be thus spoken to by a younger person (an R. C. too!), the guy threw over his chair and left the hall. Eddie was not in the least perturbed by the incident. A few weeks later the old targe came back, humbled, a better man for having been told that he didn't own the place and had the wrong idea about being a Regnalite. Eddie said what others should have said to the fellow a lot sooner in his life. I should postscript that Eddie played his part in visiting for our Stewardship (Wells' Organisation) Campaign. He painted the church for us at risk of life and limb. That was an expression of the boundless good nature which redeems that strange mixture we call 'Glesca Blood'.

Although it is not politically correct to say it, the root cause of sectarianism is denominational schools. Their very existence separates children into different camps, so that they grow up with little contact and a lot of awareness that they are divided. I once asked the headteacher of a local R. C. secondary school if he would permit me to tour the classes and answer questions from the pupils. He knew my wife, who has taught in many R. C. schools, and kindly agreed. In every single class, I was asked only one question: "Which team do you support?" I was forced to plead the Fifth amendment! Well, wouldn't you?

I am, of course, quite neutral, and I have been thrown out of both Celtic Park *and* Ibrox. Having heard that clergymen of any denomination are welcome free of charge at Parkhead, I toddled along one evening for a European game and presented myself at the turnstile with dog-collar on prominent display. An official was summoned and

I was led to the main stand wherein I expected to be seated with the compliments of the management. Instead, I was handed a ticket and told it would cost me the equivalent of a week's wages. Being unable to fork out, they bade me depart - but ever so politely!

It occurred to me that I was going about this the wrong way, so I tried again at the turnstile, this time wearing a black raincoat, and adopting a vaguely Irish accent. But I was rumbled right away - it was back to the Main Stand, the usual request for payment, followed by expulsion. I guess I had about as much chance of getting in for free as a nun would have selling rosaries at the Ibrox turnstiles. Having counted fourteen priests sitting a row, and knowing a Celtic supporter friend of mine was once asked to give up his seat to a Father Somebody or Other (request denied, by the way), I feel somewhat aggrieved to find that this 'all clergymen' really means 'some clergymen'. Having said that I feel even more badly about my expulsion from Ibrox by the other half of The Old Firm.

A person of my acquaintance wanted me to go with him to Ibrox, persuading me, against my better judgement, that I could buy a ticket outside the ground, for £12. On arrival, he approached a vendor of these so-called spare tickets and paid £18 of my money instead of the supposed £12. I grimaced and coughed up.

Seated in the Broomloan Road Stand, I was accosted by a steward wanting to see the ticket and to know how it had come into my possession. I explained. He officiously instructed me that I had bought a counterfeit, and to surrender the seat to another guy. When I asked why this other fellow's ticket was good and mine was not, I was told he had lost his ticket in the post, and been given a replacement by the ticket office. Embarrassingly taken to the police, I asked how they could tell mine was the counterfeit ticket of the two. They did not answer, satisfying themselves by stating that counterfeits were made by lasers. This did not satisfy me. To copy something, I said in cross-examination, required an original - so from what original had mine been copied? The one reported 'lost in the post', perhaps? I further asked why the youth who had sold the ticket, for which I had paid a large sum, was allowed to sell counterfeits in the open street without being arrested? These enquiries led nowhere, and I was given the ignominious 'bum's rush' by the aforementioned officious steward, and escorted to the exit. This unpleasant steward, on learning from my I. D. that I was a minister of the Gospel, asked if I knew his own minister, and when I gave an affirmative reply an expression of regret at my humiliation almost, but not quite, escaped his lips.

His minister has since told me that the steward is his church officer, and a nice fellow, but I have a mental picture of him scrutinising people's Communion Cards in search of forgeries. To conclude this harrowing story, I had just enough money to get home on the bus. To ice the cake, when I failed to turn up at our post-match rendezvous the dentist fellow, the author of my woes, had the police searching the stadium for my dead body!

Normally, in my earlier days, when I was a regular attender at Ibrox, I stood on the terracing at the Copland Road End. This presented problems: despite my attempts at concealment under bunnet and muffler, parishioners continually approached requesting my ministrations - e.g. baptism for the wean, forthcoming nuptials, references, etc. Holding my 'vestry hour' under such circumstances was not easy, but adaptability is the hallmark of my profession, and it is possible (with practice) to outline a swift resumé of the Westminster Confession of Faith in the five minutes remaining before the kick-off. At the time, I did not appreciate fully how innovative was this terracing missionary activity. Indeed, I was unaware I was pioneering the 'Church Without Walls' policy which is looked upon with such great favour by today's progressive thinkers. I have not given up hope that one day soon, a commemorative medal will be struck in honour of my experimental missionary work carried out on the boisterous slopes of Ibrox Stadium - the George Cross, or Govan Cross with Bar, will do.

These counselling sessions were amiable meetings, and I recall one in particular which reunited me with an old Club boy named Robbie; Robbie had played valiantly in the Seniors' football, and I had much valued his talents. Son of an alcoholic, he was unusual in that, of all the boys, he was teetotal. He had gone down to England, and we had lost touch, so our reunion on the Ibrox terracing was all the more cordial. However, I could see that in his absence Robbie had abandoned sobriety, and had been 'bevvying', for he was very drunk when we met. Robbie's story was tinged with tragedy: his wife had died; he had taken to the bottle; he had been in jail in Perth for crimes which he refrained from specifying. I expressed my sympathies, but he was not sorry for himself, and wanted to know if I knew the chaplain at Perth prison, a man he held in high regard. I didn't, but asked how the chaplain had helped him. 'He didnae help me at aw,' stated Robbie, 'but he was a good guy.' This reply shows that good works are not necessary for salvation: the less you do, the more grace abounds. Anyway, by this time, I found myself standing with Robbie in a wide space empty of spectators. The reason for this was that Robbie was waving a huge revolver about. He began to bellow 'S N P', and without so much as a 'cheerio', ran onto the pitch, interrupting the play.

The following morning, the *Daily Record* filled the front page with a mug-shot of Robbie over the screaming headline - 'The Face of Sectarian Hatred!' What part the S N P plays, if any, in sectarian hatreds I know not, and, I suspect, neither did Robbie. We weren't even playing the Celtic! As for the revolver, whether or not it was loaded I cannot say, but 'It's an ill-wind that blaws naebody ony guid.' One ought not draw benefits from the misfortunes of others, but I certainly did on this occasion, for Robbie left me standing all alone to enjoy the rest of the match, with a clear view unobstructed by an encroaching crowd.

Of course, there were times when danger loomed: I almost got caught in the terrible Ibrox disaster. Then there was the nasty episode over the youth standing behind me who urinated in a can and poured it out on the terracing right behind me. When I objected he totally surprised me by taking a swing at me, luckily just missing! His pals readied themselves to join in, with me for target practice. However, I had my pals too: as fine a set of former Church House boys, grown to manhood, as could be assembled. They would not stand idly by and see their spiritual guide and counsellor assaulted by some pimply youths!

One of my accompanying cronies was Gordie, a former juvenile delinquent who, in his Club days, had led the leaders a merry dance, and had oft been cast into the outer darkness of the lane for unruly conduct. Time, manhood, and marriage had turned Gordie into a respectable citizen, but not turned down his fiery nature below gas mark 9. A sure indicator that he was about to erupt was when Gordie took off his spectacles; those of us who knew him saw the red flag go up, and heard the alarm bells ringing loud and clear! Seeing I was in peril, Gordie now took off his specs, belted my assailant on the chin, and laid him out! It was a fraught situation: a general free-for-all ensued, all sorts of bystanders joining in! I visualised the headline in next morning's *Daily Record* - 'Minister of Religion Arrested for Hooliganism'. Thankfully, things calmed down - largely due to a universal reluctance to engage Gordie in mortal combat. Was I glad! I assumed the youths concerned would move off, or at least behave themselves; but they continued to make further trouble all through the game. I kept my mouth shut this time round. You needed three things at times: a blind eye, a deaf ear, and, when required, to be hell of a quick on your feet! Failing those, it was safest to stay close to Gordie and his mates.

In appearance, Gordie was no ruffian: far ftom it. Of light build and middle stature, he was well-dressed, and outwardly mild mannered. That was what made him so dangerous. After an Old Firm game at Hampden Park, five of us went for a drink in a pub in Rutherglen, unfortunately without first checking out its religious affiliations. Upon entry, the presence of a multitude of green and white scarves indicated we were in the wrong pub and the wrong company. I advised a hasty retreat, but my companions approached the bar, and an apprehensive barman.

A sturdy Celtic supporter standing there eyed us coldly and went to battle stations. Gordie's response was to give him one of his special disarming smiles and, with a kindly gesture, ask the guy what he wanted to drink. Warily, the recipient of this generosity ordered a pint. The atmosphere lightened, everyone relaxed, cordial relations developed all round. Gordie began to wax eloquent about football being only a game, something not to be taken too seriously. Warming to his theme, he condemned the evils of sectarianism, a denunciation of which everyone in the pub approved, even though none of them believed it!

Gordie and the Celtic-orientated gentleman he was plying with drinks had become bosom cronies by the time we had to depart (it couldn't come quick enough for me). Bidding the guy an affectionate farewell, Gordie extended a brotherly handshake and wished him, and his team, every joy and success in days to come. The man reached out to shake hands, and that was the moment Gordie struck with the speed of a panther, flattening his unsuspecting victim with a mighty blow in the teeth! Then, hitching up his pants, Gordie led us out of the saloon, yours truly leading the way!

There is a suggestion these days that ministers should hold Bible studies and prayer meetings in public houses in pursuit of the objectives of this 'Church Without Walls' outreach business. A good idea? Perhaps, but if you want to start a meeting in a certain pub in Rutherglen, please accept my apologies for absence!

Many people who have never been to a Rangers or a Celtic game talk as though bigotry and violence are the monopoly of the two clubs. Not so; some of the worst supporters for religious bigotry, in my personal experience, are Hibs supporters. Sitting in the old Centenary Stand at Ibrox with Ronnie Thornton, an elder of mine, during a Rangers v Hibs match, we found ourselves surrounded by about fifty or sixty Hibs fans who spent the whole of the first half chanting 'We are the Pope's men'. Strange to say, the Rangers fans nearby either did not notice, or paid no attention - at least, not until half-time, by which time the Hibs supporters had cleared off, leaving Ronnie and me sitting in a wide area of empty seats, and subjected to a great deal of unpleasant abuse.

Having stayed near Easter Road, I once followed The Famous Five with undying admiration, and Tynecastle in those days was not far behind in high class football. In Bridgeton, the Clyde attracted a big support from those who did not support either Celtic or Rangers. An original Club member, Grace Donald travels on the Clyde team bus and a presentation cushion to her is in the Hampden football museum.

As school boys, Arthur and I went by train to Old Trafford to see Preston North End play Man. United. We took the Sunday School handbell along - a big, heavy thing with a loud clang. A crane-sized Manchester docker in a polo-neck jersey ordered us not to ring the thing, but we did. "Listen, you two," this moron bellowed, "I was goal-keeping before you were born!" With his quick wit Arthur retaliated, "Aye, and I see you've still got the jersey on!" "Ask not for whom the bell tolls ... "

My father was a stubborn man who always entered a ground by the nearest turnstyle, regardless of which 'end' it took him into. On one occasion that took him (and me) into the Celtic End. He was, in spite of having been brought up near Ibrox, by no means a Rangers man ("Everybody else has a ground - *they* have to have a stadium!"). He was a Queen's Park man, but didn't care too much about which team he was watching so long as he could have a good argument. His tactic was to wait for a good long period after the start of the game, then make his move.

The idol of Celtic in those days was the immortal Charlie Tully; Pop held his fire for twenty minutes and then asked in a loud voice, "Which one is Tully?" Maybe his hearers were too aghast at this act of sacriligious daring to give it credence; perhaps they put it down to poor eye sight; most likely it did not seem possible to them that anybody not a fervent Celtic fan would be standing at the Celtic end when they were playing Rangers. A normally quiet, inoffensive man, Dad grew horns at football matches, inflamatory, provocative remarks flowing from his lips. I don't know how he got away with it, but he invariably did.

I kept a safe distance from *pater;* standing one match with a friend, a guy my friend knew joined us. After awhile he asked, "Who is that old bloke down there causing a rumpus?" With a shake of the head I replied, "That old bloke is my father." It is amazing how football can turn a philatelist into a fanatical debater! I doubt if Pop ever actually *saw* a match for arguing about games played long ago. One day, no doubt, our politically correct 'thought police', who rule the roost, will pass laws to take all the joy and passion out of football, and make us all as bland and boring as themselves. I just hope I'm not around to see that awful day.

Chapter 23

GOLF & OTHER CLUBS

Unless the weather was impossible, an old minister played every Monday with three of his elders. When one of the elders died, the minister took the graveside Service in pouring rain, and as they squelched mournfully back to the car, the minister said to the remaining two, "Och weel, he couldnae hae played the day onywey."

In my Granada, I use to drive my golfing pals to Troon on Saturdays to tee off at 9 a.m. Leaving one morning late, at 8.15, I still had them teeing off at 9 a.m. So affected by the G-forces I bring to my driving, they could not play, and I scored one of my rare victories. A Granada can shift, and they showed a distinct reluctance to get into mine thereafter.

I first played big-time golf when I became President of the Bridgeton Business Club. Told it was merely a social event, I borrowed clubs and turned up at Cathkin Braes G.C. I played Gordon Cosh, a great champion of the sport, who had never played anyone with a score of 120 before. He was very nice about it: meeting him recently at a dinner, I asked if he remembered it, and he told me he would never forget it!

Asked how a minister of religion has become a leading light in Business Club golfing circles, I remind everyone that there is a lot about golf in the Scriptures: 'The good that I would, I do not, and the evil that I would not, that I do' *(Rom.7:19),* are words which can only have come from a golfer. *(Phil. 3:14):* 'I press on towards the mark' (found written on an old papyrus scorecard) proves St. Paul was a golfer *(1 Cor. 13:12):* 'Now we see through a glass darkly,' shows he liked a Guinness at the 19th hole *(Phil.3:2):* 'Beware of the dogs' was written by Paul after he trod on it in the semi-rough. When not in the stocks, Paul played a three-ball in Athens with Timothy and Silas *(Acts.17:15).* In the Old Testament, Moses lost a ball and went looking for it in what turned out to be a burning bush *(Ex.3).*

We know that David 'played before the Lord', and after Jeremiah missed a short putt he wrote in Lamentations, 'he hath made my paths crooked' *(Lam.3:9)*. In *Job 8:12*, reference is made to the poor state of the greens, but then everybody was complaining about the greens in 200 B.C. The rules of golf were written on tablets of stone by Moses when he was Secretary of the Sinai G.C., and thereafter the Red Sea was declared a water hazard, and a free drop was permitted during sand-storms.

The earliest record of golf clubs goes back to *Isaiah 60: 17*: 'for iron I will bring silver, for wood a brassy' - these silver irons and metal woods were expensive, and a full set, with bag, would knock you back about 400 talents in the sales.

Not until Nimshi begat Jehu was the driver invented, and, according to *2 Kings 9:20*, Jehu 'drove furiously', setting a record which, since then, has only been bettered by John Daly and Tiger Woods. The 7 iron was sacred to the Jews, and no Priest or Levite would take one out on the course with him on the Sabbath Day. Special mention must be made of the Wedge. This club was first used by the Hittites (the big hitters of their day) when they played the Amalkites and the Fleabites in the Bob Hope Classic, Palm Springs. The invention of the wedge made it possible for players to keep a cuneiform score card. Many of these cards, clay tablets covered in wedge marks, have been found torn up in disgust throughout Mesopotamia. For writing in the sand, the sand wedge was introduced.

In those days, score cards were marked right to left in Hebrew, which meant players playing backwards, teeing off at the 18th, and finishing at the 1st. Only left-handed clubs were manufactured, and consequently, right-handers (see *Ps. 89*, 'high is thy right hand'), never broke a 100. Going back in time, it is not surprising that Jonah, a bloke who did not know his right hand from his left, was the only Jew ever to win the Nineveh Open.

Those early days, the dress code was strictly enforced. Changing sandals in the chariot park resulted in death by stoning. Caught girding up the loins in the bar, the offender's loins were squashed in the winepress by a barmaid. In the lounge, members were required to wear coats of many colours, ephods, and bleached, washed, shrunk, pressed fine linen garments from a list of bespoke weavers, dyers and fullers approved by Ezra when he was Club Secretary in Babylon. Raiment of camel's hair and leather girdles were not permitted in the dining room. Later, the rules were relaxed; wearing turbans on the course no longer raised Cain. Urim and Thummin machines, paying out on a jackpot of four pomegranates, were installed in the lobby to raise shekels.

Golf was, as everyone knows, introduced to Scotland by John Knox during the Reformation as a replacement for the Sacrament of Penance. There is a Ph. D. thesis waiting to be written on the theology of golf; and I might add that another doctorate is up for grabs on the theology of swearing, a related subject. I have read through the whole ninety-six volumes of Karl Barth's 'Church Dogmatics' and, you will hardly credit this, there is not a single reference to golf. Is this omission deliberate? Or did it just slip Barth's mind when he nodded off writing vol. 96? The issue is an urgent one, and must be cleared up, once and for all. The publication of a treatise to be called 'A Golf Course Without Walls' is long overdue, and I hope that Harry Reid and Sam Torrance will not delay teaming up to start work on it.

One doesn't wish to boast, but once upon a time I won the Business Clubs' Cup, after a few lessons and one or two practice rounds on the 9-hole pitch and putt in Tollcross park. This memorable triumph took place at Elderslie, where I was opposed by a young man highly skilled in the game, who turned up at the last moment, and was just recovering his breath when he realised I was four up on him. He speedily began to reduce my lead, but I hung on. At the 13th he was on the green and putting for his par, while I was many feet from the hole, straining to catch sight of the far distant pin. With a magical touch worthy of Harry Potter, I struck a long chip right into the cup - still all-square! My opponent fainted! So we battled on grimly to the end, even-steven. He drove a magnificent drive right up the middle, and I miserably duffed mine. His second hit the green for a certain par; I struck a 3-wood which sailed into the heavens in search of a blessing, struck a wall, and landed in the cup - I birdied, he parred. The coveted cup was mine, and 'running over, running over' as we sang in Sunday School.

Years have passed, but the reputation I gained that day has gone before me, and many have since said to me what General George Patton said to his favourite 'lucky' chaplain: 'Man, you must be in good with the Lord!' Golfing ministers get used to accusations of receiving Divine help. Having discovered I had great golfing potential, I sought outlets for my talents. I heard of ministers who were accorded the freedom of their local golf course, but this privilege was denied me as Brigton is golf-course-less. I tried to join a course not too far away, only to be rebuffed by the haughty Secretary. When I happened to mention this to a friend in the Business Club, he began to breath fire and slaughter! Apparently, he was the President of that particular club, and at war with the Secretary, a person who was, as I have said, a particularly unpleasant fellow.

By this time I did not want to join the said Club, but the die was cast: I was a pawn in a bitter feud. Late one night, the Secretary phoned pleading with me to play on his course for a small sum. The one condition was that I would have to pretend to being a member of the police force, so I could enjoy the privileges of that favoured caste. The ruse did not work very well, it being a well-known fact from my regular appearance in the local pulpits that I was certainly not a member of the constabulary. I cleared off *tout de suite,* while no one was looking!.

A minister in a city charge told me one day that there was some ancient rule which afforded a Glasgow minister the opportunity to play on a certain highly prestigious course for a few pence. He had been benefiting from this piece of archival research, and invited me to join him on Monday mornings for a game.

Appointing himself my chaperone, he warned me to strictly obey the Club's code of conduct: no changing shoes in the car park, no caddy cars on the tees, collar and tie at all times, even in the shower. I informed him that, like the rich young ruler, "All these things have I kept since my youth", but he made me take the oath anyway. Things went well until some old codger pulled me up for tucking my trouser legs into my socks, and threatened to report me. I indignantly replied that I was going to put my waterproofs over the pants, and thus deprived him of the pleasure of sending me to the guardhouse. But I couldn't keep out of trouble very long, and went on to commit the unforgivable sin: I entered the bar wearing a raincoat! This seemed innocent enough to me at the time, seeing it was 9 a.m., the place was deserted, I was wearing the obligatory tie, and all I wanted was to do was to buy a Mars bar. But hidden eyes were watching closely, and I was ticked off by the beak!

I am an impeccably behaved golfer, and, being much miffed by this insufferable incident, never played there again. Years passed. One morning I read a report in *The Herald* that a certain highly prestigious golf club was having a problem over the way some of its members were dressing in the club house. This moved me to write a letter to the newspaper expressing surprise at this report, believing, as I did, that the said club had solved the problem long ago when it got rid of me! I will not name the club in question, for fear of reprisals, but it is interesting to record that for many a day after I wrote, city-gent golfers I met would say to me, "Ah, you are the chap who wrote that letter about --- Golf Club." Had I blasphemed against the Holy Ghost nobody would have paid the least attention, but to smile at --- G.C, well!

Of course, public courses exist and attract all kinds ... My friend Ronnie, a retired policeman, got a job checking up on insurance claims, and called one time on a chap claiming for golfing equipment stolen from his car. Ronnie asked "What had been stolen?" - "A brand new golf bag, worth £80." "What else?" "Full set of brand new Ping clubs worth £700." "And?" "Brand new electric caddy-car, cost £500, boxes of brand new balls, new waterproof suit, glove, shoes - adding up to an additional £200." "Receipts?" No, he didn't have any receipts, lost them all. "Where was this equipment inside the car?", asks Ronnie. "In the boot." "What kind of a car?" "A Volkswagen Beetle." "All that in a Beetle boot!" exclaims Ronnie. "Erh, no, on the back seat, forgot that." Asks Ronnie "So, how much are you claiming?" Answer: "Well, £1,500 should cover it." "Do you play much golf?" asks Ronnie. "Oh, yeh, all the time." "Are you a member of a golf club?" "Sure, oor local 9-hole." "Do you play in competitions?" "Aye, every Sunday I play with my pal." "OK." says Ronnie, "By the way, what do you play off?" The guy looks puzzled. "Play aff? I play aff they wee plastic things ye stick in the grun!"

I might make a modest reference to my skills as a bowler, as well as a golfer. In fact, on the Business Clubs' outing, I won a cup. This was at the delightful Dumbarton Rock Bowling Green, which sticks out into the river; big ships sail past nearby - well, in those days they did. I was paired off with a chap who didn't turn up, so I was teamed with the green-keeper to balance the number of competitors. This elderly gentleman greeted the news that I had never played bowls before with encouraging fortitude, and he told me what was required of me: put my bowl behind that wee ball called a jack. I did this with moderate success; we won every end; I got a cup. Congrats and trebles all round! I do not wish to boast, but I can honestly and proudly say that I have not lost a bowls match since that afternoon on the bonny banks o' the Clyde.

There are many jokes about golf, but none at all about bowls. This makes it very difficult for after-dinner speaking at a bowling club, where one's speech can barely be stretched out to four minutes. The Bible doesn't have much to say about bowls either: Solomon made 'an hundred bowls of gold', according to *2 Chron.4:8*; and in *Numbers 7:85*, we read of 'each bowl weighing seventy shekels'. This would suggest that Ten Pin bowling was popular. In *Isaiah 16: 11* the prophet wrote, 'Mine bow(e)ls shall sound like an harp' but scholars cannot decide from this whether Isaiah was a bowler, a poor speller, or suffering from flatulence.

I mention the Bridgeton Business Club because it was not only formed during wartime, like Church House, but has been a good support for the Club - so have the The James Dick Benevolent Society, Glasgow Eastern Merchants, and The Trades House of Glasgow. Such public spiritedness, with especial care for the Inner City, deserves recognition, and I would thank my many friends involved.

The Bridgeton Burns Club holds its annual dinner in the city (always on January 25th), and it is the biggest in the world - some 600 attend and tickets are like gold. As chaplain for many years, and still a member, I was privileged to sit at the top table beside many prominent public figures who were proposing the toasts. They were invariably interesting conversationalists, and, as you would expect, the speaking was of a high standard, though I could name one or two who hardly mentioned Robert Burns when giving The Immortal Memory!

One who most certainly did was Willie Ross, then Secretary of State for Scotland. He was brilliant! I shall never forget how he handled the heckling (politically inspired?) which emanated from some drunks at a table at the far back of the hall. During his speech, one of these inebriates shouted out a brief Burns' quote intended to make a fool of Willie Ross. Where he ended, Willie continued the quotation in full, line after line after line, page after page, on and on and on until the hall was hushed and spellbound by this bravura display of Burns' poetry. Spontaneous applause and a standing ovation shamed and routed the heckler. Maybe the quoted passage came, by chance, from a long poem Willie Ross luckily happened to know off by heart, but if any man knew his Burns it was Willie Ross. The Bridgeton Burns' Club does excellent work in schools with competitions, otherwise I am sure Scottish culture would not survive.

I found myself drawn into the Burns' circuit when a member of the Business Club asked me, the night before the event, to propose the Immortal Memory at a Supper in Sloan's restaurant, in the Miller Arcade off Argyle Street. It was for the West of Scotland Plant Hirers Association, a society of which I had not heard, but which was, he assured me, very small. The story was that the President of this august body had been let down at the last moment by his speaker, and there was an emergency.

Arriving at this fascinating Victorian pub/restaurant, I found that half the population of the country belong to the WSPHA and the place was stowed oot! I was getting the shakes when in came Bill Thomson, an accomplished Burns speaker, who told me he was doing the Toast to the Lassies, because the President had been let down by the person allocated the job. I enlightened him as to how I had been reeled in by the same unlikely story. When the piper arrived, he too had the same tale to tell. By this time, we were at the giggling stage. So the proceedings unfolded, and the president showed no signs of having organised anything at all - but what a great night it turned out to be!

Burns would have loved it! Several hundred plant hirers "boozing at the nappy, an' getting fou and unco happy," is a wonderful sight, indeed. If you ever receive a phone call late on the night of January 24th, pleading with you to speak at the WSPHA, jump at the chance. It is the opportunity of a lifetime, believe me.

My fame as a Burns' scholar spread, and I joined some other entertainers from the Bums Club and went on tour. The oddest place was the newly opened private hospital in Clydebank, where we played to an audience of Americans who were under the impression that it was a George Burns' Supper (George was still alive but approaching immortality at the time). Explaining before every poem and song what it was about, and who Rabbie was, dampened the spontaneity value of the proceedings. The gentleman and his wife who headed the hospital came from Virginia, and having just been there I tried, unsuccessfully, to stir up a conversation with them about their native heath. Although they had been in Clydebank for a long time, they had no idea what towns existed on the other side of the river. When I mentioned I had come from 'across the water', meaning Greenock, they thought I had come from Ireland! The night was a shambles! The band and singers had been hired at great expense, but nobody paid them the least attention. One could only hope that the patients were getting their money's worth.

When I travelled by taxi with Helen Liddell to a Burns Supper, I found her extremely pleasant. Where she gets the soubriquet 'Stalin's Granny', I can't imagine, for she is nothing like that. Pulling her leg (it didn't come off), I toasted 'The Lassies' in Buckfast wine - she having just been to the Abbey in Devon to tick off the monks for making the cheap, potent stuff and exporting it to Coatbridge.

The Rev. James Currie was the doyen of Burns' Suppers and was notorious for taking down notes of other people's speeches. I recall a dinner in The Fiddlers in Largs when he wrote down Jimmy Logan's jokes during their delivery. Turning to the Reverend *amanuensis* at his side, he said, "If I'm going too fast for you, Jimmy, let me know". Jimmy was unembarrassed and carried on scribbling.

I had a lot of time for Jimmy Currie: stuck one afternoon for a speaker for the Pensioners' club, I phoned him. He came at once, all the way from Pollok. I have met a lot of ministers who would not have done that - busy, busy types. I was sorry Jimmy never became Moderator of the General Assembly. I noticed that however much on the surface his speeches at dinners were entertaining, underlying them was the Gospel message. He was a 'character', and there are few 'characters' about these days of the mediocre.

Out of the many un-mediocre characters I have met through the Business Club, let me mention just two: Frank Joyner, and Willie Anderson.

Frank was an officer in the Chindits dropped behind enemy lines in Burma. One story Frank told was of the time he and an Indian soldier stood in a narrow slit trench overlooking and observing a Japanese camp. As they watched, unexpectedly, the enemy suddenly shifted their camp, the Japanese troops encircling and trapping them. The trench was too small to lie down; they had to stand, hoping they would not be discovered, and praying the troops would go away.

Their only food was two tins of bully beef, and after a few days Frank opened one and offered some to his comrade who, being a Hindu, refused to eat it. After several more days, the Indian asked, "Sahib, what religion are you?". "Church of Scotland" answered Frank. "In the Church you belong to, you can eat bully beef? Well, I am wanting to join this Church of Scotland - open the other tin, Sahib!"

After eleven days standing in the trench, Frank was hallucinating, and began seeing himself moving about amongst the Japs. He knew they had to get out the trench, or they would die there, so they struggled out, walked right through the camp and escaped! Miraculously, not one soldier noticed them or paid the slightest attention. It was as if they were invisible! Frank, by the way, had played football before the war for both Chelsea and Arsenal. He was a fine man, but his wartime experiences had left noticeable psychological scars. Very badly wounded comrades could not be left to be tortured by the Japanese - somebody had to shoot them.

As for Willie Anderson, well, he was a real 'one-off.' Nothing upset or troubled Willie, as he weaved his way through life. Everybody liked him; he was the sort of 'clubbable man' who would have delighted Dr. Samuel Johnson. As President of various clubs, he would open proceedings by announcing that he had carried out none of his assignments, a frank disclosure which normally leads to calls for resignation, but which, in Willie's case, brought forth applause and gales of laughter. Big, stooping, amiable, Willie was just one of those men who are born naturally funny. I once told him that if he stood up and read out the telephone directory he would bring the house down! He was a totally unconscious comedian, and I am sure that like Tommy Cooper, he never really understood why people laughed at his meandering jokes.

Willie was famous for his absent-mindedness. He owned a string of small shops (dairies) and at closing up time one evening his wife, Jean, phoned him to bring her some tea-bread. On his way home, Willie stopped outside the bank, which was closed, and opened the night safe door to deposit the day's takings down the chute. When he got home, Jean asked him for the tea-bread, and he handed her a parcel. She opened it and found inside the cash takings - her tea-bread was lying in the bank's safe!

A favourite Willie Anderson story was the night the Business Club held a dinner/dance at the Royal Scottish Automobile Club in Blythswood Square. After the ball was over, Willie, ever fond of a dram, forgot Jean was with him, left her behind and drove off home in the car. While running after him, Jean fell down the steps outside the club, broke her leg, and was carried back inside. After awhile, somebody asked where Willie was. A search showed his car was gone and so was he. They phoned his house: picture Willie dozing by the fire. "Hello, that you, Willie?" came the anxious voice over the phone, "Don't you realise there has been a terrible accident?" There was a pause while this sank in. "Oh my God!" moaned Willie, "Am I badly injured?"

In fairness to Willie Anderson, I must admit to a reputation for absent-mindedness of my own. I once committed the unprecedented gaffe of addressing the great Bridgeton Burns' Club dinner wearing informal dress. Because it was me, nobody noticed!. I am also the only person in the history of Glasgow Presbytery to make a long speech seconding a motion which, as the Moderator pointed out, had not been moved. To rub it in, my three children pain me by gleefully recalling the time I went home from the kirk one Sunday to be asked by a stiffened wife, "Where are the children?" I had forgotten them and left them locked in the church! I justify this lapse by pointing out that absent-mindedness is a sign of great powers of concentration - well, that's my excuse, what's yours?

It is sad to think that the R. S. A. C. is closed, as it had a big place in the city, and happy memories for me. One such was the evening I was going to a dinner there and, being without a car, I waited in a queue for the bus in London Road. There was some hold-up in the transport system, so the waiting line grew longer and longer, until I became anxious about the time. Luckily, a taxi appeared and I hailed it, stepping forward with the eyes of the queue upon me. Many watching knew me, and everyone could see I was a minister because I was wearing a clerical collar. Just as I got in, two scantily attired ladies left the queue and boarded the taxi with me; both were well known locally as 'ladies of the night'.

'Where to?' asked the driver. 'Blythswood Square' we all three chirped in chorus. That the two prostitutes were going to Blythswood Square did not surprise the onlookers, but my accompanying them raised eyebrows. Off we went, leaving behind a line of respectable folk reflecting upon the dubious morals, hobbies, and tastes of their parish minister. Always the gentleman, at the entrance to the Club I paid the taxi and was warmly thanked by the girls - perhaps a mite too warmly for the arriving guests, who cast searching glances in my direction. A cheery pair, the 'working girls' kissed me goodbye, and expressed the fond hope that they would enjoy my company on future occasions. Rude jokes from some, and strange looks from others, followed me through the evening, but I took comfort from remembering that

Gladstone's night-time missionary visits to fallen women had been, like my own, misunderstood.

Chapter 24

I am more interested in the quality of my life
than in mere longevity.
(Martin Luther)

When our Club Secretary, and former Director of Education, Stewart Macintosh died, I read his obituary in *The Herald,* and phoned his minister in Killearn, where he had gone to live in the final years of his retirement. A pleasant man, he told me that Stewart had written his own, brief, obituary and that, although he had visited the house, he did not know when the funeral would take place. A few days later he still did not know, so, as a result, Alex Mair, Margaret Beaton and I were not able to be there. Apparently, there was a family cremation and Stewart's ashes were buried in his native Helmsdale.

It was very typical of that great and fine man that he went out of his way to avoid an elaborate obituary and an official public funeral. I suppose the old Highland insistence upon praising God, and not the dead person, had a lot to do with his attitude. It was a shame that many, who knew and admired the man, did not get a public opportunity to say 'thanks and farewell', but as the old saying goes: "Whoever builds a Church to God, not Fame, Will never mark the marble with his name."

A very private person, I remember Dr Macintosh saying that his mother told him on Sundays, "You can go out to play, but don't enjoy yourself" (said, no doubt, with a twinkle in her eye!) He was the best Director of Education the city ever had, the last of his kind. He once told me that he judged a school by the state of the toilets - the first stop on his tour of inspection. He had an impressive memory for all members of staff, including the families of the janitors. Presbyterian Scotland once bred such men and women.

I first met Stewart when he turned up at the Club in the mid-Sixties, with some other elders from Newlands South Church, to see what help they could offer. A fruitful connection was established which continues. Stewart took to Church House like a Cub Scout taking to second helpings of custard. Newly retired, he had an enormous appetite for new adventures.

I used to drive over to Pollokshields, pick him up on Wednesday evenings, and take him to the Club. There he would referee the football in the gym, standing in the middle of the floor and getting under the boys' feet as they pushed him aside. When a distinguished visitor to the Club saw this one night, he asked me with considerable astonishment, "Is that Stewart Macintosh there? I tried for years to get an interview with that man!" My wife, Margaret, appeared before him when she became a teacher in the city, during the days when to teach in Glasgow was a very great source of pride. Stewart's becoming Club Secretary was an indispensable help to me during the rebuilding period between 1969 and 1974, for he was a man of powerful influence in the city, having given so many in education their jobs.

When Alex Mair became Club Leader in 1971, we were out on the street for a long time owing to the Club rebuilding, so Stewart started visiting local homes, and each week presented me with a long, hand-written report on each family. What I was expected to do with this overwhelming volume of information I am not sure, but he gained ready access wherever he went on behalf of the Club. Such was the modesty of this man, who published books on education, that he told me he had learnt more from his experience at Church House than he had ever learnt before! The sight of him surrounded by weans while he operated the 'lavvy key' is one I treasure; his tall, rangy, figure towering over them all.

The Club gave Stewart a place, and he was highly understanding when it came to the life of ordinary folk. 'Remember, Bill,' he once advised me, 'these people have a long history of being poor.' He never became big-headed like lesser men. One night, driving him home, I said, 'Why don't you buy a car?' 'Because I can't drive,' he replied. Seeing I was surprised to hear this he added, 'Well, I always had a chauffeur.' Strange how St. Francis-in-the-East has drawn to itself so many people from all sorts of backgrounds who have found their spiritual home there. Of course, it wasn't only the place which drew all these diverse types, but the kind of people they met there.

Stewart's presence on the Management Committee during the rebuilding was invaluable. His influence in the higher regions of education was immense. There were times, however, when he forgot he was retired and twice he nearly landed Alex Mair and myself in hot water. On both occasions he sent us off to Education Department storage facilities to collect chairs (the ones in the church to this day amongst them). There we were, filling up the Club van, when we discovered we were being accused of theft! The police were called to Lambhill depot and it was with some difficulty that we extricated ourselves.

I used to say, when I became the parish minister, that ours was the only church in the world with three brass balls over the door. Everything in it was scrounged. When I traded in a Gestetner machine which I had rescued from a foot of water in a half-demolished school, the manager said to me as he handed over a new electric machine, 'Rev. Shackleton, were you born in Jerusalem?' Nothing was ever paid for. I got so used to foraging for the Club and the church that I have never got used to the idea of a minister actually *paying* for something.

Chapter 25

*"The observances of the church conceming feasts
and fasts are tolerably well kept, since the rich keep the
feasts and the poor the fasts."*
(Rev. Sydney Smith).

MISSION - A POST MODERN STUDY

Some folk have no idea what goes on in a church: once a man approached me to become a Communicant and offered me a £10 membership fee. Apparently, he had asked a guy at work how you joined a church and was told it is like joining the Masons: it cost £10 up front!

Every now and again, some sect or other would descend on Bridgeton like a cloud of locusts, and conduct an evangelical campaign. It never seemed to occur to them that we were already there, but then they didn't want to find out. These incomers were not welcome as far as we were concerned, and it angered me that they sold things to people which they could not afford - I still have a big white Bible some poor soul paid for at the door and then gave to me.

The Mormons invaded one time and made quite a stir. They made many 'rice converts' amongst the wilier elements in the community; the type who would not beware of the Greeks provided they came bearing gifts. For a short time it was all the fun of the fair, the Fourth of July and Thanksgiving rolled into one. And it was all free! It was rumoured that if you became a convert you got half-a-crown, and the Club turned Mormon over night!

Attending our Monday night Regnal Circle we had Ian, a lanky, cadaverous young man who passed his days hanging around outside a betting shop in Duke Street. There were those who saw Ian in a sympathetic light, but I was not one of them - to me he was a pest, an insufferable scrounger. Ian tapped everybody who did not know him for cigarettes, and whenever we were visited by men from other Circles, he had them in his sights. I sternly warned him against this, but during a visit from a middle-class Circle, he preyed on them shamelessly. I had had enough! ''Begone,'' I commanded. "and never darken my reputation again! Don't ever come back to this church."

He slunk off. "Well," observed one good Christian visitor, perturbed by my brusqueness, "I've never heard a minister tell somebody to get out of a church and never come back." A reassuring smile was called for, and I gave one saying, "Don't worry, Ian will be back all right, unfortunately."

He did come back to tell me he was leaving the Church of Scotland to become a Mormon. It was news to me that he had ever belonged to the Kirk, but not wishing to split hairs, I asked him why a Mormon? "My uncle is one," he replied. "Ian," said I,"are you aware that if you become a Mormon you will have to give up smoking, drinking, and gambling in betting shops?" This was news of the unwelcome kind to Ian and, as a result, his face showed considerable slippage. Pressing on, I asked him which Mormon temple his uncle attended; he paused, knitted his brows, then replied, "Oh, he doesn't go to one; he used to go but not now". "Really? Doesn't go to one?", I queried, somewhat puzzled. "No,", said Ian, "he's a lapsed Mormon." The mind boggled - a lapsed Mormon!

I recall the curious case of a carter who habitually stopped his horse and cart outside his favourite pub every day for years, until, while visiting the Carters' Mission run by my Uncle Alex in the Gorbals, he was converted, and forsook the pub. Unfortunately, the horse, not knowing of his master's change of habits, continued to stop outside the pub at the usual time, putting the new convert into temptation's way. There was only one solution: the horse had to be converted as well! This was not easy, but I believe it was finally achieved by keeping it away from socialising with the sort of horses which can lead an innocent nag astray.

There there was Isa, a fine, big, hard working woman married to Bridgeton's answer to Andy Capp - a wee runt of man called Josie Smith. Known to all publicans, sinners, and turf accountants within a mile radius of his humble tenement single-end home, Josie was a ne'er-do-well of the first water. He had turned laziness into a fine art, passing his leisure hours - which were many - parked at the telly, a can of lager in hand. You get the picture.

Visiting the house of some friends one night, Isa arrived to find two American Mormon missionaries, fine looking young men of serious purpose, sitting there, laying it on the line. After listening a wee while, Isa had had enough and rose to leave, at which one of the Mormons expressed dismay. Isa insisted she had to depart. Giving her a regretful look, the earnest young Mormon laid his hand upon her shoulder and said, "Go, if you must, Isa, but when you get home tonight, will you do something for me? Will you pray for the soul of our founder, Joseph Smith?" "Aye, aw right," agreed Isa, "but when you get hame the night, will you promise to dae something for me? For God's sake, pray for the soul of my husband, Josie Smith!"

Have I already mentioned Joe Park? He was quite a witty character. Somewhat crippled, Joe worked as a liftman in Lewis's Stores in the city centre. In the old days, soapbox meetings were held on a corner of Brunswick Street. On his way home from work one summer's evening, Joe stopped to listen to an evangelist giving it what is known in Glasgow as 'laldy'. A well-dressed, good-looking young lady sidled up to Joe in the small crowd and, in a refined Kelvinside accent, asked him if he had been 'saved'. Joe confessed himself to be unsure on that score, but tendered the information that he was a member of a church. Church membership, she clucked disapprovingly, is inadequate for purposes of salvation, and she warmly invited Joe along to one of their meetings in a nearby hall. Joe asked when these were held, and on being told "Wednesdays and Fridays", shook his head sadly; "I'm busy both those nights," he sighed, "but I really am interested. How about tomorrow night? I'll meet you here at six o'clock and we can go for a coffee and you can tell me all about it." At that point the fair young maiden seemed to suddenly lose interest in the salvation of Joe's soul. She fluttered off, leaving behind the impression that she was reluctant to accept Joe's invitation to develop a closer relationship.

My Session Clerk was that indefatigable Brigtonian Tommy Carswell, a unique individual, a man of many talents, Tommy was a school attendance officer and highly qualified for the job. Impervious to insults and criticism, Tommy hunted down truants, and by force of personality and language, returned them to the fold. It will give you some idea of what Tommy was like when I tell you that he had spent six years during the war in Burma with his beloved Ghurkas, and that he could entertain an audience at our annual Regnal Swanwick Conference concert for half-an-hour without stopping for breath. His performances held an audience spellbound, and his was pure Glasgow humour.

One evening a couple of Jehovah's Witnesses turned up at Tommy's door, expecting to have it shut in their faces as usual. To their delight, they were enthusiastically invited in. Highly encouraged, they burst into their message, while Tommy put the kettle on. Two hours later, Tommy was still talking at them. When they managed to break their very long silence and get a word in, they muttered goodbyes and stumbled to the door. Meeting Tommy had not been a part of their intensive training. Numbed, the two of them left with Tommy's voice ringing in their ears. "I fair enjoyed that; come back next week." I would just love one day to see the report of that visit which they duly made back to G.H.Q., U.S.A.

I met a convert to Buddhism recently, a guy who is right into it and has become a sort of 'lay monk'. He studies it a lot and gives much time and effort to meditating. You have to respect other people's views and all that, but after listening to him it seemed to me that three hours looking after my two grandsons, aged two and four years respectively, would teach him more about himself and human life than all the Dalai Lamas that ever existed. As for the Dalai Lama, two wee boys would enlighten him more than all his meditations, and remove the avuncular smile from his photogenic face forever!

Chapter 26

"Go to the people,
live with them,
learn from them,
love them.
Start with what they know,
Build with what they have.
But with the best leaders,
when the work is done,
the task accomplished,
The people will say
'We have done this ourselves,' "

Mrs Spam, and Barbara, and the Sovereign

Joe Hill was a live wire, a leading light at our Christian Workers' League meetings which provided a good opportunity for young adults to put their faith into action. (Sad to say, C. W. L. no longer exists.) The League operated on three principles: "See, Judge, Act". The group looked at a problem, decided what to do about it, then acted to deal with it. No 'talking shop', C. W. L. was an action group. We were out to change the world, remember!

Joe was especially diligent at exposing corruption and injustices. He drew to our attention the strong suspicion that the money boxes into which honest travellers popped their uncollected fares were being illegally emptied by certain thieving cleaners working in the local tram depot. What we did about it I cannot remember, but we were highly indignant for starters! The young are hot against malpractice, and much in favour of idealism. We were an earnest lot in those days of Socialist Revolution! However, sometimes we over did it. On one occasion Joe got me into hot water over a janitor he accused of exploiting the school cleaners. Unfortunately, the janitor got wind of our C. W. L. investigation, and I heard on the grape vine that he was threatening to knock my block off!

Joe was a great guy, and his death, owing to an accident on a building site, left Mary with a baby daughter, Tracy. From the industrial compensation money Mary received, she gave me £100 so that I could fulfil a wish to visit the Holy Land. From that trip, I brought back a bottle of wine from Cana in Galilee to be opened at Tracy's wedding. Tracy is a young lady nowadays; I recently buried Mary. How quickly in the ministry one moves from "weeping with those who weep, to rejoicing with those who rejoice".

Joe's remarkable mother, Betty Hill, deserves a mention. To myself and Joe's pals, she was always known as 'Mrs Spam', due to her feeding us spam pieces. Joe and his mother lived in a single-end overlooking the busy, bustling London Road. His brother, David, lived up the next close with his wife Jessie and their two young boys. Davie was dying of a brain tumour, but from his cheery conversation (always about football and particularly the Clyde), you would not have known it until near the end. After his death, Jessie died of tuberculosis - and one of the boys, Alan, was killed in a street accident. With Joe also gone, did any woman ever have so much tragedy in her life as Betty Hill?

Yet Mrs Spam never uttered a word of complaint, and I take my hat off to her, and the many unbelievably courageous folk I have met who have an amazing, unspoken faith! Can I forget the woman in Barrowfield whose sole concern was, not for her own life, but for those of the family she was leaving behind. Or the wee lady who said to me quite matter of fact, "Mr Shackleton, I'm not afraid to die." Neilly Hughes, another former Church House boy and Regnalite like Joe, died of cancer while still quite a young man, and his wife, Jeanette said to me "You know, he never lost his faith." What courage! The Kingdom is far wider than the church, for the Kingdom of God is without walls!

For years I used to make a long trip to visit folk in a mental hospital which had a wing for geriatric patients. I used to take my wee dog, Rags, on these visits and let her run in the very extensive woods and grounds. There was a big pond covered with green weed, and she pranced gleefully down the slope and across what appeared to be a lovely lawn. Emerging soaking wet, she looked completely baffled and rather foolish!

I felt pretty foolish myself after one visit to the same hospital. The place was way out in the countryside. If, as I was leaving, I saw someone waiting outside for a bus I made a point of offering them a lift. One day, I extended this kindness to a young woman standing at the bus stop and offered her a lift into town, which she gladly accepted. She seemed somewhat vague about where she was going, but chatted away quite normally until I dropped her off in the city. Then I realised my briefcase had gone - she had made off with it!

Enquiries at the asylum were my only slender hope of recovery, but these left me feeling very foolish. The young woman was a patient who had escaped from a secure ward and I had been her unwitting accomplice in the get-away! Everybody was out looking for her. My punishment was that the briefcase was never seen again. Later, after she had been returned and eventually discharged, she came to stay in Bridgeton and began showing a developing interest in getting to know me better. My pastoral visits to her house became increasingly hazardous and, as wives are sensitive to their husbands receiving telephone calls late at night from young women, Margaret soon snuffed out her romantic aspirations.

In the geriatric unit of the same hospital, I regularly visited a most remarkable old spinster lady named Barbara, who was a Brigtonian of the old school. Although physically unable to look after herself, she was mentally as bright as a jeweller's shop window at Christmas, and it wasn't hard to see why she had held down an important job for many years. She was totally deaf, all five feet two of her, and this had made her shy to the point of invisibility.

Before being hospitalised, she flitted far away from Bridgeton to Duntocher, and I thought that would be the last I would see of her, but no, she still turned up at St.Francis-in-the-East every Sunday. I tried racing her to the church door before she left after the Service in order to speak to her, but she always beat me to it and was gone. Barbara even turned up each year for the Christmas Eve Service at midnight. I found that she was *walking* from Duntocher to Bridgeton and back to get to and from her church - must be some eight miles each way! Our morning Service is at half past twelve, so she had the time to make it, if she set off at dawn! I never learnt her age, but she must have been in her late eighties at the time. She would not accept a lift. Tough old dame, what!

One day, when I visited her in the geriatric unit, she handed me a gold sovereign with instructions to pass it on to some young person studying for a profession. The story was that her father had given his four daughters a sovereign each when they were young girls, and this was one of them. Apparently, before they were born, their father had lent a business colleague four pounds sovereign. When he didn't get the loan back, the money was written off as a bad debt. Happily, the debtor had gone off to the Yukon and struck it rich, unexpectedly returning years later to repay the four gold sovereigns. The girls got one each, and Barbara had kept hers all her life. On her behalf, I gave it to a deserving student I knew, and she was pleased. Barbara's last words to me came from a now vanished Scotland, a land once peopled by men and women of independent character, principled, nurtured on the Westminster Confession of Faith: "Mr Shackleton," whispered Barbara in my ear, "the human heart is corrupt - never forget that."

Barbara taught me that "the true archbishops are the archbelievers". So did a jolly, likeable lady called Jessie Linden who lived in a single-end, and was one of the few real Protestants I have met. Jessie explained to me once why we have only one Mediator, and have no need of popes and priests. A shrewd and kindly judge of character, she had a phrase for describing someone she considered to be a genuine Christian: she would say, "He's got a good grasp of the faith, a good grasp." Made me think of a pair of pliers. In Bridgeton I learnt that universities aren't always the best places to meet a good theologian. Her husband, Hughie, was a gentlemanly person, as introverted as Jessie was extroverted. A deeply devout R. C., he swept the streets. When he saw me he would lift his hat and make me feel like the laird doing the rounds of the broad acres of his estate. They made a lovely couple in their room and kitchen.

Chapter 27

A. A., G. A., & N. A.

*"Everyone knew that W. C. Fields never invited
anyone into his Hollywood mansion, so Groucho was
surprised to be asked inside one day while passing. The
place was full of crates of whisky so he asked why.*

*"Because of Prohibition, " drawled Bill Fields. "But
Prohibition has been abolished," insisted Groucho. "I
know, I know," droned the famous nasal voice, "but it
might come back!"*

*"Be nice to people on your way up because you'll
meet them on your way down."*
(Wilson Mizner)

One of the happier aspects of changing times has been the
expansion of Alcoholics Anonymous into places like Bridgeton. What
had been a city centre, middle-class sort of activity spread into needy
areas where it had not existed previously. Visiting the new houses
being built in the parish, I knocked a door and found myself at such
an A. A. meeting and was greeted with open arms!

Before long, they moved into the church hall, and soon we had
two groups meeting. I came to admire A.A. greatly. Of course, there
were problems, but I saw real dedication in action many a time. The
whole outlook, that everyone involved is on the same level of need, is
basic Christianity. Those who have come up the hard way, and who
know they can easily fall again, are those best placed to understand
and to help others in the same boat.

I got to know 'Peter the Painter' very well and presumed he
was a painter to trade. He was splendid young-to-middle-aged guy,
intelligent, bright and cheerful. He led a group and would pay for a
taxi to be there if working late. Peter had some difficult folk to deal
with. One night a wild, inebriated ruffian stormed out cursing him
en route, but Peter was undisturbed and unimpressed. He simply said
quietly to the guy, "Listen, I can't stop you from leaving, but there
is something which you can't stop me doing. I'm going to pray for

you tonight, and there's nothing you can do about it!" Peter would have made a fine parish minister. I remember saying to him, "Peter, I really admire you." He smiled faintly and replied, "You don't know me." I protested that I had known him long enough to know what a good man he was - but he held up his hand in reproof; "I have been in prison seventeen times" he said. "I once tried to stab my wife. You don't know me." I refused to believe him, though I could see he was telling the truth. What is truth? Best sometimes not to know.

Great love goes into A.A., usually alloyed with very good sense. I remember a girl called Louise who had been put into the care and supervision of Jean, an older and wiser member. One evening I overheard Jean saying to her, "Louise, hen, you're no for me. I hope and pray you're for somebody else, but you're definitely no for me!" Jean had spent months trying to help Louise, in the process losing sleep and straining her own alcohol problem. Sensibly, Jean knew where to draw the line for the good of all concerned. This is a lesson all well-meaning folk need to learn well - know where to draw the line.

Uplifters and improvers abound these days; counselling is the in thing. All very well if kept within a sense of proportion. In Church House we recognised that we were only one small factor in society, and that the street, the family, indeed the world around were all bigger and had more influence than ourselves, however well-intentioned we were. It is foolish, and damaging, to bite off more than you can chew. Strangely enough, once you see yourselves as the leaven lost in the lump, you achieve far more than you expect - or rather, HE who carried the whole world on his shoulders, works miracles through your poor efforts!

Gamblers Anonymous is not as big or well-known an organisation as A. A. and I only met up with it once. That was when I took along to a meeting in the city a local man who had been coming to our Regnal Circle and who had a big gambling problem. I had tried everything, even attended games at Celtic Park (he was an R. C. and Celtic supporter) to keep alongside him - to no avail. He owed the bookies, and, when their enforcers called, Jackie would bail out the back window and run for it. When he did the dirty on his daughter and sold off her wedding presents, that was the last straw. I made him come with me to G. A.

He was welcomed and I was allowed to stay; Jackie shifted uncomfortably in his seat, as the group leader read a long list of questions which he had no option but to answer one by one. At the end of this quiz, Jackie was informed that he was very definitely addicted to gambling and eligible to join G. A. At that, I left him to their tender care.

Some weeks later, I stopped the car at Bridgeton Cross; by chance it happened to be right outside a betting shop. Jackie emerged. Catching sight of me, he looked momentarily taken aback, but swiftly recovered. "Bill! how nice to see you. You know, the best thing you ever did was to introduce me to G. A. It's great! Our Christmas party is next week and I'm helping to run it. Honest, Bill, I haven't been in a betting shop since you took me to G. A." I gently pointed out to him that though I rejoiced in his conversion, unless my eyes deceived me (or *he* was deceiving me), he had come out of one of those betting shops he had just said he never entered. He had anticipated this telling observation on my part and had his answer ready, "Och that! I wasn't in for a bet, naw, I never bet anymore - I was jist in to use the toilet!"

Ever anxious to help lame dogs over stiles, I brought along to the Regnal Circle a young man who was involved in drugs and attending Narcotics Anonymous. A very intelligent, presentable bloke, he was well read and good company, so my hopes for his reformation and future were high. Jim was a plumber to trade, and when I had a burst pipe under the manse bath, I called upon his help in fixing it - the church had no money, so it was literally 'all hands to the pumps!' The bath was solid cast iron, a tremendous weight to lift, and the bathroom was narrow and tight for space. When he and I went in and lifted the bath on end, the door was blocked. So far so good, until he became most agitated, and exhibited all the signs of a 'junky' desperate for a 'fix'. I guess he couldn't stand his exit being closed off, and soon I was as anxious as he was to leave. He started to rant and rave, and there was I - trapped! Fortunately, the window opened and out I went without delay, dropping to the garage roof and fleeing. Jim followed and ran off. I would recommend the Yellow Pages should you need a plumber - worth it.

Chapter 28

EXPLAIN THIS!

"Unless you can explain a thing to your grandmother
you don't really understand it. "
(Albert Einstein)

After John Gibbs left Preston, my home church minister was
Norman Armstrong. Spotting me in the pews one Sunday, he
announced from the pulpit that he could see I was back from
university, and how nice it was to see me again. Norman meant well,
but he got my name wrong and called me "Frank Singleton". The
following week, I returned to the Bradford college, after four years
away in Edinburgh, and immediately noticed that the top name listed
on the college Great War memorial was a "Frank Singleton". When
I told Norman Armstrong this, he was puzzled. He had never heard
of a Frank Singleton, and had no idea why he had used that name
instead of mine - weird.

At a particular spot during my visit to Gallipoli, one of our small
group visiting the old battle scenes drew me aside and said, with deep
emotion, that an uncle of his had been shot in the head at that very
spot. On seeing a faded old photograph of this uncle, dead long before
he himself was born, he had felt a sharp pain in the head. Since then
he had been compulsively drawn back to Gallipoli and visited the
place of his uncle's death many times. He had never mentioned this
to anyone before he told me, and asked me to say a short prayer in
that far-away, lonely place.

In many a church vestry you see a line of photographs of former
ministers, often going back to the days of whiskers and winged
collars. In the inner city parishes, with their shifting populations,
such ancestral memories are in short supply. When I tried to assemble
pictures of my own predecessors, I could only get back to the Rev.
Sydney Warnes and 1930. All I could discover about his immediate
predecessor, a Mr Shaw, was that he was of Hielan' background, was
fond of the bottle, and had left an endowment to the church which
brought in a very handy £300 a year towards stipend - no photograph
though. Before Mr Shaw, the minister was the Rev. Mr Turnbull who

died in 1918 after a long ministry of thirty-two years; nobody could tell me anything about him at all. I put up on the vestry wall pictures of Mr Sim, Dr. Gray, and Mr Warnes - the best I could do.

Shortly afterwards, an old man came to see me one Friday vestry hour - this was in 1983 - and gave me an envelope containing an old photograph of Mr. Turnbull - walrus moustache, hair flat parted down the middle, bulbous nose, clerical attire of the day. I was delighted, and asked him how he had heard I was looking for such a photograph for my collection. He reported that he knew nothing about my searches, and that it had long been his intention to bring the photograph. His father had been church officer in Turnbull's time, and that was how he came to inherit the picture. I gratefully received it and tramed it and put it in my 'rogues gallery'.

The following Sunday, two strangers appeared in the pews - a tall man and his teenage son. After the Service they told me they were from Liverpool, were staying in Largs on holiday, and had never been to Scotland before. The reason for them coming to my church was that they believed an ancestor of theirs had once been the minister, but they felt they might be in the wrong place. I told them the old name had been Barrowfield Parish Church, changed to St. Francis-in-the-East, and I asked their surname; it was Turnbull. "Say no more," said I, sweeping them into the vestry and showing them my picture of the old boy on the wall - they were both the living image of old Turnbull, even the same nobbly nose! The likeness was remarkable. The two of them looked bemused as I excitedly gathered folk to see this amazing look-alike comparison.

From 1918 to 1983, nothing. Then I begin asking about Mr Turnbull, and trying to get a picture of him. Then an old man who hasn't ever been in our church before walks in off the street and gives me a photo of the said Rev. Sir. Next, his grandson and great-grandson turn up from Liverpool speculating whether or not they have come to the right church. They have never seen a picture of him and have no idea what he looked like. I show them my newly obtained photograph and they are their relative's double! If you told me that the Rev. Mr Turnbull had come back from the dead, I would have believed it! It was extraordinary! Unbelievable! What a long series of astonishing coincidences. Coincidence? Or was something uncanny going on here? I cannot think it was all chance, can you?

A strange experience befell me one time I found myself making an unintended visit - at least, unintended on my part. Walking hurriedly along Bernard Street going somewhere in my usual rush, I happened by pure chance to pass the close in which a lady we all called 'Laurie' stayed. For some reason, I know not why, I found myself entering the close and knocking on her door. "Come in," she said with a big smile, "I knew you were coming to see me." The table was laid out for two for afternoon tea. Seeing I was looking baffled by the scene, and her very apparent certainty, she continued "I knew you would come this afternoon, because I really must talk to you." And there I was!

My family laugh at my 'coincidences', but I keep getting them. When the old London Road St. Clement's Church closed, our church got enough money to make it possible, with a loan, to buy the present manse for £6,000. The massive Greenhead street flat was sold for a pittance due to its situation; in a 'better' area it would have sold for a fortune.

The first phone call I got after we moved into the new manse was from a lady looking for the former occupants. The following week I met her at a party, and she introduced herself by asking if I had been taken aback by her reaction to my answering the phone. I had not, I reported. She explained that her maiden name had been Shackleton, and she had never come across another Shackleton before. I replied that neither had I for that matter. First phone call in the new manse from one of those rarest of birds: a Shackleton.

Some years later, Margaret and I went into a shop in Greenock - a butcher's and the first shop we entered in the town. The butcher was on the phone in the back shop, and eventually came out close to tears. Seeing my collar, he said he had just been told his sister had died, so we expressed sympathies. When he had recovered, he served us and offered to deliver meat to our house - he wrote down our address. Then he asked our name. "Shackleton", we said. He looked very astonished for a moment then said, "Shackleton! that was my sister's name!" She was the only Shackleton in the town; it was her married name. My first phone call a Shackleton: my first shop a Shackleton. Spooky!

The Shackletons seem to be an uncanny lot. Sir Ernest haunts the 'Discovery' moored now in Dundee. On a visit there with the Regnal men, I was told that the ship's staff see him floating around, and, in consequence, do not stay on board very long. According to an article on the subject in *The Herald*, Shackleton is haunting Scott, his old rival. Be that as it may, over the years a Shacketon has been sighted haunting Bridgeton Cross and the terracing at Ibrox, but it probably isn't Sir Ernest.

If death can be unexpected, it can also be predicted. In wartime, men seem to sometimes have a premonition of death, and the same is true also in ordinary daily life for some folk.

Visiting Foresthall (the old Barnhill Poorhouse) in Springburn, I was leaving a ward after seeing someone, when an old chap called me over to his bed. He had a well-worn, grizzled face, and an unkempt beard. He told me to sit down, which I did. "What time is it?" he asked. I told him - half past four. "I'll be deid at hauf past five," he confidently predicted, before going on to tell me he was an atheist, and giving me his life story - which, by the way, was not without variety and interest. Every so often he would ask me the time, and every few minutes I would tell him I had to go - until, about five o'clock, I managed to get away. As I left the old blether, he again asked the time saying, "I'll be deid at hauf past five."

A fortnight later I went back to the same ward and, not seeing the man, asked where he was. Sister told me he had died. "May I see when he died?" I asked. She looked it up for me - yes, there it was. He died the day I spoke to him, and he died at half past five!

I was followed as Minister's Assistant by an Australian Methodist minister, Andrew McCutcheon, tall and rangy as Aussies are required to be. He and his wife settled in a local tenement, and they were introduced to our strange ways when he turned up an hour late to take his first Service, being unaware of changing the clocks for British Summer Time. Andrew's father was the architect who built Melbourne University, and when they left, they made a film of their journey across the world for television.

Thanks to the help of Newlands South, I enjoyed having several Assistants for three days a week - the best of them being Alan Webster and Alastair Jessamine - still good friends. Alastair (presently minister of Dunfermline Abbey) has a hearty laugh, and my children were fascinated by his knee slapping mirth. My cat, Tiger Lily, and dog, Rags, adored Alastair, and would sit at his feet, listening to his every word, looking up into his moustachioed countenance transfixed with reverence. When he became minister of Strathaven, I was able to tell the congregation that though I could not guarantee that the human-beings of the town would find Alastair adorable, the local cats and dogs were in for a whale of a good time!

I also had a Dutch deaconess, Ria Platte. During her time I received a phone call from London - a stranger with a Cockney voice. He wanted me to send him a suitcase which, he said, belonged to his son working in Libya. The story was that the son had met a Dutch girl in Tripoli, and asked her to take this suitcase to Britain for him. The Dutch dame had told him that she was a student at Queen Mary College in Glasgow, and, as I was minister of Queen Mary Street Church, the Cockney father wanted me to pop round to the college, retrieve the case, and send it on to London. This struck me as an unlikely tale: how did he know I was in Queen Mary Street church? Why was he so reluctant to tell me his name? Yet, the involvement of a Dutch young lady suggested an unaccountable coincidence seeing I had a Dutch deaconess although I did not tell him that. He got stroppy and accused me of lying when I told him there was no college in Queen Mary Street, or, indeed so far as I knew, in the city. He could not tell me the girl's name, or explain why his son had given his suitcase to someone he did not know. For a moment I thought of telling him to get in touch with the police - but what if Ria was somehow involved in this bizarre business? I knew she wasn't, but you never know! When told of all this, she was as baffled as I was. Drugs-running deaconesses? 'The Dutch Connection' operating through Queen Mary Street Kirk, Bridgeton? Naw! The Vatican Bank, maybe, but surely not the Church of Scotland Offices! I thought the Kirk had stopped money laundering when the Linen Bank closed down.

The wee kirk in Bridgeton rates high in the givings-table of C of S churches. I always worked on the theory that if you explain to the people what is needed and why, you get it. Sometimes folk are over-generous: I recall knocking a door in Bridgeton and having it opened by a young woman holding a baby. Inside was a bare room with hardly any furniture, and two or three wee ones scrawling around. I explained I was collecting round the doors for Christian Aid, but that in her case, I didn't want to take anything. She took out her purse saying "It's my last 10 pence, but take it for they poor wee weans in Africa." How lucky we are, as our Lord said, that we have the poor with us always to keep us right.

Chapter 29

POP GOES THE BEADLE

"The butler entered the room, a solemn procession of one."
  (P.G. Wodehouse)

I had several Church Officers, or Beadles as they were then called. The indefatigable Tommy Carswell, helped by his darling wife Elsie, kept the place spotless, for their hearts were in the church from childhood. Tommy's replacement was Archie Shaw, a retired window-cleaner from the Gorbals. He joined the Regnal Circle and was quite a *raconteur*. Archie told us how he was almost court-martialed and shot for falling asleep on sentry duty while serving at Gallipoli with the 52nd Lowland Division. A Turkish sniper wounded him badly. He was forced to feign death in no-man's land, afraid to move lest the Turks, crackshots, finished him off. He endured the agonies of flies and pain until rescued in the night. He was just 19 at the time. I should add that there was a postman living in the Gallowgate who had won a V. C. at Gallipoli - a very modest man.

A window cleaner's tales are not always repeatable, but one night at the Regnal he had us in stitches. One story will do. He was cleaning windows at the Western Infirmary and anxious to finish and get home. Due to clean the windows high over the operating theatre table, he peeped in and, finding the place deserted, got up in the roof space and started his cleaning. To his horror, the door below opened and an operation began. Unable to give his position away, he had to cling on, poised over the gruesome scene feeling very queasy. Not a pretty sight!

Alas! excellent Beadle and fellow though he was, Archie took a drop too much one evening and came in while the ladies of the Woman's Guild were taking refreshments. The Guild President at the time was a spinster lady who was head of an important city office, a pleasant person, but not used to being cuddled by fuddled Church officers. "Miss Fleming," said Archie, "I think you are a wonderful woman!" Famous Last Words! I was sorry to see him go.

George was the replacement for old Archie. His wife, Mary, was senile, and he cared for her because "I wouldn't want to see her put in a home, Sir." I was always 'Sir' to George, and he addressed me in a remarkably similar manner to Corporal Jones addressing Captain Mainwaring in *Dad's Army* - "Permission to speak, Sir?" He also looked like Jonesy: "They don't like the cold steel up 'em, Sir," and all that.

Every Monday night after the Regnal Circle, I dropped him off at his tenement in Dalmarnock Road and he would say to me, "Will you be at the church on Friday night, Sir?" I always said I would, Friday being my vestry night as George well knew. "I must clean the brasses, Sir; you will be there, Sir?" I assured George I would. "You won't forget, Sir?" No, I wouldn't forget. This conversation went on each Monday night for years - and George never once turned up on a Friday night - a fact I could not bring myself to draw to his attention.

George was always late. On one occasion he came very late and looked frazzled. "Sir, Mary escaped from the house and followed the Orange Band all the way to Ibrox. I had to take a taxi to bring here home." Another time he explained his lateness by saying, "I was watching a very interesting science programme on the television, Sir." "Really," said I, "what science programme was that?" "Very informative it was, Sir, very interesting - I think it's called 'Spiderman'." Life was never dull with George around.

I visited him and Mary once and was horrified to see their flat was lit by a neon tube leaning against the wall. I insisted he report this to the factor, and get his lights, electric cooker, and other facilities reconnected. He said he had done all that without any results so far. Dropping in on the lady who lived below George, I waxed indignant about the neon tube, etc., but she showed no sympathy: "It's his own fault," said she, "he fiddled with the fuse boxes and blew out my cooker for a week!" This story reminds me of the time two guys hid dynamite in the cooker of the Orange Halls - yes, honest! Some ladies lit it for sausage rolls and blew up the house of a lady I knew who lived next door. I told you life in old Brigton was never dull. On that theme, I had a dear old member called Betty who was asked to post a parcel to Northern Ireland. She was arrested and jailed for six months. She was a nice old soul too! Totally suckered into it, but the Press bayed.

When George came back from holiday, he told me he had done

something he had always wanted to do - take Mary on a helicopter. "I've taken her on a boat, on an aeroplane, on a train, on a bus run, but never on a helicopter, Sir, so that's what I did, I took her on a helicopter over from Ramsgate to France." "Well done!" said I, admiringly, "Was it a big helicopter?" "Och aye, Sir, very big, it had lots of motorcars on it. The trouble was you couldn't see much becauese the windows were all wet." Helicopter? Lots of cars? Could they have been on the hovercraft? That thought I kept to myself, for George meant well by Mary at all times, when many men would not. He was a truly kind-hearted soul.

My prize memory of George was when he confronted me with a big picture of the Church of Scotland's badge: the Burning Bush. "What do you think of that, Sir?" said he, "It is the finest picture in the world." I murmured approval of his sentiments as he moved on to point out the motto beneath: 'Nec Tamen Consumebator'. "See that, Sir, that's Latin," George instructed me proudly, "It means, 'Let Glasgow flourish!'"

DAVIE

Davie was the sort of guy who has no age - my guess is that he was about forty when I first became very close to him in the Sixties. Clumsy on his feet, poor Davie finished up in a wheelchair, but appeared at every Regnal Circle meeting and was never housebound. Everybody knew Davie, because he gave out the hymnbooks in the church porch on Sundays and rang the bell. Everybody understood that Davie was prone to using ripe language very extensively - that was just the way he was - and, as a result, coming to worship after a noticeable period of absence meant running the gauntlet of Davie's tongue: "Where the so-and-so [I'm putting it mildly] have you been?" would resound through the building, as truants sidled in. He had absolutely no idea that he was swearing or being offensive; he just said exactly what he thought! There was nothing I could do about it as he didn't listen, and in ordinary conversation, as distinct from handing out threats together with the hymnbooks, he was largely unintelligible - I just said, hopefully, "Yes" to everything he said. That was Davie.

He was no fool: he was as wise as a parliament of owls! His judgment of character was never wrong, and I learnt to trust his assessment of people. Unfortunately, discretion was not a feature of his personal relationships, and it could be very embarrassing at meetings to see him point to someone present and to hear him blurt out, "Is he still here? Get rid o' that yin, he's a nae-user!" One poor guy took this from him every meeting for months - and proved Davie right by disappearing with some of our Circle funds. If Davie really disliked somebody, it was not unknown for him to go berserk and throw billiard balls at them, denting the walls in the process. Alas! His faults leant a bit too far on virtue's side sometimes, and his outspokenness became his undoing. His job was looking after the car park of a local engineering plant, and his word there was law! Unfortunately, the Big Boss's wife tried to park some place Davie did not sanction, and he called her many names which had not been given to her at her baptism. She insisted upon his departure, and, sadly, he lost his job.

In some ways, I like to compare Davie and Dr. Samuel Johnson, lumbering figures; odd, but kind and profound. Getting him around could be a problem, of course, and when our Regal men went on an outing to Dollar to visit Castle Campbell on the hill above the gorge, it took all our efforts (we had no block and tackle) to get him up there! On our annual trips down South to the Swanwick Conference Centre in the Peak District, he had a disconcerting habit of coming into the sessions half way through some uplifting speech, crunching gravel signalling his approach (filling me with dread), banging open the doors, and booming out, "What the blankety-blank is happening?" The sedate English audience was somewhat flustered by this sort of unaccustomed behaviour until they got to know Davie better. Indeed, for about 25 years, Davie was greeted at Conference by an English clone of himself named Willis Oliver. Willis was exactly the same height and Falstaff shape as Davie; when they met it was belly to belly. Willis described himself as a 'garbageologist', in other words he was a street sweeper in Kidderminster. Like Davie, he was shrewd in his own way, and his conversation was as unintelligible as that of his Scottish counterpart. They loved each other like brothers, and spent most of their weekend deep in conversation, though I am certain neither had the faintest idea what the other was saying, what with Davie's Brigton and Willis's strangulated "Argghs", and "Oiys"!

One night at the Regnal Circle, an earnest young man spoke to us about "The Global Village". "How can I get in touch with my neighbour in this global village?" was a refrain he kept repeating over and over again, each time growing more and more anguished. Davie looked more and more puzzled by the question, and the questioner's failure to provide an answer. "How can I get in touch with my neighbour in this global village?" he cried once more, whereupon Davie helped him out by saying "You should go roon and chap his door". All along Davie thought the guy was talking about his neighbour, the man next door! In his innocence, Davie was always down to earth!

Davie was renowned for two things: his tea-making, and his answers at quizzes. On Monday nights at the Regnal, he made the tea, which was to be served up at 9 p.m. On the dot Davie rattled open the kitchen hatch and bellowed "Tea". If the bloke chairing the meeting did not stop instantly, cutting the Speaker dead, Davie ensured he did by creating by dropping trays of pots and pans. Everybody jumped when Davie spoke *ex cathedra*. At a quiz he had a genius for nearly getting the answers right. When asked, "What was the name of the famous Battle of Britain fighter in the film "Reach for the Skies?", Davie replied, after much prompting, "Baden Powell." Asked "What is the Common Market" he felt on surer ground and answered ... "The Barras."

The post of bell-ringer in The High Kirk of Queen Mary Street was a highly prized appointment for life. Davie officiated in this vocation with boundless pride and, Sunday after Sunday, the dull clanging of our bell issued its call to worship, and indicated that our bell ringer was in good health and pulling well. The crisis arose when the widow of a dear friend of mine donated a sum of money to the church. The amount was just enough for me to think about fulfilling a dream, and installing a system of electrically operated tune playing bells. Instead of clang, clang, I would then have cheerful hymns sounding out over the parish - it was a dazzling prospect. Other, wealthier, kirks had them and I wanted them as well. A tape-recorder was purchased, a recording of enticing tunes from the finest carillons obtained, and, by good fortune, I acquired four loud-speakers from Kings Park Church. These were not in prime condition, having been on the roof there since 1939 before being replaced, but they worked, so we installed them in the steeple. These proceedings did not meet with the approval of the pigeons in residence, or, for that matter, with Davie either.

The great day came at last, and at precisely 15 minutes before the

Service, the system was switched on for the first time. The sweet sound of "Onward Christian Soldiers" floated across the sleepy parish (it was early, not long after noon), and was music in my ears. Everything had gone well, Davie having been notified, with the utmost tact and sensitivity to his feelings, that his services were no longer required. I believed we had heard the last bong of the old bell.

My expectations were premature. *Bong! bong! bong!* went the old bell, raking through the melodic chimes like a broadside from HMS Victory! A hasty switch down of the loudspeakers resulted. For several weeks we attempted to persuade Davie to abandon his bell-ringing in favour of the new system - all to no avail. He was not a man to budge. A plan had to be devised to make it impossible for him to ring the bell, and one presented itself: the long rope from the bell fell all the way down the well of the staircase and right down into the porch where Davie stood to pull on it. I reckoned that if the rope were cut high up, so that it did not reach into the porch, Davie would be left ropeless. So the rope was duly cut, and the short bit remained tied tightly round the banisters of the upper landing, making me confident that victory was mine in the battle of the bells.

Sunday came, the tape was switched on, all was going fine, and then *bong! bong! bong!* as usual. It was most baffling! How on earth (or rather above the earth!) was Davie ringing the bell? After the service Davie came shuffling up to me, burning with indignation. "You'll need tae dae something wi' that effin bell," he complained bitterly, "every time I pull the rope, the banister rails keep going up and doon!" The force of the heavy bell's swinging had torn the iron banisters out of their moorings and left them dangling in mid-air! Oh Davie, the Quasimodo of Queen Mary Street Church, if only thou hadst untied the rope round the banisters. In thy memory, dear old boy, the old bell still rings out Sunday after Sunday, my new-fangled electric bells long since consigned to the scrap heap.

I should add that I got the musical bells idea from a Mr Sellars, minister of Flemington Kirk, one of those inventive clergymen left over from the 18th century. He had made up and installed bells in his church steeple, and proudly set them off one Sunday morning. His story was that a young woman heard them playing "Safe in the Arms of Jesus" while visiting a local graveyard where she had just buried her mother and a sister who had committed suicide. Filled with despair, she lay face down on the muddy grave, until some music from the skies caused her to sit up and listen ... "Safe in the Arms of Jesus". She followed the music to the kirk, and told Mr Sillars her story. A real-life miraculous resurrection from the grave if ever there was one - or so the young woman thought, and who would doubt her?

Visiting Stonelaw Church recently, the beadle turned out to be an old Club boy, and he mentioned the day we took down and sold the Church House bell. The steeple was very high, the bell very heavy, but we needed the scrap value. The beadle reminded me that the bell fell from a great height, crashing through floors in a great cloud of dust and feathers, nearly wiping us all out. It was the Kaiser who described bells as 'the artillery of the Church' and you can see what he meant. I had forgotten, but he remembered.

In the Sixties, congregational meals were popular as part of a Stewardship Campaign. We held one of these in the St. Mungo Halls, Gorbals, for 450 people! The band was behind a curtain and, thinking St.Francis-in-the-East meant we were R. C.s, they played Irish music all night. Reg, our church pianist, was blind; as he played in pubs and was to come late to the dinner, I asked Davie to stand by the door to meet him and bring him in for his food. The speeches and meal over, there was no sign of Davie and Reg. When they turned up, I asked them in bewilderment, "What on earth made you so late?" "We weren't late," Reg replied, "Davie met me at the door and we've had a lovely meal - food was first-class." "Well, you haven't had it here," said I, looking at their unoccupied places. At this point, Reg grew thoughtful, and I grew suspicious. "Where did you take Reg, Davie?" "Doon stairs, I took him in wi' the rest of the big crowd." I set off 'doon stairs' to investigate - there, in another hall, a wedding reception was going on! Davie had taken Reg to it and they had had a fine feed, with wine to wash it down, at somebody else's expense! "Right enough," commented Reg. "I didn't seem to know anybody, and nobody seemed to know us!" Shows how easy it is to gatecrash a wedding reception; the bride's people think you are with the groom's lot, and vice-versa.

Reg had always been blind, but he could tell whether or not the paint on the walls was gloss or emulsion. One very dark, very dank night I offered him a lift him home to his flat near Queen's Park and as 1 wiped the misted windscreen, muttering "I can't see a blooming thing!" Reg seconded the motion saying, "Well, that makes two of us!"

I got on great with Reg, but he had one big fault: he was always late. I entered the pulpit one Sunday, gave out the opening hymn, and nothing happened - no pianist. His excuses were enough to bring tears to the proverbial glass-eye! "Bill, I fell in a hole in the street" - or down the subway, etc., etc. Reg never fell down anything in his life, but it sounded good. 1 was sorry to see him move on, for he was a 'character', and so good at imitating Frank Sinatra that nobody could tell the difference. I wish him well.

Chapter 30

"There arose a reasoning among them, which should be the greatest." (Luke 9)

"It is a certain, though a strange, truth, that in politics all principles that are speculatively right are practically wrong."
(Soames Jenning)

Arthur Gray had held political forums, and so did John Sim. I continued that on the understanding that all candidates be present, or it was off. There was real political interest in those days, and audiences turned out in numbers.

The platform party formed a full spectrum of Bridgeton's political allegiances: we had Labour (always won), the I. L. P. man (always the best educated and articulate), the Socialist Workers' Party, and the Communist Party. Occasionally, we had a Liberal, even a rare Conservative like Ross Harper, and there was once a famous victory for the S. N. P. over Labour by Isobel Lindsay (now Labour herself).

The audiences were ever so polite and good natured. Men would rise from their seats and apologise for leaving to go to work on the night shift! One Labour man was so hopeless a candidate that he was a bag of nerves and kept dropping his papers all over the platform. The ever helpful audience picked them up and sorted them out for him, with expressions of sympathy at his predicament. I think people voted for him because he was a nice guy and they felt pity for him, but the S. N. P. defeated the poor chap because pity, like patriotism, is not enough.

The Conservative candidates were well received by everyone, and not only the Unionist element (ever present in a Brigton audience). They were bosses and, as such, to be held in respect. Besides, they were modest men, each of whom began his speech by saying that he had no hope of winning, and was only there because he had been challenged by colleagues in his office to stand up for his beliefs in public. This he was doing (applause!). Perhaps sensing I might understand what they were doing standing in Bridgeion, they would draw me aside and say they were doing it for a dare and a wee bet (wink, wink, nudge, nudge). Anyway, everybody was happy and we had a "rare wee night", which, when you think about it, was why we were all at the meeting.

The ones who fitted the least comfortably into the East End scene were the Liberals - they adopted the wrong approach. One day, a thin young man walked into the church hall dressed in sandshoes, a knitted bunnet, and one of Lieutenant Colombo's old raincoats tied round the waist with a bit of rope. He was unshaven and wore spectacles held together by fuse wire. I asked this spectre his business and he declared, in an Oxford accent, "I am your Liberal candidate, meeting the people and all that, don't yah know". As our cleaning lady commented after he had gone, "Och weel, he wis hairmless, so he wis, the poor sowl!"

A proud moment was the night the Community Council was formed at the completion of the new housing around the church. The one or two churches left had formed a sort of *ad hoc* Community Council during the long drawn out seven years of rebuilding, and it was time, we thought, to hand it over to the people moving in. We met in our church hall, and I had to take the chair until an election could be held. For many years the wee Queen Mary Street Church had enjoyed a very good name amongst the people, and I was pleased to see that continue when someone, an R. C. at that, asked, "Why is it that this church is the only one to take an interest in the people here?" It wasn't strictly true, but that we met in our hall, and I was in the chair, said a lot about our long tradition of social involvement. Yet it was also a sad night for me as well; I was nominated treasurer (a job I did not want), but sectarianism crept back in, and I was kept out. I guess expecting the whole life of the community to take its central inspiration from the Kirk was asking more than was possible. Thomas Chalmers could not manage it, so what chance had I? But we came near it! Very near.

CONCERTS:

Socials and concerts seem to have been replaced in the churches by Bible Study and Prayer meetings - which is all very well, but where has all the fun gone? In our wee church hall, with its tiny stage, we had shows (often unrehearsed) which went a treat. Folk packed the place for a 'good wee night oot', and if the on-stage performers began to flag, then the members of the audience contributed willingly. The men of the Regnal put on an annual pantomime - a minister is expected to be a comedian/tragedian as well as a great preacher and pastor - and I much enjoyed writing it and putting it on. Every organisation contributed to the concerts, and the ladies of the Guild did sketches. The Club had its own Christmas Panto and there was talent around to be tapped then - boys played guitars and girls sang solos!

My version of 'Snow White and the Seven Dwarfs' was particularly memorable, as two dwarfs failed to turn up (despite many rehearsals), and I had to amend it to "Snow White and the Five Dwarfs". Even the most difficult kid could be found some part to play and such things are never forgotten. A congregation is a family. When folk get together and lose themselves in the wider family, hearts are warmed and minds set free. Today, those who govern the churches seem to have forgotten that Jesus was a sociable man, a man with time for children, a friendly soul. How he would have enjoyed one of our Guild Hallowe'en parties - the ladies all dressed up in the most colourful, creative costumes, having a good feed while John Webster and I told them terrifying ghost stories - but now I am not being politically correct, am I? Hallowe'en! Tut-tut!

The best after-dinner speaker I know is Andy Cameron, who, in the early days, worked in Bridgeton at the Sunblest bakery (a huge proportion of Scotland's bread was made within a mile of Bridgeton Cross in those days). Andy was still making his way to the top of his stage profession when I asked him one day to entertain us at one of our concerts in the church hall. Always ready to help a good cause (and being a 'blue-nose' as well), Andy came along and had the audience convulsed with laughter in no time with his Glasgow humour.

The seating was in rows of metal stacking chairs, and half way through his act, a tiny, very old lady rose up to leave, choosing not to take the short route to the exit, but the long one *via* a line of chairs. This meant shifting all the occupants about, and making the maximum amount of clanging noises as she crawled her way out. Completely ignoring Andy, who was busy performing on the stage, she then shuffled right in front of him on his way to the door. As she pulled it open and was about to leave, Andy stopped his act, and made one of his unforgettable *ad lib*s. Addressing the old dear he said to her, "Tell yer Mammy I wis askin' fur her, wull ye, hen!"

That reminds me of one of my flock, the petite Mrs Ogilvie, a lady of great age. I met her, one day, wending her way slowly along the street and enquired if she was going to visit a neighbour or friend. "Och no, I'm away tae see my mither," said she, and toddled off, leaving me wondering what Jurassic age her mother must be!

The Christmas Pensioners' Concert was preceded by a dinner and, at the first one of these my new fiancée attended, melon was served. Melon was a great innovation in those days, and the old ladies regarded their plates with some suspicion. The waiter came round asking who wished ginger with their melon, only to be thanked and told that they would have a glass of 'ginger' later. They set about the melon; the sight of eighty old ladies chomping their 'wallies' through those melons (rind and even the labels consumed!), is something my wife remembers vividly!

Talking of melons reminds me of Lady MacLeod getting a bill for forty melons from Miss McLean, proprietress of Iona's tiny and only shop. Not having ordered or received any melons, Lorna, knowing the shop's pricing policies, politely declined to pay up, but the diminutive Miss McLean merely persisted, persuasively saying, "What are a few melons between friends?"

Chapter 31

"For all the gifts of childhood lent,
That gift more prized is than gold,
Which saves a soul from growing old.
(Anon.)

"If the end of the world were coming tomorrow,
today I would plant a young apple tree."
(Martin Luther)

'LET US RISE UP AND BUILD'

The histories of St. Francis-in-the-East Church and its offspring, Church House, are stories of resurrection. Who in 1929 would have imagined that the derelict wee kirk in Queen Mary Street would be the only one left today out of all the many churches then in Bridgeton, not a few of them far better off in every way? And looking back myself on the rebuilding of Church House in the late Sixties and early Seventies, what a remarkable achievement that was.

The story of how the Rev. Sydney Warnes transformed the old Barrowfield Church, in his brief four year ministry, into St. Francis-in-the-East has often been told; but the church's flourishing continuance during the desolate years of demolition, when the population dropped from 28,500 in 1971 to 15,049 in 1981, is no less remarkable a tale. It would be wrong to say the church and club 'survived' this period, for they actually prospered and in many ways advanced where others faltered.

In the mid-Sixties, I reckoned that I could lose half the congregation of some 600 members and stay self-supporting. My part of Bridgeton was the poorest housed, so I knew it would go first - but I could stand it, because I knew the other churches were already too small to lose 50% once their turn came - by which time I would have a rebuilt parish. Sounded easy, but it was 1976 before the GEAR (Glasgow Eastern Area Renewal) project began, and prior to that much of the increasingly dilapidated old housing persisted, while the building work of the Direct Labour Department of the old regime was plagued with strikes and go-slows which made it seven years before the new housing started to appear. So far as my parish part of Bridgeton was concerned, for a long, long time, you could see all the way from the church to Church House, some quarter of a mile away. It was odd to see a rabbit one summer's evening outside the church, and not a human-being! It was even odder to notice how local folk in Bridgeton and Dalmamock who had not been around the kirk for a long time started attending again because it was all that was left standing in their old world. Nevertheless, it can be depressing to see obliteration and desolation all around during year after year of frustrated hopes; worst of all to see your best people going off to benefit other congregations and leave you weakened.

One personal incident maybe puts it well: a fine couple I had moved two miles away, but as transport was no problem for them, I thought I would not lose them. I met them in the street and they told me they were 'lifting their lines'. I wished them well, said all the right things, but they detected the dejection in my eyes - yet another blow! They later phoned me to say they had changed their minds and wanted to stay on. That helped keep me going no end! Others kept attending even though moved quite far away - I suggested to one lady she go to her nearest kirk, but she replied, "No, no, I like coming here - you never know what's going to happen during a Service!"

High ideals and good intentions were one thing, but money was the problem. What happened in 1964 determined the future, not only of our congregation, but of a Church of Scotland presence in the whole area. That year, I persuaded the Congregational Board to borrow £1,500 from the bank, and bring in the Wells Organisation, professional fund-raisers. It was a great act of faith. The amount was huge sum in those days, greater than our entire annual income. The treasurer naturally baulked, and I had to offer him, on the quiet, an assurance that should it fail, I would personally make good the debt. On my minimum stipend, without any other income, and with a new wife and baby, my guarantee was not worth much, so the treasurer was committed to seeing it would not fail. We had to succeed - no ifs or buts.

The organiser arrived from the Wells Organisation and immediately found himself facing a disastrous situation: his initial meeting of visitors, to go round the congregation with the message, consisted of myself and the treasurer. It was a Monday night, Regnal Night. I took him to the church hall where sat some 25 men in our

Circle. I explained matters to them. I knew that being Regnalites they would not let me down, and they didn't. For three weeks, every night including Saturdays and Sundays, they visited homes and asked for pledges. Climaxing with the great dinner aforementioned, the campaign was a triumph. Our finances shot up and have never fallen below standard since. The church is no longer self-supporting (something upon which I insisted for reasons of self-respect and ecclesiastical politics), but to this day is today up in the top bracket of giving per head in Scotland. Considering this is a 'deprived area', not bad at all. It worked only because it absolutely had to work. Others had the same challenge to face but shirked it. That is why they no longer exist. It is as simple as that. And who are to be thanked? The men who, that Monday night, stood up to be counted - some of whom I had only recently brought into Regnal and were not church attenders! 'Big Eddie' was an R. C.! By George Orwell's doom-laden 1984, St. Francis-in-the-East was doing very nicely, thanks to 1964. No risks, no faith!

Looking back, the rebuilding of Church House still amazes me. In 1969, left with no leaders, a building in a dangerous condition, and coffers emptied by throwing money away on useless attempts at dry-rot eradication, rebuilding seemed impossible. Fortunately, the Home Board at that point had as its Secretary Horace Walker, and later Ian Doyle, two men of whom I cannot speak highly enough. Horace only asked one question of a friend of mine, a question about myself: "Is he committed?" When he got an affirmative, Horace backed me up, always, of course, while pretending the very opposite! It was a beginning. I was also blessed with a fine treasurer, Mr Duncan Martin of Giffnock South Church; the newly arrived Dr. Stewart Macintosh; and Jim Herd, a former Club boy high up in the B.B.C.

The Home Board produced an architect who told us we could rebuild for £27,000 - hopes rose! It didn't seem too bad after all! We were soon up and running, with very positive encouraging financial responses from the Scottish Education Department. Other offers of support came in. Everything was coming up roses, until we found out the architect did not work for the Home Board - he would have to be paid - and that the Quantity Surveyor privately predicted the work could not be done for anything like a paltry £27,000. Tenders went out and the lowest was £56,000. Had I known that at the start, Church House would never have been rebuilt. The Lord conned me into doing it, and very successfully at that!

The work finally cost almost £100,000 in 1974, when the Club reopened. That was, what - a million pounds - today? The money did not come knocking on the door - it had to be raised, and what an effort that turned out to be, through some five years, during which we began employing Alex Mair and Margaret Beaton, which meant adding salaries etc. I promised myself that when it was all finished, I would get an armchair, place it opposite the Club, sit in it sipping a glass of *The Macallan* whisky and having a puff of the most expensive cigar I could buy ... but, alas! as Jonathan Swift said, "Promises are like piecrusts, meant to broken." That is one promise I still have to keep.

When problems arose with the architect, an unknown man telephoned me and asked what I needed most - I answered "a lawyer". Whoever he was, and whatever his motives, he supplied one at no expense. Not that it did much good - it never does, but it was encouraging. Many people helped during those fraught years of rebuilding - and I had a stroke of luck! Peebles Hydro ran 'mid-week weekends' (free for children), so Margaret and I took advantage. By the grace of God, a conference of Glasgow Councillors was going on, and I 'mingled' at the bar. The subject of Church House and its need of cash 'happened' to come up, arousing much sympathy amongst my all-powerful hearers. Had I not gone to Peebles that time, I wonder if Church House would exist today?

The rebuilding was not only an agonisingly slow process, but also a haphazard one. The back section was to be little altered; the old church section was to have the very high steeple removed, the outer walls cut down to gallery level, and re-roofed. There were to be other minor changes, but that was all our money was going to get us. The architect said the wooden (and well-worn) floor of the church would be left as it was. He intended taking off the enormous roof without it falling inside the building. Some hopes!

Within a couple of days of the work starting, the floor was matchwood and a bulldozer stood inside the building amidst the debris from the collapsed roof. This alarmed me no end! A new floor would be required and would have to be paid for. Then, there being no Clerk of Works or watchman on the project, vandals bumed down a large part of the rear halls section of the premises - no insurance because nobody would insure Church House owing to the countless break-ins (my sorrow at having my beloved, beautiful, half-size billiard table burnt is beyond tears). Then no provision had been allowed for new drains - more money again. The surveyor gave up and opened a tea-room in the Borders. Then a remarkable 'coincidence' occurred: I got talking to the only other spectator present while I was watching a boys' football match, and the man told me he was a joiner. I complained to him bitterly that the the joiner hired to work at Church House had not turned up for months - and lo and behold! the guy was the very joiner in question! He speedily put me right - he had received no drawings from the architect, and his original estimate would need to be considerably upped. He was the one to complain, not me! The scales fell from my eyes - with quite a clang! And what was worse, the debts piled up.

But it's an ill wind ... In the end, we got a fine asphalt floor for the old wornout wooden one. The burnt out area I turned into a girls' club - something they had never had before - separating one half off for cookery, the other for hairdressing, relaxation, etc. I named them the "Martha and Mary" rooms and the names have stuck. With the approval of a very helpful Scottish Education Department, a new office with a foot thick concrete roof and walls was installed. All pipes were under concrete, all doors made of steel and opening outwards so they couldn't be kicked in, no windows; in other words, a building resembling Fort Knox: steel and concrete - virtually fireproof. The old gym had its roof repaired, and was later re-floored by the generous Newlands South congregation. Provision was made for a corner with seating for evening prayers. A sanctuary for small gatherings was made and dedicated to Dr Gray's memory - "The Upper Room".

Out in the street for three years, we were like the those poor souls who, according to the writer of the Hebrews *(II Verse 37)* "were stoned, sawn asunder, slain by the sword, went about in sheepskins and goatskins; being destitute, afflicted, tormented, wandering in deserts and in mountains, and in dens and caves of the earth" (OK, I'm exaggerating, but not by much!). But the great day finally arrived, and I picked up Dr. George MacLeod to open the new Church House in all its finished splendour. He said he had only been twice to Church House, to dedicate it at its opening in 1942, and back again to rededicate it in 1974. At the original dedication, 'Tubby' Clayton, founder of Toc H and a Regnal member, blessed the occasion by saying that he had never seen a building so desecrated to the glory of

God! It was from Tubby's "Upper Room" in Talbot House (Toc H) in Belgium, that I took the name "Upper Room" for the Club chapel.

Jim Herd, one of the first Club members, collapsed while giving the vote of thanks during the opening ceremony, and died a few hours later. This cast a deep shadow over the large company gathered for the occasion. As my father-in-law died the same weekend, in Inverness, I was in a pretty shaky state and shot through a red traffic light, almost crashing into a van - you can get so tired as to be past caring. I must have looked really inert because the van driver felt sorry for me.

During the long time rebuilding, Sammy Whitelaw turned up at the manse bringing in his lorry two enormous cast steel Iona crosses which he had 'acquired' from an old church being demolished in Garscube Road. They were, he said, his gift to the new Church House. A small, vivacious, likeable man, Sammy ran the Bridgeton Waverley football team, and supplied local shops with bleach he produced with small regard for the rules of health and safety. His wife, Molly, was a lady of considerable quality, and an elder of mine; but interesting as all this information was, it did not help me know what to do about the two crosses.

Happily, Sammy was not offended when I agreed to accept only one cross, after I pointed out that it would take an enormous crane to lift it out of the lorry and I hadn't got one handy. He said he would store my chosen cross until such times as required. From then on, again and again for two years, Sammy would ask me when to deliver and unload the cross at Church House. Finally, I sent him the long-awaited signal to spring into action; The cross was to be bolted to a very thick interior stone wall strong enough to bear the weight, but the only way to do this was by lowering it into place with great care and precision - a hole was left in the roof to permit but this was about to be covered over by the roofers. Urgency was my message to Sammy. Needless to say, he did not turn up on the day. The great cast steel cross was later positioned by reopening the roof, and, in the process, bending some of the steel trusses. However, I look upon it now and take pride in the knowledge that it is the one thing in the Club which cannot possibly be stolen by thieves. It is a memorial to Sammy.

First-time visitors to the Club are always surprised at the contrast between the beaten-up outside and the very fine facilities inside. Church House must be not only the longest existing youth club in Scotland, but also the best equipped. In the late Seventies, by 'coincidence', Alex happened to go to speak at a Women's Guild in Dumfries (something he almost passed up on doing because of the distance involved). There he met the Guild National President, Dorothy Dalgleish - a gem! This dynamic lady weighed in at National Mission (so I'm told), and the Guild made Church House its project for 1983, raising money to install the new canteen, etc. It involved speaking at many Guilds all over the country - although I had just left for Greenock, I did my bit with some twenty engagements. While speaking at Balshagray Guild, an old lady told me she knew the late Rev. Dr. Arthur Gray. When I asked if they were school together, she said that they had been; when I further asked if they had been in the same class she answered, "No, I was his school teacher."

It is very rewarding to see youngsters, and even mothers with children, sitting at the tables in the brightly decorated new canteen (sorry, 'soda-fountain'). Nearby is a big mural which was painted for the reopening of the rebuilt club; it is a copy of a mural in St. Nazaire, which I had noticed on a visit to the French Protestant Industrial Mission. I brought back a picture of the mural, and because it portrayed children playing around a figure holding up a Bible with a background of shipyards, it suited Glasgow fine. The shipyard bits have since been painted out - no yards anymore, alas! - but still people, and weans, and games, and a Bible.

The years of running around for the rebuilding programme had its funny side, too. I was to meet the architect one night at a Presbytery meeting in Hamilton Old Parish Church. Unfortunately, this was during one of those electricity blackouts we had at that time. I arrived in a totally dark town and couldn't find the church. After driving round and round its notoriously circuitous one-way system, I saw the church at the end of a short lane - marked 'One Way'. Desperate, I chanced it, only to meet a police car halfway up. They were very nice and I followed them, in hope, miles round. But I was still lost when they left. Then I passed a notice saying 'Presbytery' - I was delighted and got out.

The vestibule of the church contained a group of folk standing around waiting, I presumed, for a break in the Presbytery business in order to enter without causing a disturbance, so I joined them. After some five minutes, I decided to go in, business or no business, swung open the door and entered. In a second I was back out again! I was in the R. C. chapel, and the folk waiting in the vestibule were going to Confession! To see me enter and reappear so rapidly must have left them astonished at the brevity of my penitence, and lightness of my sentence.

Confession, they say, is good for the soul; but it isn't any good for finding your way round Hamilton in a blackout. I never did find Hamilton Old Parish Church. I know it exists, because it appears in the Year Book, but I have my doubts if it is in Hamilton at all.

Chapter 32

*"It took me fifteen years to discover that I had no
talent for writing, but I couldn't give it up because by
that time I was too famous."*
(Robert Benchley).

"C'est magnifique, mais ce n'est pas la gare!"
*(Dorothy Parker on being taken by taxi to the Louvre
instead of the Gare du Nord).*

TRAVELLING ON

I should record how much I learnt from the French Protestant
Industrial Mission. The 'Mission' is not 'Industrial' in the sense we
think of Industrial Mission, *i.e.*, relating Christianity and Industry
through industrial chaplaincies. Nor, for that matter, is it 'Mission',
in the sense we use the word in this country, as campaigning. The F.
P .I. M. is much more like our inner city 'Settlements', community
centres with a Christian core. The idea was originated in Paris by a
British clergyman named McColl, who was caught up in the siege of
Paris (1870-71) during the Franco-Prussian War. Twenty thousand
Parisians were massacred, when the French army recaptured the city
from the left-wing Communards. McColl was shocked, not only by
the violence, but also by the poverty in the devastated city. The F. P.
I. M. is also known as the McColl Mission.

For several years running, the Secretary of the Mission, Georges
Velten, stayed with us at the manse while on his annual visit here
to raise support through our own Industrial Mission Department
of the Home Board. A tall, highly intelligent, typically fastidious
Frenchman, Georges took a close interest in our kirk, and Church
House, both moving along the same theological lines as himself.
He taught Margaret and myself to understand much better our
relationship with the people we served - it made us to realise how
'bourgeois' were some of our attitudes and expectations. Above all, I
think I was able to take my Iona experience a step further into seeing
how all our communicating has to start with the world we know and
where we are, rather than with the Bible and working down from on

high.

I became very interested in this way forward, and travelled to France to visit their centre in Rouen. As in the Highlands, the main meeting began about 10 p.m., and was held in a big room filled with choking smoke from a hundred-plus folk puffing Gauloise cigarettes. Georges, in the chair, had the local priest sitting on his one side and the Communist mayor on the other. The subject was immigration, and there was much mentioning of 'Le Rive Droit' as opposed to 'Le Rive Gauche' - we were on the 'Gauche' side of the Seine, the poor side, and much was made of this by the left-wing inclined audience (which puzzled me, as I didn't see all *that* much difference between 'Droit' and 'Gauche'). The current French politics of student revolt were in the air, and the discussion became heated - at which point, an English Methodist minister beside me whispered. "I've been in France four years, and I still don't understand French politics. Politics here is a living thing, a sort of animal, not a subject!" I took his point.

What intrigued me was the way Georges handled the boisterous discussion. He was like a goalkeeper fielding shots and high-balls! He never answered questions, but directed them skilfully to somebody who could deal best with them - the priest, the mayor, members of the audience. What had 'mission' to do with all these questions about immigration in France? He rounded things off by asking, "Does the Bible have anything to say about all this?" I expected silence to greet this, but no, quite the opposite! A coloured guy started things off. "Well, what about Joseph? He was an immigrant, wasn't he?" Similar Biblical references followed thick and fast - I was amazed at how many knew relevant scraps of scripture, which they applied. At the end, no resolutions were passed, no decisions taken, but Georges left folk feeling Christianity was about the real world they knew, and to which they had to respond positively. That seems to me to be exactly what the churches exist to do in the modern world - like Our Lord, to make folk think, to raise issues of everyday concern, to make ordinary folk feel they can find answers if they ask, seek and knock, to free them from fatalism, to empower them. I remember asking what someone had to do to become a church member here, and was told they must simply say that they believed in the Resurrection.

On one occasion when back home, Georges asked if some of us would drive groups of his own folk on day trips to see something of the Scottish countryside. I landed up with a *voiture* full of Frenchmen who spoke not a word of English! For several painful hours I stuttered at them in my schoolboy French. Looking at them I realised that they could have been my elders, working blokes. I also realised that France is not, as is commonly supposed, a Roman Catholic country, but secular, with few churchgoers. In Rouen, and indeed, in Normandy in general, there is a sizeable Protestant community - presumably the left-over remnant from the Revocation of the Edict of Nantes by Louis XIVth, when the Huguenots were driven out of France (some of whom brought to Calton and Bridgeton their weaving skills, to France's great loss of quality people and skills). The Normandy Protestants I met were not by any means discouraged about the future of the Faith. The Bible is of great importance to them, and they found the Word of God in the historical parts of the Old Testament, which they looked at, not in terms of personal piety and salvation, but in terms of the politics of God contrasted with the politics of men.

As we move more and more into a secular society, the churches here have retreated into a played-out Victorian theology of the type rejected long ago by my father's generation. The criterion for success is numbers - you hear it so often said, "Look at such and such an 'evangelical' church, full of people" Impressive, but numbers are no substitute for faith, We do not need a change of vocabulary, but a change of heart. By the way, when I invited Georges to speak at our Regnal Swanwick Conference, he did his stuff using lots of diagrams and posters stuck up with Blu-tack - he loved Blu-tack, and sighed over the lack of it in La Belle France! To my disappointment, Georges did not go down well with some of the Englishmen in the audience (some of whom mention him with disapproval to this day!). The English do not really like the French. When I remarked to Georges that the Scots find the English personality to be a Teutonic mixture of hard-headedness and sentimentality, he very, very warmly agreed - so the dislike is mutual! Mind you, the "Auld Alliance" brought Scotland disaster upon disaster, and it is hard to know why people speak admiringly of it when the reality is that the French used us for their own selfish ends.

If you ask me, (go on, ask), the tragedy of France is that she never became a Protestant country (Calvin was French, as were so many other Reformers), because a Frenchman is a natural born Protestant. Eli Halevy, the great French historian, wrote in his book "England in the Nineteenth Century" that the glory of England lies not in its grand cathedrals, but in what he called 'its tin chapels'. On the continent, the grand churches stood for suppression of thought - it was in Britain alone that freedom was born, and born in the Nonconformist 'tin chapels'. It took a Frenchman to see that clearly. It was from the much derided Calvinism that the belief came that a man is innocent in law until he is proved guilty. From what I read in the 'quality' English newspapers, your average Anglican clergyman lies awake at night, chewing the blankets for fear John Calvin will murder him in his bed! Even Scots journalists these days can issue no greater denunciation than to call someone a 'Calvinist'. A trip to the F. P. I. M. will soon educate them over that - if they can be educated at all, which is unlikely.

To add an anecdote to this diversion into deep waters: In Rouen I met a charming, widowed, English lady who had married a Frenchman. She took in students, all from West Africa. After awhile, she felt something evil was in the house, and began going to church after a long absence. Voodoo was being practised in her home, until she put her Nigerians out. She said she hadn't realised the power of evil until this had happened to her, and how much she needed the greater power of God to fight it. As my wife, Margaret keeps telling me, evil is very real in Africa, and this woman experienced it right there in Rouen.

Chapter 33

"The most anxious man in a prison is the warder."
(G.B.Shaw)

PRISON CHAPLAINCY

There was this girl who was accused of murdering another lassie. She was placed on remand and I visited her in prison awaiting trial at the High Court. The trial took the best part of a week. She had had a troubled history; regarded as a strangely detached girl at school and in the Girl Guides, she got pregnant very young to a no-user and had had an abortion. Her mother was a kindly, pleasant, weak lady, who was dominated by the daughter. A quiet, gentle man, the father suffered all sorts of physical and psychological problems due, I guessed, at least in part, to his being almost excluded from the mother/daughter relationship. The trial traumatised the parents severely.

It was one of those 'did she fall or was she pushed' trials, and the result was an acquittal. The interesting thing was to see the girl's attitude and posture during the proceedings - a sort of chilling, blank detachment. Years later Margaret and I were in a restaurant in the city centre when the waitress came over all smiles and I recognised her as being the girl I had last seen on trial. She was filled with pleasure at seeing us; she was a different person! The change was astonishing: gone were that blank look and those dead eyes - instead she was bright and attractively outgoing. She told us that she was very happily married, had a family, and was living in clover! People can, and do change.

I noticed the same transformation with some difficult boys taken out of their environment and given, say, a job looking after horses; they became quite different in the countryside, away from the city. Standing in the Club gym with Alex, he pointed out a boy who was banging his head off the wall while playing football - "He's a psycho," said Alex. Later, this boy, with some others, committed a terrible rape with extreme violence. We must not think such badly damaged and dangerous people can be wished away, but you never know - with God, all things are possible.

The only time I have truly seen real evil with my own eyes was when I visited a wee, weird guy, in a dirty cell in the prison. He looked like Charles Manson; bearded, hunched up. He asked me if I believed in demons, and I thought, "Here we go, he's winding me up as the inmates usually do to chaplains!" But I soon sensed he was not questioning me but attacking me. A very chilling and scary thing began to take place: his face changed. If Auld Nick has a face, then I have seen it! A terrible evil someone - something - was looking at me, and he wasn't acting or putting it on. He was a very evil wee man. In a prison, you meet very few evil men - I only met a handful, and I never felt really threatened even by them - but this guy was something else. I got out that cell at the double, believe me, and was shaken in a way I had never experienced before.

When Manuel, the notorious serial murderer, was hanged in Barlinnie, a Mr. Anderson was the chaplain who had to attend all hangings. Understandably, he was a strong opponent of capital punishment, but he told me that when he saw Manuel hang he felt glad the world was rid of an evil monster. We must not revert to the days of witchhunting, seeking evil spirits and the Devil's hand in every sin and sickness (alas! some 'Christians' go in for that sort of medieval nonsense), but evil is real and we do not live in a theological discussion group.

I have the highest respect and admiration for prison officers. I never met a bad one, and found them great company. From Governors down, I found a team working together to a positive end, loyal to each other, each doing what they were paid to do without interfering and meddling in things which did not concern them. Everyone respected the boss, and he did not shirk responsibility. (Ah! what a lot the Kirk has to learn).

What did a prison chaplain do? Well, I felt it was my job was to help the boys out, but I found that whenever I helped one out the cops always helped him back in again. I'm sorry to say that my sermons were blamed for the high rate of escapes from the jail, the inmates reporting that my powerful preaching had them climbing the walls (things became even more serious when even the prison officers started trying to escape). I don't wish to boast, but even the most hardened criminal could not withstand my preaching for longer than five minutes without begging for mercy. As for my Services, these were ecumenical affairs, with the R.C.s sitting at the Celtic

End and the Proddies at the Rangers End. After hearing me preach, none of the prisoners became recidivists, every one of them becoming extremely anxious not to go back to jail again. Part of my duties was to keep everybody happy, so when I was not preaching, I ran the ice-cream van captured during the famous Ice-cream Wars. The prison sports day was popular, but I had to cancel the pole vaulting for obvious reasons, and the marathon runs as well, because none of the starters ever finished. It will come as no surprise to you, dear reader, to learn that during my years as a chaplain, the numbers in prison fell dramatically.

You meet a lot of interesting, clever people inside. There was the big, likeable fellow I got on with very well who had escaped three times, and had been in the infamous cages of Inverness prison. If it had been me I would never have figured out a means of escape, so I had to admire him. Unfortunately, his record, what with one thing and another, meant he was doing many years. He fell out with me because he thought I wasn't a kosher Christian fundamentalist like himself, but he forgave me later.

It is easy to forget you are in a prison as you go around treating men just like every other guy you meet. But a jail is not a club or a pub, nor is it a school. A prison is a sort of castle turned inside out, the walls around it are there not to keep people out, but to keep them in. Folk pass it every day without giving a thought to what goes on inside - much as we do when we pass a hospital. A prison is a dustbin for all the problems society cannot solve and wants to hide away. So far, nobody has come up, with anything to replace it, and I doubt if anyone ever will - more's the pity.

It is easy to land up in prison; in a jail you meet men who never dreamed it would happen to them - professional men from the top drawer, and tradesmen of previous good character, who put a foot wrong. The picture painted by sections of the media that prison is some sort of holiday camp for the undeserving is a very false one. It is an awful place, especially for the type of man who does not keep the sort of company prison provides. The loss of freedom is the major punishment, and shame and guilt compound the misery for many. Bravado characterises the young offender under peer pressure, but apart from the institutionalised old lags (who cause no trouble), nobody, but nobody, wants to be in a jail. At best, for those who see crime as their 'profession', prison is an occupational hazard; and because something like one third of prisoners have been brought up in children's homes, prison to them is an extension of institutional existence. It takes all kinds, and the strangest group to meet (a small group at that) are the sex offenders. These are usually gentle spoken individuals, and it is very hard to figure out what motivates them. Called 'beasts' by the lower element of the prison population, they have to be segregated for protection. They give no trouble and come from all walks of life.

It is conventional wisdom these days to say that drug addicts should not be put in prison, but I have met young men who were more than happy to be inside and unable to take drugs, otherwise they would be dead. The only experience I had of drugs in a prison came about when a young sex offender told me he was being forced to collect drugs from the visiting room, which he cleaned, and bring them to the hall. If he didn't do that, he would be in danger, but if he did, and got caught, he would be in deep trouble with the authorities. I had no wish to get myself involved, seeing I had to stay 'neutral', so I passed word on to the Governor. However, I was required to vouch for what I had been told by the prisoner so, while everybody was 'banged up', I accompanied some officers to the visiting room. There, behind a loose panel in the ladies toilet, they found a very valuable haul of drugs! It struck me as exceedingly easy to bring drugs in, once past the gate! The staff were delighted! Of course, pretence was made that sniffer dogs had found them, but just in case somebody had seen me earlier talking with the source of our information, I decided to keep well away from the prison. Confident that my part in all this was unknown, I went back a week later, only to have the officer on the gate say, as he gave me my key, "Dae ye think ye'll find ony drugs this week?" With maximum apprehension, sure the entire jail knew of my part in the sore loss, to some gang of crooks, of what must have been several hundred pounds worth of illegal substances, I went into the halls. Nothing happened! No reactions! The Governor speculated that what we found was just a 'blind' for another parcel of drugs, but who would want to throw away so much money? My informant was not questioned by the gang either. All very odd. I still await my O. B. E. for my services to my country on this one - I ought to have brought it up the day Princess Anne visited the prison.

A few minutes before her arrival, I was asked to introduce her to the assembled local dignitaries imported for the event. In a panic, I tried to memorise their names so I could introduce each one in turn, but she did the job for herself, to my great relief. She was in excellent spirits, presumably because of her forthcoming Scottish wedding, so I took to her right away. She asked the usual questions. I explained I was in the job because her mother had written to me to say the jails were running short of hostages and ask if would I help out - H. M. rated me highly as hostage material, which was very flattering. I assured the Princess Royal that I would stay at my post until either ransomed or paroled, and that she need have no fears for the safety of the realm. Annie took all this it in good part before gliding on to the next mug in the line.

We had a lot of illegal immigrants awaiting the results of appeals to the Home Office against deportation. Some had been in Britain for years, until 'shopped' by some disgruntled rival or ex-girl friend. We had so many Singhs that I called the jail 'Sing Sing'. They had broken the law, but it was sad to see them behind bars. Nowadays they would not be called 'illegal immigrants' but 'asylum seekers', and housed by the local authorities instead of kept in prison. The appeals system was as slow as could be. When one Nigerian lad got fed up waiting, and knowing he would be deported anyway, he tried to withdraw his appeal, but was told he couldn't! The very tall, very cheerful Gambians said they would just turn around, and come back to Britain anyway! The Sikhs said they would be arrested by the Indian police as soon as they flew into Delhi. I didn't see why, but that is what they told me. Their religious leaders were permitted to wear their traditional daggers when holding meetings, which I made a point of attending as chaplain, and they liked that.

I was not impressed by one mullah (if that's what he was), who when I phoned him about a Pakistani chap who wanted to see a Muslim for spiritual guidance, asked me for a fee. I pointed out he would get travelling expenses, but he refused to come without a fee. We had Pakistani young men from time to time, often married to R. C. lassies, and they sat very loose in their religion - except for one thing - pork. Pigs they abhorred! Even Lord Emsworth's beloved "Empress of Blandings" would not, I fear, have overcome this distaste for all things porcine.

I learnt a great deal during my days of prison chaplaincy. For instance, how to empty fruit machines undetected; how to sell software to I B M (their own); how to fire a shotgun outside a pub in

Campbeltown; or enjoy a good Saturday night brawl in Rothesay. In Port Glasgow, assault is always 'serious assault' (never 'light-hearted assault'); the rest of Inverclyde prefers shop-lifting and car theft (what might be called the 'light industry' of crime). Bearsden, Milngavie, and Newton Mearns usually have to import their criminals from Dumbarton, Paisley, and, of course, The City of Culture itself, their own being restrained by Neighbourhood Watches. Stealing from trout farms, getting rid of unwanted vehicles, delaying the theft of your Mercedes for four whole minutes, poaching in the Clyde - all these and many other skills I acquired in the education department of Cell 99. If you get all your kitchen scraps, put them in a container and hide it under the floor for a few weeks, you can get an alcoholic beverage fit for a king - a dead one, that is! All it takes is ingenuity!

A few true stories exemplify a prison for me, so I'll tell them. A young chap, doing 15 years for murder, struck me as being highly intelligent and well presented, so I persuaded him to take Highers through the small Prison Education Department. Once a week I took him for History, and we got on fine, until one day he admitted not having done the 'home work'. Forgetting to whom I was talking and where I was, I took him to task over this and he blew up on me. It was an ugly moment. I had forgotten the tremendous stress on a prisoner; easily done when you are trying not to think badly of someone. Mistake!

Another young guy was from Edinburgh - jailed for I know not what. He was highly educated, good-looking, mild natured - a very fine person in my eyes. His story was that he spent his days sitting at the top of the steps up the Mound, above the National Galleries, reading books. He did not beg and sat in all weathers, day after day. People passing to work often gave him sandwiches. Some ruffians eventually drove him away. He did not seem to be mentally ill or disturbed. He showed no interest in analysing his behaviour. He said he was a Christian, and I'm sure he was, in the best sense of that much abused name. I hope he got his place back on the steps on the Mound.

A young chap used to hurl abuse at me from one side of the gallery to the other - he was a Celtic supporter and I won't repeat what he called me at every opportunity. One night I was called in to see somebody in the suicide cells - it was him! In that totally bare place, lying on a canvas sleeping bag on a concrete base, he looked the very opposite of the cocky, aggressive ned who had given so much trouble. How appearances mislead. I might add that the same applied to a prison officer (the only one who was 'dry' with me) who met me after his retirement and surprisingly asked for help with his depression - outwardly one person, inwardly another. "Judge not that ye be not judged" comes to mind.

Then there was the guy who had his cell covered with his daily weather forecasting tables! It was his hobby, and he made all his observations through the bars! There was 'Robin Hood', one of the nicest young men, a kleptomaniac who kept coming back again and again, though he gave away everything he shoplifted! There was the tall, handsome Spanish hit-man, a gun-for-hire killer of five other men, a smoothie who wanted me to get him compassionate leave to see his pregnant 'partner' in London (the boy in the cell with him kept indicating behind the Spaniard's back that he thought he was 'loopy'). The Chinese boy, who was inconsolably cast into despair, having been involved in a Triad gang attack on a restaurant owner in Glasgow - the Triads would see he had no future if he got off and went home to Hong Kong. Then there were the cases of blokes who simply did not care whether they lived or died - like Colin, a young Paisley drug addict, for whom an elder in a kirk there did all one man can do to help another, in spite of being constantly used, lied to, and let down. Such behaviour is inexplicable, for even self-interest doesn't come into it. Colin asked me to notify this elder he was being released and to meet him outside with his car. After a long drive early in the morning, the elder waited in vain. When Colin was next in jail, I asked him why he had deliberately gone out earlier than the time he had asked the elder to pick him up. He couldn't tell me why. Soon afterwards, he was killed by a train walking along the lines - a not uncommon thing. I met another guy who did the same and lost his legs.

There seems to be a sort of built-in badness in some people - whether due to their environment or genes, who dare say? The joinery department made benches for sale in garden centres, and I got some of the scrap wood to give out to pensioners for firewood. Two huge, heavy bags were too much for me to lug all the way to the gate and load in my car, so I was grateful when three of the younger fellows offered to carry and unload it for me. As we walked back to the hall, behind the accompanying officer just in front of us, I saw them lift up stones and try breaking the office windows as we passed. My gratitude evaporated; they just could not do the right thing without spoiling it.

Two things are absolutely essential in a prison: chips, and snout (cigarettes to you and me). If chips were not provided, the customers simply refused to eat the meals, and the food was thrown out. Chips were essential. What concerned the prison doctor was that chips lack fibre. What concerned me, as chaplain, was that the diners lacked moral fibre!

If I ever met a guy doing time who did not smoke, I don't remember who, when, and where. Everybody smoked. The fags were roll-ups, matchstick-thin things which flared up and disappeared as soon as they were lit. I offered a young inmate a cigarette one day, the genuine article out of a packet, and he refused it saying, "I only smoke roll-ups". "What kind of tobacco do you buy?" I asked him. He seemed startled to be asked such a question, and replied, "The best, only the best." Being untutored in the qualities of the various brands of roll-up snout, I leaned forwards and asked out of curiosity, "The best, eh? What kind is the best?" He regarded me with a degree of disdain, "The best? Golden Vagina, that's the best." I could hardly disagree with that.

The vast majority of guys, when you entered a cell for the first time, were very glad to see you: somebody to listen; a link with the outside world. Anxiety and depression were never far away - especially amongst Dundee United supporters - OK. that's facetious, but you have to lighten things up at times. Lightening things up was first base for a chaplain.

Of course, everybody was innocent. You went into a cell during the recreation period and a half-dozen guys would be crowded in playing cards and, you know, not one of them was guilty of a crime! I know that's true, because they told me so themselves. Hearing their sad tales, I sympathised with them and told them the story about Frederick the Great, King of Prussia - I'll tell it to you now, just in case you are innocent as well ...

His Majesty visited a prison and went round asking each man in turn, "Are you innocent or guilty?" One after another, each declared his innocence. Finally he came to one guy and asked the same question, "Innocent or guilty?" "I am guilty, your Majesty," answered the man. Frederick turned to the jailer. "Release this prisoner immediately." he commanded, "His presence here is corrupting all these poor innocent men!" This story always went down well in the telling; grins and chuckles indicating that they got the message. I expect the story is still doing the rounds of prisons all over Britain, enjoyed by the sons of my original listeners.

The faces of arriving young offenders were often familiar enough for me to ask, "Your name so-and-so, son? You stay in Brigton? My, you're awfully like your Da! How is your Da, by the way?" Such pleasantries smoothed life's journey for all concerned especially for a lonely chaplain.

Last story? Yes: a quiet, dreamy young man in his twenties told me he had always been in an institution, ever since his family deserted him as a two-year-old. They were Irish tattie-howkers and when they went back to Ireland they simply left him toddling around a street in Whitlawburn! He never saw them again! Who said "truth is stranger than fiction"?

Last, last story - you're getting it anyway ... While playing golf with a friend I mentioned a certain 'character' I met in the jail. To my embarrassment and astonishment, he said, "That's my old man!" Moral: be careful what you say to people about their relations, especially if you are talking to a judge, an Archbishop, a Moderator of the General Assembly, or even a golfing partner.

Chapter 34

COURT CASES

Years ago, during a case on the Munster Circuit, the judge asked one of the leading members of the Bar, "Is your client not aware of the legal maxim 'de minimus non curat lex'?" To this learned counsel replied, "M'Lud, I can assure you that in the obscure Irish village from which my client comes, there is no other topic of conversation."

I spent a good deal of time in various courts as a character witness, by request of the accused. These requests were of the sort which can't be refused. It gave great offence not to go to the aid of a local miscreant, so I always went along, hoping not to be called by the Sheriff to testify. In the strange world in which these things operate, I found that I could get out of going by saying I was going to the pictures that day. Why this most feeble of excuses was acceptable I cannot say, but it was! A dying mother was no let-out - but the movies were OK. No wonder Jonathan Swift left his money to provide a lunatic asylum for this crazy world!

Sheriff Irvine-Smith and the dreaded Sheriff Langmuir were, in their hey-day, the scourge of Brigton. Great lawyers, like the famous Dowdalls, pitted their its against them in vain. The entertainment was great and the attendances at the shows in the High and Sheriff Courts never flagged.

The case of Dobi came up; the Sheriff welcomed him into the dock, most cordially if somewhat sadly. "Ah, Dobi, Dobi, you here again, Dobi? What you here for this time? How many times have you appeared before me?" "Aboot 136 times, m'Lord, drunk and disorderly" "Och, Dobi, Dobi," sighed his Lordship, "what will I do with you? It will have to be sixty days, I'm afraid." Dobi stiffened. "Och, here, wait a wee minute, that's a bit much intit?" The good Sheriff weighed matters as judges are supposed to do. "How would thirty days do then, Dobi?" he inquired, considerately. "That's a loat be'er. I wisnae expecting sixty days!" "Well, let's leave it at that for now," said the obliging Sheriff. "Look after yourself, Dobi" "You tae, my Lord." This agreeable encounter shows the glory of British justice at its best, and I am sure that as you read it, you felt as uplifted as I did myself when I was privileged to be present at this exchange of goodwill and pleasantries between the majesty of the law, and a humble citizen.

Mr Bumble's pronouncement, 'the Law is an ass', seemed more than likely to be true the time one of my members was arrested for attempted murder. Driving home from work, he was stopped by the police because there was a building on fire and hoses lay strewn across the road. At the head of a line of waiting traffic, he was eventually waved to come on ahead by a policeman, and did so. Some fifty yards on, the arm of a police sergeant shot through his open window, grabbbed him round the throat, forced him backwards, and caused him to push down on the accelerator. As the car shot forwards, the police sergeant let go and fell onto the road. John was accused of attempted murder!

The trial at the High Court lasted the best part of a week. The Q.C. was Hugh Morton (later Lord Morton), son of Ralph Morton, Deputy Leader of the Iona Community, and known to me personally. Hugh was the dry, lawyer, type: the sort who, when you were in the middle of a conversation with him, would suddenly and disconcertingly leap on an invisible bicycle and pedal away! "Hugh," said I, "why are you trying this man for murder? He was sober at the scene, he has no criminal history, he drives for a living, he did what he was told at the time, and, most baffling of all, why should he want to murder a man he not only did not know, but could not even see! Hugh was unimpressed and unmoved, 'cycled' off and the case continued, until John was found 'not proven'. After the trial, which completely shattered him and his family life, the police sergeant kept making anonymous phone calls to his house, threats which John felt he could not report. Well, that's what John told me, and I have no reason to doubt his word - or, indeed, that 'the law is an ass'.

I never had much time for Nicholas Fairbairn, after one trial in which he was to defend one of my men accused of embezzlement. Ian had been urged, as every good Christian should, to 'get into trade unionism and politics', so he became Treasurer of a very big union in a very big factory. His predecessor in office had been convicted of corruption, and it was no secret that the union was riven with strife (along R. C. *vs* Masons lines, I was told). Ian was dead honest, but sadly inexperienced in the ways of the world in which he was moving. His wife would take the union dues, several thousand pounds at a time, along to the local bank hidden for safety under the baby in a pram! £200 was missing - not surprisingly given the banking system! - and he was charged. Presumably the police were on the look out for misconduct in the light of their previous dealings with the union officials.

In the entrance hall of the High Court, we awaited the celebrated lawyer, Sir Nicholas, and a few moments before the case was called, he appeared hurrying through the entrance. I raced alongside him, offering to be a character witness, saying why I thought Ian was innocent, and drawing attention to Ian's readiness to pay back the £200 he had muddled in his chaotic books. In court, Nicholas Fairbairn repeated my every word, it being obvious he had done no work on the case at all. Ian was given 6 months. The judge, spotting my clerical collar, kindly invited me to speak, and I did so quite forcefully, angry at the feeble defence. The sentence was reduced to 3 months. I went to see Ian in Perth prison, and have retained a bad impression of Sir Nicholas Fairbairn ever since.

Standing in the entrance hall of the Sheriff Court, old friends would shuffle up and ask me, "You here wi' Sparrow?" (a well-known Brigtonian); or "Ony fags oan ye?" It was quite an 'old boys reunion'!

One exceedingly glaikit young man's mother asked me to speak on his behalf before the Sheriff. He had been 'lifted' while staggering along, in broad daylight, under an assortment of stolen goods, on his way to a second-hand shop in the London Road - that should give you, dear reader, some idea as to his intelligence. Asked by the Beak to present my character witness statement (without taking the oath), and enter my plea for mercy, I began: "My Lord, you see before you in the dock a sight which would move the stoniest heart to pity. There stands a poor, cretinous creature, a complete moron, a slack-jawed, slobbering idiot, a repulsive youth, fat, ugly, disgusting, incapable of performing the simplest of crimes involving the slightest degree of intelligence." The Sheriff looked closely at the figure in the dock, shook his head, and airily dismissed the accused with an admonishment uttered in a weary voice. Afterwards, fearing the youth's mother would assault me for what I said about her beloved son, I was pleasantly surprised when, instead, she thanked me with all her heart!

Being asked for a reference could be tricky; I found it best never to refuse, to say the best I could, and to stretch it a little to get the poor guy a job! However, with the best will in the world, that sometimes proved impossible. I did a reference for a young fellow in the Club which read: "Under no circumstances employ this person. He is a thief, a liar, and totally untrustworthy." When he opened my letter and read it he said, "Whit's this?" I could only reply, "You asked for a reference. Well, there it is - you didn't say it had to be a good one!" Abraham Lincoln's solution to the references problem was to weigh them. He got loads of references with each application for one of the countless jobs in the patronage of a President, so he weighed them on scales and the heaviest got the job!

Chapter 35

"There is not the least use in preaching to anyone unless you catch them ill."
(Rev.Sydney Smith).

DOCTORS & HOSPITALS

I recall visiting a sickly-looking stranger who had moved into Bridgeton from the Gorbals. This poor guy had every ailment known to medicine, with a few unknown ones for good measure. He went through each of these for me in detail, and concluded by expressing boundless admiration for the Rev. Cameron Peddie, a minister in the Gorbals famous for his healing ministry. I said how pleased I was that he had been to Mr Peddie for faith healing and that it had done him so much good, to which the patient replied, "That Mr. Peddie's a wonderful man, wonderful, but, naw! he never did me ony guid!"

Anyone asking my father-in-law, Dr James Brown, for a 'line' soon discovered his request being closely cross-examined. One time a chap entered the surgery, and when asked what were his health problems, simply replied, "There's nuthin wrang wi' me, doctor, I'm here for a line - I'm taking a few days aff to go tae the Wembley." Such an approach to Dr Brown was not one to be recommended. "Oh, you are you, are you." observed he coldly, "A 'line' to go to a football match, eh? - and what will I put on it?" The petitioner blundered on; "Och, jist pit onythin' at aw on it." The 'line' was duly written, handed it over, opened and read: "Whit's this? 'Jimmy Smith is suffering from onythin' at aw', Signed Dr. James Brown." "Well, that's what you told me to put down," said the doc, "'onythin' at aw'!"

My father-in-law was a man of few words and he used those sparingly. I read a book by the journalist Cliff Hanley called "Dancing in the Streets", in which he said he was born in Soho Street off the Gallowgate, and to make conversation, I alluded to this. My information was received in silence; after a very long pause he said, "No, he wasn't". "But in his book, he says he was." I persisted. No response ... I passed another long spell in the waiting room, until finally he spake. "He was born at 1000 the Gallowgate, and I ought to know because I brought him into the world - and I wish to God I hadn't bothered!" It gave me considerable pleasure to have the opportunity to relate this anecdote in Cliff's presence at a book launch at Thins in Edinburgh. I had waited a long time to tell it.

A chemist as well as a doctor, Dr. Brown was a family doctor of the old school, one of the last of the Dr. Cameron type, straight from Dr. Finlay's Casebook. He had had to buy with his East End practice, the house and even the furniture of his predecessor so that his wife had to live with that furniture all her married life, though she disliked it. The pre-war health of his patients, like their income, was in a poor state, and it took all his skill and experience to cope. To him, medicine was an art, and he used to say that the more doctors came to rely on drugs, the more the standard of nursing would fall. As a doctor he commanded total confidence. He was pre-bureaucracy, and from him professors and consultants received no deference. We shall not see his like again, I fear, neither in medicine nor, for that matter, in the ministry.

His contempt for those he called 'red rebels' knew no depths. Driving his Humber one Saturday evening to see a child with diphtheria, his way was blocked at Bridgeton Cross by a crowd listening to man on a soap box - one of those 'red rebels' in action. Honking his way through, he worked into the small hours, saving the child's life. Mother was there, but no father - at least not until he arrived after the worst was over. The father was, you guessed it, the 'red rebel' at the Cross. "I never said anything," Dr Brown told me, "I just looked out the window to see if it was raining. It wasn't raining hard enough, so I waited till it was pouring buckets. 'Here', said I, 'you're the father, take this prescription right away to Boots in Renfield Street'. I knew the last tram had gone, and he'd have to walk it. I didn't tell him it was only a prescription for aspirins. I hope he got drowned!" Lenin would never had got far if he had had to deal with Dr. James Brown, instead of that wimp, Dr. Zhivago!

Hospital visiting had, of course, its sad moments, but its happier ones as well. Like every minister, I spent a great deal of my time going to hospitals. My first experience of a death came when I was a complete rookie. who had never been in such a situation before. A young mother of three died and I was shaken up. Her husband came away from the bed with me; as we walked down the corridor, he put his arm around me to comfort me! Here was a guy who had just seen his wife die, who was left with three wee kids, and instead of me comforting him, he was comforting me! Sometimes, the courage and faith of ordinary folk leaves you speechless and very, very humble.

Peter and his wife were an old couple in the congregation. Maimie suffered a severe stroke, and was in hospital. Peter, an old-fashioned gentleman, always mild-mannered, polite, considerate, visited her every day for several months until she died. He was at the hospital at 10 a.m., and left at 10 p.m. He fed and nursed her personally; so much so that the staff left him to it. I never heard him complain, or say he was tired. It all happened long ago now, but I have never forgotten Peter's devotion to Maimie. Just to remember that one ordinary man is to receive a blessing. "Love suffers long and is kind ..."

Of course, it had its daft side as well! I once visited a girl, called Miller, in Rottenrow Maternity. I did not know her, just her mother, and after church one Sunday she asked me why I hadn't been to see her daughter. I protested that I had indeed seen her, and enjoyed my visit. It turned out I had spent half-an-hour talking to the wrong Mrs Miller, and the silly lassie never once asked me who I was, or why I had come to see her! Much the same happened to me with a male patient in another hospital. Records sent me to this chap because he had exactly the same (and unusual) name as the man I went to see. How he could be so dopey as not to tell me he hadn't a clue what I was talking about most of the time. I cannot imagine!

A young lady I knew had had her baby when I visited her. She told me that she had just overheard a conversation, through the curtains, between the lassie in the next bed, the sister, and the doctor. The lassie was in tears. When the doctor came, he asked the sister what was the matter; "She can't breast-feed the baby, and she's upset, doctor" sister explained. "Well," said he, "you know what to do sister. It's just hardening of the nipples; get some olive oil soaks and put them on." So saying, he departed. Sister said, "Don't worry, hen, doctor says I've to get you some olive oil soaks, and put them on, and they'll help you." The lassie looked puzzled; "Olive oil soaks? - OK. I'll gie them a try, but wull they no make an awfy mess o' ma feet?"

On an equally cheerful note, I knew a man in his eighties who had an amazingly boyish face - not a wrinkle. He suffered a massive stroke, and I went to see him in hospital. He was so changed in appearance that I walked past the bed without recognising him. As he was unconscious, all I could do was ask the staff how long he was likely to live. They gave him little hope. Three days later, I went back, and this time the bed was empty. Assuming the man had died, I was astonished to be told he had gone home! The doctors were baffled by his amazing recovery, not merely because he had survived, but because he showed no effects of the stroke. I saw him at home, and he looked younger than ever - I pondered the possibility that the stroke had done him a world of good, because he lived for years after that.

Then, as there always is, you had the 'creaking gate' type. One old guy I remember because he had five daughters who fussed over him. He was always on the point of death, but the point never seemed to do more than give him a wee prick. After I had buried the last of his daughters, he was still going strong!

The uncertainty of life was underlined one day, when I visited a very old man in hospital who was dying and nearly gone. When I spoke to the ward sister about him, she said the family expected to be notified of his death any time; then she added, "Don't you remember me?" I had to admit that I did not, so she filled me in. "You married me fourteen years ago". In uniform, folk look different, but when she told me her name, I remembered her and that pleased her no end. I said I would come back the next day to, see how the old man was doing. On my return, he was still alive, so I asked to see sister again, and was told some terrible news. After leaving me, she went off duty, left, and was knocked down and killed outside the gates of the hospital. I couldn't believe it! The old man was alive, and she, who just been talking to me about his death, was gone herself. It was very very sad.

Visiting an old lady in a Home, the matron told me that she would say, as soon as I met her, that she would die that night. I was told that she was havering, had nothing wrong with her, and that I should tell her so. As soon as we met, she predicted her death that night, and I, of course, pooh-poohed it, as instructed. Staff came in from time to time and called across, "Tell her to stop talking a lot of rubbish - there's nothing wrong with you, Bessie!". The following morning, having had some experience in these matters, I phoned to see how she was. She had, of course, died during the night, and apparently of no known causes!

Annie died of a broken heart. She was a delightful, middle-aged, lady who had been referred to me by her doctor because she was depressed. So she joined the Guild, came to the church, and having found company, picked up no end. Then one day I heard she was ill and went to see her in her single-end. She was in a melancholy state, wouldn't eat, and claimed she was too ill to get up from the bed. Next day, I returned with my two young daughters, and tried a wee trick. I turned my back to the bed to light her fire, and took sly looks over my shoulder. Annie could not resist the charms of two wee girls at her bedside, and she was smiling and sitting up, giving them sweets. When I came, of course, she slumped down again. It was all psychosomatic, and I later learnt that she had been bad-mouthed by some spiteful woman who had turned Annie's innocent friendship with a man into a scandal. It broke her heart and, in otherwise good health, she gave up and died.

In extreme contrast, the jolliest death I ever witnessed was that of an elderly chap I knew slightly, through his wife. He was an unpleasant, dour fellow, and I can't say I fancied him much, but as I sat with the family, round his deathbed, he was a different guy altogether! Anyone passing the bed must have thought it most inappropriate for us to be in stitches laughing, but he was tremendously funny, spinning jokes, calling out marvellous *ad lib*s to the nurses, giving us a great comic performance! Could this be the man I had known as a sourpuss? If any man ever died laughing he did - and he nearly took us all with him. Make of it what you will, but then, as my dear old Uncle Alex said when his end drew nigh, "Who wants to be a miserable looking corpse?"

Chapter 36

A Chaplain's Creed:-

"Take a box of fags in your haversack, and go with them, live with them, talk with them. You can pray with them sometimes, but pray for them always."
(Rev. Studdert Kennedy, 'Woodbine Willie', Great War Army Chaplain).

"Millions of tracts have been written. Tommy does not read them. We are still wearing the second-hand intellectual garments of the Middle Ages and they fit us as the armour in the Tower of London would fit the fighting men in Flanders."
(Alexander Irvine, chaplain, 1918).

Regnal

"There are no great men. Just great challenges which ordinary men, out of necessity, are forced by circumstances to meet."
(Admiral Wm. F. 'Bull' Halsey, 1942)

There was a remnant of Sydney Warnes' "Old Pals Club" still going when I took over as minister in 1960. It was as dead as Third Lanark Football Club. Church men's clubs were dying out everywhere in the new age of television. I was not sorry when the few members left in my own club gave up. But what to replace it?

It was a disappointment to me to begin to realise that the Iona Community was not focused on the men missing from our churches, but upon a bourgeois agenda. George himself often spoke of the idea of the Community coming to him when he was trying to relate the Faith and the working man. In the early days, craftsmen and ministers worked side by side as a Community; there was an Industrial Secretary, Penry, and there was real concern for men amongst Community ministers - indeed, amongst many ministers who were not members of the Community. But that began to evaporate. Today the churches are even more feminised than they were in the days when men said that Christianity is a good thing for women and children, but not for them. I used to think that men are not interested in the Church, but the truth is that the Church is not interested in men.

Men will only respond to leadership - and just as business relies on good managers, so the Kirk relies on good ministers who will lead from the front. Of course, ministers are just like any other group of men, but one wonders what some of them are doing in the ministry at all. At the end of the American Civil War, Lincoln wrote, "What has occurred in this case must ever recur in similar cases. In any future great national trial, compared with the men of this time, we shall have as weak and as strong, as silly and as wise, as bad and as good". It takes all kinds in the ministry - "horses for courses" - and I have made as many mistakes as the next man, but we can do without weak, silly, bad ministers in this our time of national trial.

I was meeting many good men every day. I met them at weddings and baptisms, on visits and through all sons of contacts. I would look around at the thousands attending football matches and wonder what the Gospel had to say to them. Seeking answers, I asked older ministers what they were doing about it, and got blank stares. They replied they were either too busy to do anything about the problem, or were running a successful Men's Association (I liked to 'go see', and found they were just 'talking a good game' on that one). When men met me, especially young married men, what had I to offer them? Come on Sunday? Nice if they did, but they didn't. I long ago learnt the wisdom of understanding that *a minister needs men more than the men need him.* I needed something to offer men which would be attractive and, above all, worthwhile.

One of my coincidences turned up the answer in the unlikely form of Phil. Phil came to Church House through Voluntary Service Overseas, an organisation started by a visionary chap called Alex Dickson, who wanted to send young people abroad to assist poorer nations. No placement had been available, so Alex asked me to take Phil for a year, telling me that he was a former head boy of Manchester Grammar School who had played rugger for English Schoolboys at Twickenham, and was the son of a wealthy businessman. A fine, big, handsome young man of about twenty, I showed Phil how to get around the city, and he quickly fitted in at the Club. He was a very good leader, easy-going, and brave with it. He had to be when he was not much older than some members; he had some teeth knocked out one night. I liked Phil, and he was popular. For some reason, Mancunian males look like Albert Finney, and Phil was no exception.

Hearing of my search for something to offer men, Phil mentioned a thing called a "Regnal Circle" which he had seen in Manchester. He offered to get me information about it, an offer which usually means 'sometime never', but Phil was as good as his word. I read the literature he had sent to me and liked it. The General Secretary of the Regnal League was the Mayor of Kidderminster, David Samuel (Dai Sam to everyone), a Welshman from the Rhondda. I invited him to come to Glasgow, met him at Central Station; and took him to a meeting I had called. The hall was pretty full with men who came because they knew me, or because I had told their wives to send them. Dai went down a treat. Twenty men followed my call to begin a Circle. What tipped the decision for me was Dai's offer to send a bus-load of men from Gateshead Circle to start us off, and to do it within a fortnight! It showed the sort of enthusiasm I was not finding elsewhere.

While all this was going on, Phil's story unravelled: he was not what he claimed to be, was not leaving us for University, had a sister in Glasgow and he knew the city well before he came to us. Believing his story that he was suffering from a brain-tumour, he came and stayed at the manse, but there was no brain-tumour and he left suddenly, taking my alarm-clock with him. Next thing I heard was that he was working at the Kibble Approved School in Paisley - no references sought from us either.

Concerned for Phil, and the reputation of the Kibble, I phoned the place, and was put in touch with the psychologist, a very helpful Australian chap, to whom I related the story in detail. He undertook to do whatever he could to help Phil, whose mental health worried Margaret and myself. I had several conversations with this psychologist and we became quite chummy on the phone. One day when I phoned my call was passed on to the Head of the Kibble. He told me I could no longer speak to the psychologist because he had left. I wanted to know where had he gone, only for Head to admit that he no idea - the guy had disappeared, leaving his luggage behind! This was the psychologist who was supposed to be solving Phil's mental problems, and he was completely potty himself!

As I have already pointed out, St. Francis-in-the-East, and therefore Church House, would not be here today were it not for the Regnal Circle. Of course, many others, especially the ladies, contributed greatly, but it was the Circle which carried through the vital stewardship campaigns. The influence of the Circle in Bridgeton went far beyond the local scene: out of it sprang Circles all over Scotland, for Regnal is essentially a missionary movement, its aim being to serve the Church by bridging the gap between men outside and those few already inside, who are almost all officebearers. In Regnal, the saying goes that the most important member is the man who was last in through the door.

Ninety-nine ostriches buried their head in the sand. Along came the one hundredth ostrich, looked around and said, "Where's everybody gone?" (Robert Benchley)

With the churches retreating into fundamentalism (a 'fundamentalist' is a neurotic who does not know what the fundamentals of Christianity are), the gap between the Church and the people gets ever wider. A 'martyr complex' prevails, and the leadership on offer is 'cauld kail het'. The most striking feature of many ministers today is their lack of curiosity. 'Seeking', 'Knocking', 'Asking' - these do not feature in their programme. We are in the age of mediocrity.

From our original Circle, others began in Linwood, Gorbals, Govan, Easterhouse, Bargeddie, Hawick, Kinlochleven, Rutherglen, Burnside, Partick, Dreghorn, Greenock, Kilmarnock, and, more recently, Auchterhouse/Murroes by Dundee. Some of these have vanished due to church closures or lack of ministerial interest in the men, but Regnal is still being found by those who are seeking, asking, knocking.

The word 'Regnal' simply means 'The Reign of a King', and it was first used by the Rev. Donald Standfast as a new word free from the bad associations the word 'Christian' had in the minds of the men he served amongst when he was first a private soldier, then, after being badly wounded, an army chaplain in the Great War. The earliest Circles sprang up in the trenches, and continued after the war when The Regnal League was founded in Rouen in 1919. Outstanding ministers like 'Tubby' Clayton (Toc H), George MacLeod, and

'Woodbine Willie' emerged from the war realising the existing religious formats were tainted and distorted in the minds of men, and a new relationship had to be begun with a whole new vocabulary. This is still true today and, being the ultimate challenge, is avoided.

The Kirk has nothing to offer men today and doesn't give them a passing thought! Freemasonry remains the major outreach to men by the Kirk. To deny that is to be blind to reality. In so saying, I have nothing to say against any man choosing to become a mason. Very many fine men are masons, just as in Rotary, but though some of these give their prime loyalty to the church, the time and energies of many others are not directed at winning men for Christ. Even the easily despised (by those who don't know the men in it) Orange Order provides men with something they need, and which they do not find in the churches. These points are possibly debatable, but debate and discussion are suppressed in an increasingly irrelevant Church.

Some years ago, after visiting a committee at the Church Offices in Edinburgh ('121') to try to interest them in supporting the creation of a national movement along Regnal lines, one of the men with me from Easterhouse said, "Bill, you're wasting your time - you wouldnae get through tae that lot wi' a nail-gun!" Things are worse today (if that's possible) because the 'Policy & Resources Committee' refuse even to discuss the subject with us. It crosses my mind when I encounter such 'Christians' to think of becoming a Jew!

I had a dream once, in which a ghostly Co-op undertaker appeared to bet me that I couldn't arouse the Board of National Mission to show some kind of emotion - sympathy, interest, curiosity, anger, any sort of response would do. He offered my spirit free Air Miles for when it soared 'through tracts unknown', upping the wager by even throwing in an extra couple of curtain calls for my cremation. Wisely, I did not take him up on the bet because there was no way I could win in.

Will Rogers' son came home from University and said, "Dad, that old Greek philosopher Socrates. taught us all we need to know - he said, "Know thyself".

Will thought awhile and then said, "Sure son, know thyself - then get to know the other fella, there's two halves to a whole."

A Regnal Circle is not another men's club. I would describe it as 'Alcoholics Anonymous without the alcohol'. Misrepresented, damned with faint praise, I have been trying for forty years to interest the national church in the fact that, like my father, men think that the church is a good thing but it is not for them. As the Kirk becomes increasingly feminised, this impression is not helped. As one very good lady minister told me, "I like the Regnal but I'm a woman, so how can I start a Circle?" I have often heard the objection to Regnal that it is aimed at men, when what is needed today is a grouping together of both sexes. I always then ask where they are holding such groups, only to find they exist only in the mind of the objecting speaker! There is undoubtedly a place for mixed meetings, but despite the present supremacy of trendy, theoretical political correctness in these matters, men and women will always want time to themselves, as anyone can see if they go to a party and watch the company divide. This may outrage the 'unco guid' of today, but it is a fact of life. At one time, apprentices listened to and learned from good tradesmen not only their skills, but also about behaviour. I have seen young guys doing the same in the Regnal.

"Travel narrows the mind" (Oscar Wilde)

One of the things we say in Regnal is that if we are asked to go anywhere and speak about it to a group of men, we will go. This has taken us far afield - but I never thought we would be asked to Orkney! Alex Mair and I set off in the van, drove all the way from Glasgow to John o' Groats, and crossed the Pentland Firth in great peril of death by drowning. The weather was glorious, so what the Firth is like in bad weather I cannot begin to imagine!

My father's mother being a Sinclair from Orkney, I was interested in seeing it for the first time. During the weekend trip, I met an old lady who told me she had a ball of thread from my grandfather (he upholstered Glasgow City Chambers), and she was still using it! Ancestral memories right enough! She remembered playing with my father in 1902!

Alex and I were fed by the welcoming session clerk at his fine, modern, farmhouse, and then taken to the manse of the minister who had invited us. This was a big, old, stone pile, which in the darkness of the night looked forbiddingly haunted. The door was opened by a tall, silent lady who led us into a sparsely furnished sitting room with half the floor tiles missing, so I asked her if they were just moving in.

No, they had lived there quite some time, reported our hostess. On hard chairs, we awaited our host's arrival, and he turned up around midnight. A medium to small figure, his mind seemed elsewhere, and he made no enquiries as to our long journey, nor did he refer to his asking us to come. Instead we were presented with a good deal of information about the locals and their genealogies. And so to bed. As we went up the stone staircase, I said to Alex, "I'll see you in the morning," to which he replied, "I hope so!"

My small room had a comfortable bed and nothing else - no curtains, carpet or chair. A night-time toilet trip down dark corridors proved scary. Morning viewing was of a field with cows mournfully gazing in the window. We went for breakfast. In daylight the house looked as if it had been stocked up for an Arctic winter: boxes of baked beans, and the like, lined the corridors. Working our way to the table, we were offered porridge. By this time, I began to take a great liking to the lady of the manse; something 'fey' about her, a quiet demeanour with an underlying intelligent mind and a sense of humour. No sign of him.

Producing the porridge took longer than it would to roast an ox whole, so Alex and I were exchanging giggles by the time it reached our plates, in the form of a glutinous mass of inedible grey stuff. It was becoming clear why he had not joined us for breakfast. When he did appear he offered to take us for a drive round the islands to see the sights. It was perfect weather for seeing Orkney ...

The car was in a barn which was house and home to the hens. Chasing them out, he installed the missing back seat into the vehicle, then bade us get in. Having noticed the car bore 'L' plates, I asked, "Is your wife learning to drive?" "Oh, no," said he. "It's me, I'm learning to drive." Helpfully I said, "Well, both of us have licences, so you'll be all right driving." "Oh, they don't bother about that here; I drive about all the time." "When is your test?" I asked. "Haven't fixed another one yet," he replied. "I've failed it nine times - jump in."

It was a wonderful day, heavenly blue skies and a bare, table-top landscape dotted about with prosperous dairy farms. We saw the sights: Skara Brae, the Italian chapel, the barrages, etc. The one thing lacking in all this, though, was any reference by our host to the purpose of our visit. Discreet enquiries revealed that he had arranged a meeting for some men that evening to hear our *spiel* about the Regnal.

After dinner, we began looking at our watches - no word of where and when this meeting would be came from the convening minister. Finally we made a move: "Will we be starting the meeting soon?" we speculated. "Ah," said he, "the meeting is off. It is a fine evening, so the farmers will be out making hay while the sun shines." His nice wife smiled like the Mona Lisa. Alex and I raised our eyebrows in astonishment! Apologies that we had driven hundreds of miles, crossed the high seas, and spent our own cash on travel, all for nothing, did not spring to the lips of our host. He hurriedly left us, sitting on his hard chairs in his empty sitting-room, and disappeared, presumably to bring in the hay.

Before boarding the morning ferry, leaving him on the quay with the seals sunning themselves on the rocks, the Reverend suggested that he and I exchange pulpits for a few months. For all the attractions of this offer, I respectfully declined, and we parted on the shore, as the song says. Why he asked us to travel from Glasgow I know not, and how he could then cancel the meeting is beyond me; but we did our bit, and fulfilled our boast to go anywhere, any time, for the sake of Regnal - the Reign of the King. Crossing the Pentland Firth, tossed about on the deck of the small boat, I remarked to Alex that this was how St. Paul must have felt as he travelled far and wide during his missionary journeys. An indoor faith is not enough; you have to go out to find "high adventure", fulfilment, fun. That's how you also find yourself.

Monday night is Regnal night! That's long been our slogan, and it has been kept by the St. Francis-in-the-East Circle for forty years. How many men have passed through the Circle I can only guess, so many men have gone to the Unseen Circle, or simply moved away, going on their pilgrim way freer and stronger men for having been in Regnal.

It is the custom to end our meetings with a silent prayer. One night I could not resist the temptation to ask a rather rough young guy what he prayed about during the silence. "I thank God for the Regnal," he replied. He had pawned his suit one year so he could come to our annual conference at Swanwick. One night, he and a pal of his had gone off, on their own initiative, to visit another church to try to start a Circle there, and when they returned I shall never forget what they they said to us: "The minister sold us down the river". At the meeting, the minister had not spoken a word of welcome or encouragement to these two laddies who, with no church background, were sadly discovering that many of those who lead the church, ministers and elders, are all too often modern day Pharisees - guys desperate to argue that Christianity doesn't work. I never knew what Pharisaism was until I went about trying to interest church leaders in the Regnal. "The rank is but the guinea's stamp, The man's the gowd for a' that."

Having travelled to an East Coast church (pre-motorway days) on a Saturday afternoon, with a dozen men who were giving up their precious leisure time to speak about Regnal, the minister there welcomed us and then started to leave. I pulled him back, asking where he was going. "I've to get ready for tomorrow's Service," he replied, in that infuriatingly bland way many ministers have. I explained to him some facts. Firstly, our men had come to help him, and come a very long way at their own expense and on their day off. Secondly, I had to stay the afternoon, in his church hall, *and* I had to drive all the way home, *and* prepare for my Sunday Service. This persuaded him to stay - for a short while, that is. His church no longer exists.

This isn't the place to go into how Regnal works, but behind it lies the word. 'Wholeness' - body, mind, and spirit. The whole of life in Christian discipleship. It takes men as they are and where they are, in mutual acceptance and friendship. No 'talking down'. Only rarely do we have a speaker, because we provide our own. The games period is just as essential as the discussion and short opening devotions - and we sit in a circle. All are equal. No long term office-bearers either - one year and you are out! When we were trying to begin a certain circle, an elder there was dead against Regnal coming to his patch. When he visited our own circle and saw one of our members, a poorly dressed, wee lost soul called 'Jolly' Miller showing his home-made movies he changed his mind completely. It was 'Jolly's' night, and everyone sat for an hour through the worst film show in history - upside down, flickering hairs, you name it. At the end, 'Jolly' got great applause and praise, and went home that night feeling a better man. So did the critical visitor who said afterwards what he saw that night taught him what Regnal is all about. He went back and started a Circle. Regnal is 'better felt than telt'.

It is amazing how little we know about each other! Folk bounce off each other in our churches like billiard balls. I have known men for ages and yet not known them until a Circle night. John gave us a talk on Christian Aid and revealed he had been court-martialled in India during the war for giving cookhouse waste food to the Indian people. Robbie, an old-stager, starchy and formal in manner, gave us a hilarious night singing and reciting his heart out - how wrong your assessment of a guy can be! Then there was the chap whose programme consisted of taking our piano to bits and cleaning it - while I prayed he could put it back together again. I've seen men teach us how to sole and heel shoes, or turn out to be short-wave radio buffs. One bloke brought a suitcase of bird's eggs.

Our best nights have always been when some guy has simply told us his work-a-day problems - the honest foreman who has to make his squad work on a Friday afternoon when they would rather laze about in order to get Sunday overtime (knowing they needed the extra money makes it really hard to know what is the right, Christian thing to do in such tricky situations). We have no answers, but we can listen and a man is satisfied with knowing somebody cares whether he lives or dies!

Matt was elected the Steward of our Circle one year and gave us a talk I shall never forget: 'My Life of Suffering'. He had been in and out of jail all his life, and saw it as his 'Suffering'. He was amazed to be elected to the Chair, and accepted into our Circle of Friendship. Of course, probably inevitably, once back in his old environment, bad old associates pulled him down again, and he drifted away ftom the Circle, but like others I knew, he would always wear his Regnal badge and talk as if he still attended when I met up with him in the street. It was all poor Matt had to hold on to. As we say, you can join Regnal, but you cannot leave it.

We have had some speakers over the years, and they invariably say they have enjoyed coming because we didn't let them speak! Questions keep things down to earth: when a Pakistani minister came he put up his hand and said, "Please, gentlemen, vould you speak in English so I am understanding your questions". Glaswegian is not English, it seems!

One night I brought along an American negro minister ftom Montgomery, Alabama. It was at the height of Martin Luther King's campaign for Civil Rights, and this young minister had been active, entering segregated premises, etc. He had cigarette burns on his neck where segregationists taunted him in restaurants. He dined at the manse and I gave him a dram. He asked for another, and another. We had practised singing 'We Shall Overcome' for his visit, and started it off, but he held up his hand and cried, "No, no, that's all wrong guys!" He proceeded to sing it to a tune unknown to anyone else in the world, and in words I suspect he made up as he went along. The Spirit certainly moved him that night!

A prominent business man, Walter Hibberd, still tells of the night years ago he was invited for tea at the manse, then found himself a guest at the Regnal Circle being introduced as the Speaker for the evening! He received this news with astonishment and trepidation but this soon turned to pleasure as he fielded questions about his business - later I told him that had I told him in advance that he was to be Speaker, he would have worried, prepared, and forfeited spontaneity!

SWANWICK CONFERENCE

"The Hayes" conference centre is the largest in Britain, and it is situated in the Peak District of Derbyshire. My first visit there was in 1954, as a student, when I attended a conference on 'Men and the Bible' organised by the Student Christian Movement. The main speaker was the Rev. Ted Wickham, founder of the Sheffield Industrial Mission, a tiny man with a powerful personality. All I remember of his talk was that it opened with him saying, "This will be a short talk because men know nothing about the Bible". It is sad to think there are no Ted Wickhams about these days, or such as Bill Gowland, leading light at the Luton Industrial Mission. I visited both Sheffield and Luton. Ted later became Bishop of Manchester. Sheffield became the land of that tragic film, 'The Full Monty'.

I remember that 1954 Swanwick conference was run by two prominent individuals of the day - Jim Blackie and Nancy Anderson. During the night, one of my fellow students, an engineer, was awakened by the sound of the heating pipes rattling ominously. He got up to tell Jim Blackie the boiler was threatening to burst. Entering Jim's room, he found him in bed with Nancy, and hastily retreated with apologies, thinking he had stumbled upon an illicit liaison, unaware that Nancy Anderson was Jim's wife!

The Regnal Annual Conference is held there and the men from the Bridgeton Circle have attended since 1964 - some 20,000 miles travel in total over the years. It always amazes me that we take such a large contingent so far each year, and everyone looks forward to going (bit of the old 'Trip to Wembley' spirit about it, perhaps). Our first visit was pre-motorway, and took us twelve hours via the Pennine moors. The somewhat douce English were awakened by the sound of a big drum, bugle, etc. We were housed in the cubicles of a wooden building, outwith the main house, built for German officer P. o. Ws. It was from one of these rooms that the only successful German escapee dug a tunnel, made his way to an airfield, and almost took off in a Spitfire, A film, *The One the Got Away*, told the story. The German pilot eventually escaped by swimming across the mighty St. Lawrence River into the neutral U. S. A., and got back to Germany only to be shot down and killed later.

Our second trip was better planned: we went down the A1 in several cars. All went well until my own car ended up in a country lane at 2 a.m. Totally lost, the only thing to do was wait until somebody came along and ask where on earth we were. After a long wait, car lights approached and, as it passed, we waved it down. The driver stopped and walked back towards us - it was Danny, one of our guys stopping to ask us where *he* was!

One year we borrowed an ancient bus from the minister of Garthamlock Parish, an enthusiast for doing up old vehicles. It chugged along not too badly, then broke down. The A A got it re-started but by then the door wouldn't shut. As it was early March, and blowing a gale of freezing rain, we almost died of exposure! The following year, I had a Morris Minor van, which could take seven in the maximum discomfort. It was restricted to doing 40 m.p.h. in those days, so the cars with us sped ahead. One of the men gave me a rest from driving, and promply knocked out my two headlamps. My passengers had to be at their work early next morning, so I had no option but to crawl back home ninety miles, in pouring rain, with only the side-lights working on a night as black as the Earl o' Hell's waistcoat! 40 m.p.h. was no problem!

Much the same happened another year when my old Triumph took seriously ill near Gretna during our return from Swanwick. Towed back to Carlisle, the R A C man searched his garage for the needed spare part, and by 3 a.m. found an old dynamo. Overjoyed, we pursued our course, only to lose the registration plate *en route* when it fell off. I took some of the men straight to the next work morning.

The motorway improved matters, and we had our own minibus by then. Alex's driving, which rivalled that of Stirling Moss, got us there in half the time. But not without occasional difficulties: breaking down at Shap, we called out the A A seven times, until they refused to come again. So we pushed the van most of the road to Derbyshire, no mean feat, assisted greatly by the sympathetic police. Coming back, we were transported as far as Carnforth by the A A and left to our own devices. The possibility of our having a trouble tree journey to Swanwick was pretty remote in those days - on our first trip John Webster had ended up in Blackpool, but then he would! I look back and wonder how we ever found the place and got there at all.

One year, miles from our destination, a radiator hose burst; steaming our way into a village in torrential rain, we stopped at a pub looking for water. It was late on Friday night, the pub was noisy and crowded, and as we invaded the place, twelve Scotsmen wearing tammies, etc., there was complete silence. An apprehensive barmaid was approached by Alex MacDonald. "Could we have a bucket of water, please?" he asked. The idea of twelve Scotsmen entering an English pub and asking for a bucket of water (presumably with twelve straws!) was an unanticipated novelty for the locals, and doubtless to this day, the tale is told throughout an unbelieving village.

The theme of the conference one year was 'Grasping the Nettle' and I gave it the works from the platform. At 2 a.m. my room was raided by a pranksters offering to sell me a battleship - the formula used on these occasions. The surprise was not, however, on me, but on my assailants, for they found me, not asleep, but sitting in a chair and giving them a heartfelt welcome! I was covered in a blazing nettle-rash, and had been lying in a bath of cold water seeking relief At 8 a.m., when the local chemist's shop door was pounded upon by a horde of Glaswegians carrying their wounded leader; the alarmed apothecary responded with alacrity. I survived by sitting at an open van window bare chested in the cooling breeze. 'Grasping the nettle' is not a subject which I would recommend to a speaker, as one never knows the undesirable side-effects.

The Warden of The Hayes, an archetypal Englishman, was a look-alike for the T.V. actor Geoffrey Palmer. He took a dim view of the Scots in general, and those from our Regnal Circles in particular. One can hardly blame him; every year, he found himself accompanying Alex and me to the Casualty Department of Derby General Hospital, seeking treatment for one or other of the younger members of our party. Saturday nights in casualty are long-drawn-out affairs in gloomy circumstances, and the thought that we would be returning to his conference centre next year further dispirited the poor soul. Broken legs and ankles, received at the annual England *vs* Scotland soccer match in a cowpat field, were high on the list for treatment.

For variety, a Church House boy managed one time to fracture his skull putting! This takes some doing; my guess is that you have to lie with your head over the hole. The Warden conveyed us to the hospital, his annoyance tempered by the grim satisfaction of knowing one of his tormentors might leave this world. The news was that the boy would have to be kept in for at least a week. This meant Alex staying; I had to take the bad news home to Bobby's mother upon my return to Bridgeton. I went up to the house where I found the family watching television and eating crisps. Holding my hat to my chest, I broke the sad news. "Mrs B, I have to tell you that Bobby has fractured his skull and is lying in hospital in Derby, where he will be for quite sometime". "Oh aye," commented mother. The circumstances merited, in my opinion, a more concerned response but none was forthcoming, so I slipped away leaving them absorbed in their viewing and stoically munching their crisps.

Another, and stronger reason for the warden's antipathy towards us was the tendency for some of our younger group to rob the place. The trusting Christians, earnestly conferring and praying in one or other of the several conferences going on at The Hayes, were unaware of the viper in their midst. Tea and coffee was on supply at all times, and payment for this was by placing money into a saucer - a glittering prize for a 'tea-leaf'. Orange juice bottles were also easily acquired. Accusations of theft were levelled at us on one fraught occasion before we could leave. The van having broken down, we were left behind after everyone had gone, and the enraged warden pounced upon us demanding the return of his orangeade. A big man of military bearing, he was not lacking in either provocation or courage, but he had not reckoned with Big Cammy. A native of Burnside, Cammy was built like a lumberjack, and therefore bigger than any warden. Towering over our accuser, Cammy uttered the memorable words: "These boys are my friends from Bridgeton, and if you want to have a go at them, ye'll need tae go through me first!" Discretion being the better part, the warden withdrew to fight another day. The orange juice made a mysterious reappearance in the repaired van on our way home.

On a more serious occasion, Alex took some guys to Swanwick against my advice (I had seen them acting suspiciously outside a pub). The office was broken into, and precious items were taken from visitors' rooms - the daft thing was that the perpetrator of the crimes was bound to be caught if searched getting into the van to go home. So it transpired: the odd thing was that the most likely suspects turned out innocent and the least likely, guilty. What to do? Call the police? Spend days travelling to a court in Derbyshire? The Law had never figured prominently in our dealings at the Club, and Alex solved the problem in the usual manner - he felled the young culprit with one right on the jaw! With goods restored to their owners, God was in His heaven, and all was right again with the world. "I knew it was him," said somebody later, "he brought a jemmy with him." "Thanks a bundle for telling us," was my dry reply.

Lest you begin to think that our trips to Swanwick for the past forty years have been a trail of pillage, let me assure you that is not the case. *Joie de Vivre* has been our contribution to the somewhat ethereal approach to religion practised south of the border, and the Scots are very popular. And on each visit, our men have visited all the beauty spots of the Dales, as well as the truly marvellous tramway museum, and places like Lincoln Cathedral and Chatsworth. Meeting people from all over the country and all walks of life is what Regnal's Swanwick Conference is all about. In the lunch queue I met Colonel Campbell, and he invited my family to stay at Talbot House in Poperinge, Belgium, the Great War base for Tubby Clayton's Toc H. This is a wonderful place to visit, and we have been often, thanks to Regnal. You should go.

Persuading men to go places isn't easy; I once tried repeatedly to get a nice, shy man called Ronnie to come to Swanwick without success, so I deviously asked his nice wife why she wouldn't let him go. This she indignantly denied, and guaranteed he would be there next time - he was. Like many men, Ronnie thought a conference was all Bible reading and prayers (OK for some but not for him), so he was surprised to find himself under no such pressure when he got there. He evidently enjoyed the holiday atmosphere and warm frendly spirit, for when I asked him what he remembered about the weekend, he answered, "A man came up and shook hands with me - a stockbroker from Cheshire". Not the talks, not the worship, not the food, not the accommodation - no! What he remembered was a handshake! Surely it is such simple things which count the most - we forget that as Christians we are not in the business of winning arguments, but winning men. And it is done by a handshake. Well, isn't that how Our Lord operated?

These days I continually hear that such and such a minister cannot come to a meeting of men because it's his day off and he keeps it strictly for himself. Fair enough, I suppose, but somehow I cannot picture Our Lord saying to some paralytic, "Sorry, mate, can't heal you today, the Sabbath is my quality time for leisure" ... Or Paul saying, "Sorry, Macedonians, I can't come over to help you because it's my day off." ... Or the early Christians calling to Nero, "Hail Caesar! Before throwing us to the lions would you please keep off Mondays, because that's the day we don't witness." Nor can I imagine Pal Warnes, saying to the man who asked him for shoes, "Come back tomorrow, Jock, this is a Monday night and I only meet people on Tuesdays." But then, as I am often told, I am out of date, behind the times.

Years ago, the Monday after a weekend down at Swanwick Conference, I took a funeral and met members of the family, all strangers, at a meal in a restaurant. They were Glasgow folk who like countless others, had gone to work and live in England. When I asked them where they were going to after the funeral, they replied, "Oh, to a place down South - but you will never have heard of it". "Where's that? I continued. "It's in Derbyshire" they said. "A wee place called Swanwick." Another coincidence! They were astonished and delighted to hear that I had just come from Swanwick the previous day, and knew it well. Small world, right enough!

Last Chapter

"General Sherman said, 'War is hell', so I got the hell out of it."
(Mark Twain on leaving the Confederate army after one week.)

"I only have one very brief thing to say as I leave my job after all these years, and it is this: friends: if you have seen it, I have slipped on it!"
(Glasgow 'Green lady' infant health visitor in her retirement speech).

I was constantly pressurised by the Presbytery 'planners' to leave St. Francis-in-the-East to facilitate a union with Bridgeton Parish - a thing I strongly resisted, feeling, rather than knowing, that it would be fatal for both parties. Bridgeton Parish Church was very low in numbers and aid-receiving. I finally agreed that should my own church lose its self-supporting status, I would move, but that put me under a great strain - one year we finished in the black, but with only £2 in hand! Had the minister of Bridgeton Parish, John Lang, left, there would have been a union, and doubtless we would have then moved into his, at the time, better premises. However, he did not go until after I myself had left. This turned out to be providential, because had we moved into Bridgeton Parish and closed Queen Mary Street Church, there would be no church at all in Bridgeton today. Bridgeton Parish building was found to be unsafe and had to be demolished.

It truly broke my heart to leave St. Francis-in-the-East, but the pressures from both the 'cowboys' (Unions & Readjustments), and the 'Indians' (Community Education trying to take over the Club), added to paying off the last of the huge rebuilding debts, and keeping the congregation self-supporting, were exhausting. The struggle to save the Club and the Kirk had worn me out, though I didn't realise it. The place needed a change too, yet had someone said to me, "Don't go", I would still be there. I guess nobody did because it never occurred to them that I would ever leave (when a church in Dundee approached me one time, they wrote saying they hadn't the heart to take me because I, and my congregation, looked so happy together!

I agonised over accepting a call to Wellpark West in Greenock, then took the plunge and decided to accept for weal or woe. At my valedictory, the congregation presented me with £250 (£10 a head, at a time when £10 was a lot of money). In return, I presented the congregation with £400 which I had accumulated over the years from weddings and funerals (my 'petty cash') so, on balance, they gained £150 on the deal - something which pleased me no end, for such is Christian economics!

Speaking of Christian economics, I was working very late one night with some of the men wall-papering the Session House, when one of them, Neil Hughes, was reminded by the treasurer, Willie McGowan, that he hadn't paid in his freewill offering envelopes. Neil looked up and said, "Some place this - you have to pay to work!" That's the strange thing about the church - it is the only place on earth where you have to pay to work! But then, that's how Christianity turns the world upside down!

This is my story about my ministry in Bridgeton, and so the twelve years Margaret, Scott, Alison, and Joy spent in Greenock, before I was given 'the black spot' and forced to retire (to make way for a younger woman), do not figure in this book. We and the family had some happy times, made many good friends. I started the first B. B. Company formed in Greenock since the war, began a big Regnal Circle for men (still going), and amongst other successful ventures, formed my pride and joy, the Youth Fellowship. We had a great Y. F. and did the Christmas Eve plays I had done in Bridgeton. The young folk of the Y. F. have a special place in my affections. Yet for all that, I guess a big slice of my heart was still in Brigton, and I continued to raise funds for the Club, and to keep up my involvement in the Bridgeton Business and Burns Clubs.

Church House is full of spirits for me: "gone, gone, all are gone, the old familiar faces". The story goes that when talking pictures came in, Buster Keaton, the great star of silent films, found himself suddenly dropped by the studios. In the rapidly changing Hollywood scene, he was soon a forgotten man, out of work, in poor circumstances. Some years later, a Hollywood hostess ran a swell party in her mansion, and an old friend took him along. When the beaming hostess noticed him standing all alone in a corner, she wanted to know who he was, and what he was doing in her house, so she went over and asked him a little suspiciously, "Have you been here before?" "Yes, lady," Buster

Keaton replied dreamily, "I've been here before. I used to live here. I built this house."

I hope by writing this, I have preserved the memory, and some of the names, of many fine, courageous people. New generations are entering into a goodly inheritance, but as the saying goes, "The father's finding is only the son's search warrant".

While on holiday in Virginia, I heard a very intelligent, 'classy' lady (in her sixties I guessed), being interviewed on the radio. I gathered she had been in the music business in her younger days. She spoke of her grandson telling her excitedly about a new band he had heard and which he recommended highly. She asked him the name of this band, expecting to be told the name of the latest pop-group; instead he told her it was called 'Glen Miller's Orchestra.' "You won't have heard of it, Gran", said he. There was a pause, then she said softly in her beautiful voice "As a matter of fact, I have heard of it, son. I was Glen Miller's lead singer."

How did you ever become a minister, Bill? That is a question I am often asked, especially following my after-dinner speeches, which arouse frenzied standing ovations. Well, I often wonder myself how I ever became a minister, for I had other ambitions in life. Truth to tell, I always wanted to be a concert pianist in an Orange flute band, but I had to give that up as a career choice after being told I would have to learn music. Becoming a bull fighter was another ambition which always attracted me, but on my income I couldn't afford a bull. So I guess I have ended up in the ministry, not by choice, but by that pure coincidence called 'prevenient grace'.

I spoke well of a certain old minister one time to Alex MacDonald, one of my elders, and Alex agreed saying, "Aye, he's a good yin, and there's no mony guid yins!" - whether he classified me as a 'guid yin' I can but guess.

Aged eighteen, I took my first Service at 6.00 p.m. in a village church. My school pal Arthur accompanied me and tells me that we were back home at 6.30 p.m. After this early success, I have continued where I started - short and cheery. A lady phoned just the other day to ask me to take her father's funeral, "Get Shackleton," said Bob with his last breath, "he will be short." So now you see that brevity has been the secret of my success in the ministry.

Let me leave you with this final thought from one of the great philosophers of our time.

"We stand today at a crossroad: one path leads to despair and utter hopelessness. The other leads to total extinction. Let us hope we have the wisdom to make the right choice." (Woody Allen).

I can't think of a better reason for keeping cheery than that - can you?

Printed in the United Kingdom
by Lightning Source UK Ltd.
106041UKS00001B/124